England's Anglo-Saxon Heritage

A County-by-County Exploration

Geoff Marshall

Matador
Unit E2 Airfield Business Park,
Harrison Road, Market Harborough,
Leicestershire. LE16 7UL
Tel: 0116 2792299
Email: books@troubador.co.uk
Web: www.troubador.co.uk/matador
Twitter: @matadorbooks

ISBN 978 1803131 641

British Library Cataloguing in Publication Data.
A catalogue record for this book is available from the British Library.

Printed and bound in Great Britain by 4edge Limited
Typeset in 11pt Adobe Garamond Pro by Troubador Publishing Ltd, Leicester, UK

Matador is an imprint of Troubador Publishing Ltd

Contents

Introduction

The Anglo-Saxons held sway in this country from the time the Romans departed until the Norman Conquest: a period of over 600 years; in other words, the same length of time from the present day back to late medieval England, at the time of the War of the Roses. By any standard, a considerable period. The era used to be known as the Dark Ages, a term now largely discredited, considering the substantial achievements of the age. The exquisite workmanship of the discoveries at Sutton Hoo is one such example.

The Anglo-Saxon legacy has endured. They gave us our language, place names, an English identity and an administrative system of dividing the country into shires which – apart from recent boundary changes – is still with us today.

England's Anglo-Saxon Heritage: A County-by-County Exploration brings the tremendous accomplishments of the Anglo-Saxons to life. It is not intended as a work of scholarship but rather it is aimed at the general reader and written in an accessible and clear way. It could, however, act as a springboard to more advanced study. The book is presented in two parts. Part One is an overview of the course of events in Anglo-Saxon England. Its purpose is to put into context Part Two, which is a richly illustrated place-by-place exploration of what there is to see and enjoy today of the Anglo-Saxon world. Part Two is designed to be used in the field by those who enjoy exploring our country with guidebook in hand, as well as by the armchair reader. All well-known places are described, from the magnificence of Bede's Jarrow and Monkwearmouth, to the wonderful churches at Brixworth and Earl's Barton. The Anglo-Saxons' ability to execute the most intricate of sculpture is explored, everything from the Bewcastle Cross, standing in idyllic and remote countryside close to the border with Scotland, to the beautifully carved grave cover at Wirksworth in the Peak District. The accomplishments of the Vikings are included, such as their splendid hogback tombs and unique sculpture. There are stories as well: St Guthlac, and his meeting with a Mercian prince in the solitude of the fens at Crowland in Lincolnshire; vivid tales from Norse myth such as the exploits of Wayland the Smith and the impish Loki; the saintly Aetheldreda and her flight from her unwelcome husband. But there is much more. As well as the famous, more secret and hidden treasures are described, places ranging from the fells of Cumbria to the South Downs in Sussex. The simple but breathtaking architecture of Anglo-Saxon churches, their intricate sculpture and captivating historical associations are all waiting to be discovered.

All places listed in Part Two have been visited personally. I owe a great debt to and acknowledge those who have studied and written before. In particular and first, Sir Nikolas Pevsner and his fellow authors of *The Buildings of England* series. These splendid books accompanied my wife and me on our travels and were consulted throughout. Those who wish to investigate architecture further should, as I did, consult the standard work of H.M. Taylor and Joan Taylor, *Anglo-Saxon Architecture*. The standard work on Anglo-Saxon sculpture is the magnificent *Corpus of Anglo-Saxon Stone Sculpture* published under the guidance of Professor Rosemary Cramp at the University of Durham. The weighty volumes, first begun by a team of experts in 1977, can be consulted in the British Library or online. Other excellent sources are Leslie Webster's *Anglo-Saxon Art* and Richard Bailey's *Viking Age Sculpture*. Guy Points has also produced an excellent series on Anglo-Saxon architecture and sculpture.

I would also like to acknowledge the very many authors – many of whom do not give their names – who have produced splendid local histories the length and breadth of the country. This book would be the poorer without them. Thanks are also due to the staff of the British Library for retrieving heavy volumes so efficiently. I would also like to pay my appreciation to Dr Michael Bintley who has offered many helpful suggestions and encouragements.

Part One

Early Settlement

The story of the Anglo-Saxon settlement in Britain begins with the Romans. By the 4th century their hold on Britannia, the outermost province of their vast empire, had seriously weakened. Roman Britain faced increasing raids by Picts from the north and by tribes from continental Europe, typically Saxons or Franks. To add to its troubles, Rome itself was faced with increasing attacks by barbarians from the east and it was inevitable that pressure would be exerted to recall forces from Britain.

The course of events in the final years of Roman rule was recorded by Zosimus, a pagan Greek historian and official of the eastern empire.[1] In the early 6th century he wrote *Historia Nova*, a record of Roman Emperors.[2] Zosimus tells us that, in 408 or 409, in response to barbarian raids on Britain, the Britons rebelled against their Roman overlords:

> The Barbarians above the Rhine, assaulting without hindrance, reduced the inhabitants of Britain and some of the Celtic peoples to defecting from Roman rule and living their own lives, independent of Roman laws. The Britons therefore took up arms and, braving the danger on their own behalf, freed their cities from barbarian threat.

To what extent the Britons freed their cities and how permanently, it is difficult to say, but barely a year later, in 410AD, the Emperor Honorius 'wrote letters to the cities of Britain, bidding them to take precautions on their own behalf.' Therefore, even though the Roman army had begun leaving Britain over a period of years in a piecemeal manner, the year 410 is generally accepted as the date when Britain was left to its own devices to look after itself with no protection from its Roman masters.

In what amounted to a last-ditch attempt to elicit help from the Roman Empire, as the 6th century monk Gildas tells us, a letter was addressed to Flavius Aetius, leader of the Western Roman Empire in 446. It has become known as the 'Groans of the Britons' and laments: 'the barbarians drive us to the sea, the sea throws us back to the barbarians and so two modes of death await us, we are either slain or drowned.'

There followed a period, often referred to as the lost centuries, an era of two hundred years where accurate history is, at best, sparse. But we do know that Britain was Christian at the end of Roman rule. Constantine was proclaimed Roman Emperor at York in 306 and in 312 won a famous victory against his rival, Maxentius, at the Battle of Milvian Bridge, north of Rome. There are various versions of the story, but it seems that Christ appeared to Constantine in a dream, in consequence of which he placed the chi-rho symbol (the first two letters of Christ's name in Greek) on his soldiers' shields. Constantine was victorious, and Christianity was henceforth tolerated in the Roman Empire and formalised by the Edict of Milan in 313. Within a year, the first Council of Arles was held, attended by three British bishops, including Restitutus, Archbishop of Londinium.

How firmly Christianity took root in Britain is open to question, but archaeologists have excavated many sites where it was practised, for example the Roman villas at Lullingstone in Kent and Hinton St Mary in Dorset. It survived after the Romans left for, in 428, Bishop Germanus of Auxerre visited to discourage a trend towards Pelagianism (questioning the meaning and consequences of original sin) and to impose orthodoxy.[3] During his time in Britain, Germanus visited the shrine of St Alban, the first Christian martyr in Britain, and in consequence Verulamium (modern-day St Albans) has often been proposed as the place where the power of Germanus's rhetoric overcame the Pelagians.

For our sources of information about the lost centuries we have only four: the Anglo-Saxon Chronicle, the writings of Nennius, the Venerable Bede and Gildas. The Anglo-Saxon Chronicle was first compiled in the 9th century and deals mainly with the history of Wessex. Nennius, a 9th century Welsh monk, may have written *Historia Brittonum* (History of the Britons). It has had many revisions and it is generally accepted that its accuracy should be treated with caution. Bede takes much of his information from Gildas and it is Gildas, a 6th century monk, whose work is our only contemporary source.

So, who was Gildas? To answer, we must be content with the word 'may'. He may have been born in North Wales in about 500. There again, some say

Strathclyde. He is said to have died in Brittany at Rhuys or maybe at Glastonbury Abbey.

Gildas's major work, *De Excidio Britanniae* (Concerning the Ruin of Britain), was written in the 540s. It is not history as we would understand the term today – more a tirade against what Gildas saw as the evils of the time. Gildas rails against the sinfulness of British kings, in particular Vortigern, whom he labels a proud tyrant. His condemnation of British rulers was the purpose of his work and so conventional historical interpretation must be viewed with this in mind.

There were also errors in his work, for instance, he was mistaken on the dates of the reign of the Emperor

Vortigern's Stone, Carmarthen Museum

Tiberius and the revolt of the British queen, Boudicca. Gildas describes events leading up to the Anglo-Saxon settlement. He first describes a time of famine, followed by the expulsion of the enemy by the Britons, after which was a period of prosperity and then of plague. At this time, the main threat to the Britons came from the Picts and Scots in the north. According to Gildas, it was Vortigern who invited the Saxons to come to Britain as mercenaries to help to repel them. (In Carmarthen Museum there is a stone slab, inscribed 'MEMORIA VOTEPORIGIS PROTICTORIS', otherwise known as Vortigern's Stone.) In chapter 23 of his work Gildas takes up the story:[4]

> Then all the councillors, together with that proud tyrant Vortigern, the British king, were so blinded that, as a protection to their country, they sealed its doom by inviting in among them (like wolves into the sheep fold) the fierce and impious Saxons, a race so hateful to both God and men, to repel the invasions of the northern nations. Nothing was ever so pernicious to our country, nothing was ever so unlucky. What palpable darkness must have enveloped their minds – darkness, desperate and cruel! Those very people whom, when absent, they dreaded more than

death itself, were invited to reside, as one may say, under the self-same roof… they first landed on the eastern side of the island, by the invitation of the unlucky king, and there fixed their sharp talons, apparently to fight in favour of the island, but alas more truly against it.

Then comes the defining moment when the Saxons, aggrieved at their lack of pay, rebelled and, rather than return home, brought reinforcements and stayed for good:

Yet they complain that their monthly supplies are not furnished in sufficient abundance, and they industriously aggravate each occasion of quarrel, saying that unless more liberality is shown to them, they will break the treaty and plunder the whole island. In short time they followed up their threats with deeds.

It was the brothers Hengest and Horsa that Vortigern invited in as leaders of the mercenaries. They are shadowy figures – probably mythical – and are thought to have been either Frisians or Jutes. According to the Anglo-Saxon Chronicle 'they turned on the British, destroying through fire and sword's edge'. Some years later at the Battle of Mons Badonicus (Mount Badon) the British gained a temporary respite with a famous victory. Many say the resistance was organised by Ambrosius Aurelianus, a Romano-British war leader. The legendary character King Arthur has also been cited as its leader. The exact date of the battle is unclear; between 490 and 517 has been suggested. As for the site of the battle, there are many contenders, but in any event, although the invaders were stopped in their tracks for a while, the victory had no lasting effect in stemming the tide of Anglo-Saxon invasion and settlement.

It is worth noting at this point what evidence there is for the life of King Arthur. The great bulk of our information – true or false – about this legendary figure comes from Geoffrey of Monmouth, a 12th century Welsh clergyman who wrote much fanciful history. Another source is a poem known as the Gododdin (an area in south-east Scotland) which was written in about 600. It tells of a battle the king of Edinburgh fought at Catraeth (probably Catterick) against the Angles of Northumbria:

Though he was no Arthur
Among the powerful in battle,
In the front rank, Gwarddur was a palisade.

Arthur is also referred to in the writings of Nennius who says he fought in twelve battles including the Battle of Mount Badon, 'carrying the cross of our Lord Jesus Christ for three days and nights and that he died at the Battle of Camlann in 537'.[5]

Pattern of Settlement

It is to the Venerable Bede that we look for information about the pattern of settlement of the Germanic invaders. So, who was Bede? He was born on Tyneside in about 673 and spent all his life as a monk at the twin monastery of Monkwearmouth and Jarrow. He wrote in Latin and his output was both learned and vast. He was fortunate to have at his disposal the library of the abbey's founder, Benedict Biscop, who had amassed an enormous collection of books from his travels abroad. Bede's most famous work was *A History of the English Church and People*, which describes this country from the time the Romans left to the year 731.

Bede, obviously familiar with Gildas's writing, tells us that 'the newcomers were from the three most formidable races of Germany, the Saxons, the Angles and Jutes.' The Jutes came from the Danish peninsula (Jutland), the Saxons from within the area of present-day Germany to the east of the river Weser, and the Angles from the land between Saxons and Jutes. Bede continues:[6]

> From the Jutes are descended the people of Kent and the Isle of Wight and those in the province of the West Saxons opposite the Isle of Wight who are called Jutes to this day. From the Saxons – that is, the country now known as the land of the Old Saxons – came the East, South, and West Saxons. And from the Angles – that is, the country now known as Angulus, which lies between the provinces of the Jutes and Saxons and is said to remain unpopulated to this day – are descended the East and Middle Angles, the Mercians, all the Northumbrian stock (that is, those people living north of the river Humber), and other English peoples.

Without doubt, apart from Angles, Saxons and Jutes, it is certain that there would have been migrations of Frisians, Franks and even reverse migration of Britons to Gaul. It is appropriate to point out that many archaeologists have questioned the precise nature of Bede's pattern of settlement. But we should be careful not to dismiss Bede's work too easily; he is accepted as a scholarly historian. It is likely, however, that in the absence of further historical sources, new interpretations will come from archaeologists.

But what happened to the native Romano-Britons? Were they absorbed into Anglo-Saxon society? Were they slaughtered, were they driven westwards by the Anglo-Saxon advance from the east? The strongest argument against survival of the Britons is the quite remarkable lack of British influence on the Anglo-Saxon language. Also, while it is unwise to generalise, place name studies show a marked lack of British names – particularly the names of small streams – east of a line drawn from the Humber estuary to Southampton. Then further west, British place names increase until in Wales and Cornwall they predominate.[7] Interestingly, and in contrast to Britain, the Frankish influence on Gaul was different. The Franks seem to have readily assimilated Gallo-Roman culture and Christianity.[8]

The Anglo-Saxon Heptarchy

The term heptarchy is a loose expression to describe the seven kingdoms outlined in Bede's account of the early Germanic settlement. Although it is justifiably criticised as being too generalised it is nevertheless a useful aid in the otherwise difficult task of describing events. The seven kingdoms – within which were many sub-kingdoms – were the South Saxons, Wessex, Kent, East Anglia, Northumbria, Mercia and Essex.

The South Saxons (Sussex)

Ælle is recorded as an early king of the South Saxons. He landed near to Selsey Bill in 477 and forced the Britons – probably the Regni tribe – to seek refuge in a wooded area called Andredes leag – identified today as the Sussex Weald. Later, in 491, he won a decisive battle at Andredes cester (present day Pevensey) and 'killed all who lived there; there was not even one Briton left there.'[9] Ælle must have gained great prestige from his capture of Pevensey, a fortress of the Saxon Shore. His victory could explain why he was the first king said to hold 'overlordship' over other Saxon kings.[10] The term 'overlordship' later became identified with the term Bretwalda, or Britain Ruler, and referred to the king who was dominant amongst the many Saxon kings of his time. Once again, Bretwalda is a loose term. It was certainly not a formal title and whether the

Bretwalda had any real authority over territories apart from his own is far from certain. In the case of Ælle, the most credible conclusion is that he was a distinguished warrior who held sway over a wide area. After Ælle died there is no further record of Sussex until about 600.[11]

The West Saxons (Wessex)

As with so much of the period, the birth of Wessex is confused. There are other explanations but by tradition and according to the Anglo-Saxon Chronicle it was founded by Cerdic and his son Cynric who landed in three ships near Southampton in 495 and defeated a British king at a site in present-day Hampshire.

Ceawlin – probably the great grandson of Cerdic – was a later king of Wessex and was the second of Bede's overlords or Bretwaldas. Rather than in Hampshire, his people were settled in the upper Thames valley. He fought and was victorious against Aethelbert of Kent at Wibbandun (probably Wimbledon) and so won control over Surrey.[12] He also won an important battle against the Britons in 577, the Battle of Dyrham, and occupied Cirencester, Gloucester and Bath. The Battle of Dyrham, the site of which is identified with the Iron Age hill fort at Hinton, north of Bath, was strategically very important for the men of Wessex because the Britons of Wales were now cut off from their kinsmen in Devon and Cornwall.[13]

Ceawlin, or indeed the native Britons, may have constructed some of the defensive earthwork, the Wansdyke, which runs for about 20km through the Wiltshire Downs. Ceawlin was finally defeated and killed in a rebellion in 592 by Ceol at Woden's Barrow, probably near Alton Priors in North Wiltshire.[14]

Archaeology has revealed a large settlement of Anglo-Saxons at Dorchester-on-Thames. It later became the place of the first Wessex bishopric under Birinus. Birinus led a party of monks who landed at Hamwich (Southampton) in 634 and converted Cynegils, then king of the West Saxons. He founded his see (the area of a bishop's ecclesiastical jurisdiction) at Dorchester. In 675 it transferred to Winchester under Bishop Haeddi.[15]

Kent

As we have seen, Hengest and Horsa are by tradition considered to be the founders of Kent and from them – if indeed they existed at all – the royal dynasty descended. But of more significance was Aethelbert. He was the third king named by Bede as Bretwalda and the most powerful king considered so far. Aethelbert was the son of Eormenric and because of his marriage to Bertha, a Frankish princess and daughter of Charibert, king of Paris, had trading and other links with the continental Franks. Many Frankish imports have been found in Kentish graves. It was during his reign that coins began to be minted once more in Britain at a mint in Canterbury. He is best known to us because in his reign he received Augustine and converted to Christianity.

The Mission of St Augustine

It is as well at this point to emphasise that Augustine's mission was a reconversion of this country. The Emperor Constantine, after his victory over Maxentius at the Battle of Milvian Bridge, permitted the practice of Christianity in the Roman Empire. It was therefore practised widely in Britain, but to what extent it survived amongst the Britons when the Romans left is open to debate. What is certain, however, is that the Germanic invaders were pagan.

The reconversion of the English was planned in the pontificate of Gregory the Great (590–604). At the time, Rome was in ruins following the Lombard invasions of 568 and Gregory realised that if the Imperial Church was to survive the barbarian invasions, the barbarians themselves must be converted. Therefore, in order to establish the Church's rule – even in the remotest parts – he determined to reconvert the English.

It was Gregory's original intention to educate English slaves in the monasteries of Gaul and then dispatch them to England to convert their pagan countrymen. Instead, he sent Augustine, a prior from his own monastery of St Andrew, together with forty monks. At the same time, Gregory was aware that Aethelbert, king of Kent, was the most powerful of the disparate collection of English kings and furthermore was married to a Christian. She was Bertha who came to Britain accompanied by her priest, Bishop Liudhard. Aethelbert provided her with a chapel to the east of Canterbury, the present-day church of St Martin.

Augustine was at first unwilling to undertake the mission – after all, he spoke not a word of English – but his vow of obedience compelled him to follow Gregory's instructions. And so it was that Augustine, his party of monks and their Frankish interpreters arrived in England at the Isle of Thanet. Aethelbert soon heard of their arrival and instructed the party to remain where

Statue of Queen Bertha, St Martin's Church, Canterbury

it was. Bede takes up the story: 'Some days later, the King came to the island and sitting in the open-air commanded Augustine and his companions to come thither to talk with him.' Aethelbert promised to make a safe passage and accordingly they made their way to Canterbury and established themselves at Bertha's St Martin's Church. There 'they first began to meet to chant the psalms, to pray, to say mass, to preach and to baptise, until when the king had been converted to the faith they received greater liberty to preach everywhere and to build or restore churches.'[16] Later, Aethelbert helped found the bishoprics at both Rochester and London.

Theodore of Tarsus

In about 664 the Archbishopric of Canterbury became vacant. Wigheard was nominated by Pope Vitalian and he duly made his way to Rome to receive the pallium. While in Rome he was struck down by the plague and so, with post still not filled, the Pope looked to Hadrian, abbot of a monastery near Naples. Hadrian declined but recommended his friend Theodore who accepted and so was born a remarkable period of reinvigoration for the English church. Theodore was born at Tarsus, in the Byzantine Empire, and studied at Constantinople. He found himself in Rome in 667 when the see of Canterbury became vacant. Few Romans were prepared to come to England but eventually Theodore agreed and at the age of sixty-seven left for Canterbury.[17, 18] Hadrian joined him and became abbot at the monastery of St Peter and St Paul at Canterbury with Theodore as Archbishop. Theodore set about reorganising the church, imposing canon law and enforcing orthodoxy. Theodore filled many vacant bishoprics, including those at Hertford, Dunwich and Winchester, and decreed that a national synod be held twice every year at Clofesho (the site of which is unknown but Brixworth

– see Northamptonshire – has been proposed). He was recognised as a great scholar and together with Hadrian founded the famous Canterbury School where Aldhelm, later abbot of Malmesbury and Bishop of Sherborne, studied. Theodore's impact on the reorganisation of the church can be appreciated if one considers that on his arrival there were only seven dioceses – and some of them unoccupied – but when he died, fourteen had been established.[17] Equally, there were only a dozen or so monasteries but a century later the number had increased to over 200.

The Law Codes of Aethelbert

It is to Aethelbert that we owe the first English law codes.[19] His Kentish law codes, and those that followed, were the first writings of the Anglo-Saxons and furthermore they are written in English. They deal with penalties for crimes committed by all social ranks, the punishment depending on the social standing of the victim. It is significant that the most serious crime was that committed against the church – more serious than a crime against the king.

For a better understanding of Anglo-Saxon law, it is appropriate to discuss wergild and kinship. Kinship was all important to the Anglo-Saxons. Family members would demand justice for any member of the kin who suffered wrong. Wergild literally means man payment and was the payment made to the victim's family or kin by the person guilty of the crime. Wergild was later extended to many crimes. The laws of Aethelbert confirm that Anglo-Saxon society was hierarchical. Wergild paid on killing a nobleman was 300 shillings, 100 shillings was the value of a ceorl's life, a freeman was between forty to eighty shillings and for a slave, compensation was paid to his owner. Compensation was paid for injuries, depending on their seriousness. For example, if an eye was put out it was fifty shillings, a big toe cost ten shillings and a big toenail, thirty scaetta. There were ninety sections in Aethelbert's laws; some examples are:[20]

- If anyone kills a freeman, he is to pay fifty shillings to the king.
- If anyone lies with a maiden belonging to the king, he is to pay fifty shillings compensation.
- The property of God and the church is to be paid for with twelve-fold compensation; a bishop's property with eleven-fold compensation; a priest's property with nine-fold compensation; a deacon's with six-fold; a cleric's with three-fold.

- If a freeman steals from the king, he is to pay nine-fold.
- If a freeman lies with the wife of a freeman, he is to atone with her wergild and to obtain another wife with his own money and bring her to the other's home.
- If anyone kills a man, he is to pay ordinary wergild of 100 shillings, twenty shillings at the open grave and within forty days the whole wergild.

After the death of Aethelbert, Kent lost influence and power shifted to Raedwald of East Anglia and to Northumbria.

East Anglia

Wuffa was the legendary founder of East Anglia. Raedwald, a descendent of Wuffa, was the fourth king to be named Bretwalda. He is forever remembered and associated with the treasure at Sutton Hoo. Raedwald was king of the East Angles from 600 to 624 and was baptised into the Christian faith in Kent, almost certainly at the court of Aethelbert. He later apostatised under the influence of his pagan wife and according to Bede 'had in the same temple an altar for the holy Sacrifice of Christ side by side with an altar on which victims were offered to devils.'[21] As well as ruling East Anglia, Raedwald was instrumental in installing Edwin as king of Northumbria.[22]

Northumbria

Northumbria, as its name implies, included all territory north of the river Humber and was settled by the Angles. It wasn't until the late 6th century that the Germanic invaders brought the native Britons under their sway. Two kingdoms then emerged, Bernicia in the north and centred at Bamburgh, and Deira situated to the south of the river Tees in the area between the Yorkshire Wolds and north Nottinghamshire.[23]

Mercia

By tradition, kings of Mercia are descended from Icel. He was an Angle and according to *Flores Historiarum* (a chronicle of English history up to 1326 and written by a variety of authors) led a group of 'pagans (who) came from Germany and occupied East Anglia… some of whom invaded Mercia and fought many battles with the British…'. Creoda is recognised as the first king of Mercia and was the great grandson of Icel. He lived in the late 6th century and made Tamworth his capital. In contrast to the other kingdoms of the heptarchy, the pattern of settlement of Mercia is less well defined. The name means 'boundary folk' from which it has been inferred that Mercia developed between Wales and the other existing Anglo-Saxon kingdoms. An alternative explanation is that it evolved between the boundary of Northumbria and the Trent valley.[24]

Essex

The Kingdom of the East Saxons completes the seven kingdoms of the Anglo-Saxon heptarchy. It encompassed modern-day Essex, Hertfordshire, and Middlesex. Settlement began in the early 5th century as is revealed by excavations at Mucking. As elsewhere, there was an amalgamation of minor kingdoms. The first king mentioned in history was Aescwine who reigned in about 527AD. Saebert reigned in the early 7th century. His uncle was the powerful Aethelbert of Kent whose influence induced Saebert to convert to Christianity. London fell within the kingdom of Essex and received Mellitus, first Bishop of St Paul's Cathedral, in 604AD. Essex reverted to paganism a number of times thereafter despite the mission of St Cedd from Northumbria.[25] He founded the tiny church at Bradwell on Sea, still there today.

References

1. Johnson, *Late Roman Britain* (1980), p. 104–107
2. Buchanan and Davis, *Zosimus: Historia Nova, The Decline of Rome* (1967), Book VI, 5, p. 252
3. Stenton, *Anglo-Saxon England* (1971), p. 1
4. www.vortigernstudies.org.uk
5. Campbell, John and Wormald, *The Anglo-Saxons* (1982), p. 27
6. Bede, *A History of the English Church and People*, Book One, Chapter 15
7. Loyn, *Anglo-Saxon England and the Norman Conquest,* 2nd Edition (1991) p. 6
8. Higham and Ryan, *The Anglo-Saxon World* (2013), p. 105
9. Stenton, p. 17
10. Bede, Book Two, Chapter 5

11. Bede, Book Two, Chapter 5

12. Stenton, p. 55

13. Stenton, p. 29

14. Venning, *The Anglo-Saxon Kings* (2011), pp. 28–29

15. Love, in Lapidge, ed., *The Blackwell Encyclopaedia of Anglo-Saxon England* (1999), p. 67

16. Bede, Book 1, Chapter 25

17. Lapidge, *Archbishop Theodore, Commemorative Studies on His Life and Influence* (1995), p. 26–9

18. Wormald, in Campbell, ed., *The Anglo-Saxons* (1982), p. 72

19. Griffiths, *An Introduction to Early English Law* (1995), p. 32–42

20. Whitlock ed., *English Historical Documents* (1979) Vol 1, p. 391

21. Bede, Book Two, Chapter 15

22. Higham, in Lapidge, ed., p. 154

23. Fisher, *The Anglo-Saxon Age c400–1042* (1973), p. 39

24. Venning, p. 33

25. Venning, p. 30

Northumbria

Two kingdoms emerged in Northumbria: Bernicia in the north and Deira in the south. Aelle was an early king of Deira. We hear of him in the famous story of how Gregory, later Pope Gregory, heard that slave boys for sale in Rome came from the land of the Angles, whose king was Aelle. According to legend, Gregory was inspired to convert these 'angels' to the Christian faith – hence the mission of St Augustine, not, as it turned out, to Northumbria, but to the people of Kent.[1]

Bede tells us that Ida was the first king of Bernicia, reigning from 547 to 559.[2] Later came Aethelfrith, who was to unite the two royal houses of Bernicia and Deira when he married Acha, the daughter of Aelle of Deira, so becoming king of a united Northumbria. Aethelfrith is depicted as a fearsome warrior, 'peopling with English settlers more territory of the Britons after exterminating or subjugating the natives'.[3] In 603 he defeated the Scots under their warrior king Aidan mac Gabrain at a place called Degstastan in the Border Country. By so doing he removed the threat of Scottish incursions for over 200 years, Bede writing that 'no king of the Scots ever dared to make war against the English in Britain'.[3] Aethelfrith made other conquests, notably against the Welsh at the Battle of Chester in 616.[4]

Meanwhile, Edwin, son of Aelle, the former king of Deira, went into exile and it is upon Edwin that we concentrate. Edwin may have been brought up in Gwynedd. Here he would have surely met and lived alongside Cadwallon, son of the king of Gwynedd, and soon to be his most formidable enemy. It is certain he was soon in Mercia at the court of King Cearl, where he married Cearl's daughter, Cwenburg. Edwin's next place of refuge was in East Anglia under the protection of Raedwald.[5]

Edwin posed an obvious threat to Aethelfrith and accordingly, on hearing of Edwin's presence in East Anglia, Aethelfrith bribed Raedwald to kill him.

Bede then records that a 'loyal friend', probably the Italian missionary from Kent, Paulinus, appeared in a vision and advised Edwin that all would be well if he adopted the true faith. As it turned out, Raedwald, at the instigation of his wife, came to Edwin's aid and fought alongside him to defeat Aethelfrith at the Battle of the River Idle (between Gainsborough and Bawtry) in 616. In so doing, Edwin was installed as the king of Northumbria.[6]

On Raedwald's death, Edwin became the fourth of Bede's Bretwaldas. He had friendly relations with the people of Kent and married Aethelberg, daughter of King Aethelbert and Queen Bertha. According to Bede, the marriage was only agreed with the proviso that Edwin converted to Christianity. Accordingly, Aethelberg travelled north accompanied by her priest, Paulinus. The influence of Paulinus, Aethelberg, and the vision Edwin had while in East Anglia, all contributed to his acceptance of the Christian faith.[7] But it was his victory in a battle against Wessex to avenge an attempted assassination that sealed the matter. It seems that Cwichelm, king of Wessex, had dispatched an assassin to kill Edwin with a sword soaked in poison. The attempt was unsuccessful, but it had to be avenged and accordingly Edwin marched against the West Saxons, put them to the sword and defeated them.

Paulinus duly became the first Bishop of York and Edwin was baptised there in 627. Paulinus went on to found many churches and baptised the saintly Hilda of Whitby. It is likely that he baptised many more at Ad Gefrin, now identified with Yeavering in the Cheviots and since excavated by Dr Brian Hope-Taylor. Edwin's time was truly a time of peace in Northumbria, so much so that Bede said that 'a woman with her new-born child could walk across the whole island from sea to sea and take no harm'.[8]

Although insisting that idols should be destroyed, Pope Gregory was wise enough to allow certain pagan symbols to remain. Pagan names were retained for the days of the week, for example Tiw (Tuesday) and Thor (Thursday). Pagan temples were permitted to be converted to Christian churches and Goodmanham in the Yorkshire Wolds has now been identified as the site of Deira's foremost shrine. Here it was that Coifi, Edwin's chief priest, came to renounce the gods he had previously worshipped. In the presence of Edwin and Paulinus, Coifi 'girded with a sword and with spear in his hand mounted the king's stallion and rode up to the shrine… and cast into it the spear he carried and thus profaned it… and full of joy at his knowledge of the worship of the true God, told his companions to set fire to the shrine and its enclosures and destroy them'.[9]

Peace was short-lived. Northumbria became embroiled in a series of wars with Mercia and in 632, at the Battle of Hatfield Chase, Edwin was killed by the pagan forces of Penda of Mercia and of his brother-in-law, the Welsh Cadwallon of Gwynedd. Hatfield Chase is about eight miles north of Doncaster, but Edwin is reputably buried at Edwinstowe (Edwin's resting place) in Nottinghamshire. Edwin's defeat forced Paulinus to flee south with Aethelberg and her young daughter. He later became Bishop of Rochester, leaving James the Deacon behind at York. Cadwallon continued his devastating raids and, according to Bede, ruled Northumbria for one year.[10] Despite the courage of James the Deacon, it is difficult to say how viable the Christian faith would have been after Edwin's death. A warrior-based society would not have reacted favourably to the defeat of a newly converted king!

Meanwhile, during Edwin's reign, Oswald, the son of Aethelfrith, was exiled in Dalriada amongst the Irish who had settled in the west of Scotland. Oswald converted to Christianity at Iona and determined to regain Northumbria from the pagan Cadwallon. Before he gave battle, Bede recounts how he instructed his army to 'kneel together and ask the true and living God Almighty of His Mercy to protect us'. It was at the Battle of Heavenfield (the Heavenly field) – thought to be near Hexham on 'the northern side of the wall which the Romans had built from sea to sea' (Hadrian's Wall) – that Oswald, probably with the help of his friends from Dalriada, defeated and killed Cadwallon and so united Northumbria once more.[11] Oswald's rule in Northumbria now extended from the Humber, north into Scotland to the Forth of Firth and west to Strathclyde. He also had overlordship of the kingdom of Lindsey south of the Humber and must have had good relations with Wessex. He married Cyneberg, the daughter of the King Cynegils of Wessex, and was present when the Cynegils was baptised at Dorchester-on-Thames by Birinus, the first bishop of the West Saxons.[12]

Oswald was instrumental in spreading Christianity in Northumbria by inviting the Celtic monk Aidan to Lindisfarne (see later) and was the sixth Bretwalda identified by Bede. In his *History of the English Church and People*, Bede has nothing but praise for Oswald. He tells of an occasion when Oswald was feasting with Aidan, he heard that a group of poor people were begging outside. He immediately gave his 'silver dish full of dainties' to them, prompting Aidan to respond by taking Oswald's arm and uttering 'may this hand never perish'.[13] But conflict with Mercia continued and Oswald was killed in 642 at the Battle of Maresfield (thought to be near Oswestry or Winnick near Warrington) by the army of Penda of Mercia. That Oswald had conquered land south of the Humber (the kingdom of Lindsey) is confirmed by the refusal of the monks of Bardney Abbey in Lindsey to receive his relics 'because he was originally of another province and had ruled over them as a foreign king'. It took a miracle to persuade them to change their minds.[14]

Oswald was succeeded by his brother Oswy, who in the early years of his reign was under the domination of Penda. To cement his position in Deira, ruled at the time by a sub-king, Oswy married Enfleda, the daughter of Edwin, who, as we have seen, had fled south on her father's death and was living in Kent. Oswy then allied himself with Penda. A double marriage took place: Oswy's daughter married Peada, Penda's son, and his son married Penda's daughter. Significantly, Oswy's daughter's marriage to Peada was conditional on Peada becoming a Christian, thereby introducing the Christian faith to Mercia.[15] But the marriage pact did nothing to dissuade Penda from continuing his assaults on his northern neighbours. In 655, with a large army under his command, he invaded again. At first, Oswy tried to buy him off with 'an incalculable quantity of regalia and presents as the price of peace.'[16] Penda was unimpressed, and it has been speculated that this treasure is the Staffordshire Hoard discovered near Lichfield.[17] But against all the odds, Oswy was victorious in the following Battle of Winwaed, which took place near Loidis (Leeds). Oswy's surprising victory gave him overlordship of Mercia and much of Britain as well, and he became the seventh Bretwalda of Bede. But his ascendancy was short-lived. Within three years, prominent men in Mercia rebelled against Oswy and installed Penda's youthful son, Peada's younger brother, Wulfhere, as their king. Oswy died in 670 and was succeeded by his son Ecgfrith.

Ecgfrith campaigned, successfully at first, against the northern Picts and for a while held all the land between the Tweed and the Forth. He also defeated the Mercians in 674. But the Mercians sought revenge at the Battle of the river Trent in 678 and Ecgfrith's brother was killed. It took the intervention of the Archbishop of Canterbury, Theodore of Tarsus, to prevent further bloodshed.[18] The headstrong Ecgfrith was still intent on extending his rule on the Picts. In 685 he marched far into their territory but was defeated at the Battle of Nechtansmere.[19] By now, Northumbrian power was in decline and ascendancy was passing to Mercia.

The Northumbrian Church

It is generally accepted that Britain was Christian when the Romans withdrew in the late 4th and early 5th century. The degree to which the country remained Christian during and after the Anglo-Saxon onslaught is less clear. We do know, however, that at some time in the 5th century, Patrick, a Romano-Briton, was seized while still a youth from his family in Wales and taken to Ireland as a slave. He remained there for six years before escaping back to his family but later returned to Ireland once more to begin his missionary work. Monasteries were established in Ireland and it is from Ireland that the Celtic Church spread to Northumbria.[20]

Columba was an Irish monk, born in 521. He was a pupil at the famous Clonard Abbey on the river Boyne and founded many religious houses in Ireland. In 563, Columba set sail for Scotland. He settled and founded a monastery on the tiny island of Iona, off the west coast of the Isle of Mull, itself off the west coast of Scotland. By so doing he became the catalyst for the establishment of the Celtic Church in Northumbria. But there were differences between the Celtic Church and the Church of Rome. In contrast to the Roman Church, which was organised and hierarchal, there was no one Celtic Church, it was rather a series of independent monasteries, each led by an abbot.

It was while in exile amongst the Irish at Iona that Oswald first embraced the Celtic Church, and once king he determined to bring it to Northumbria by inviting the monks of Iona to send missionaries.[21] Corman came first but with little success, finding the Northumbrians an 'uncouth people'. Afterwards the monks sent Aidan, who in 635 became Bishop of Lindisfarne, a remote island off the north-east coast of Britain and near to Oswald's royal palace at Bamburgh. Aidan was a saintly man and stories abound about his good deeds. Once, in 651, Penda, in one of his assaults on the royal stronghold at Bamburgh, was successful in setting the place ablaze. But prayers were offered by Aidan and according to legend the wind immediately changed direction, blowing the choking smoke towards Penda's men, forcing them to turn tail and flee. Aidan hence became the patron saint of fire fighters.[22]

Lindisfarne was more a headquarters for Aidan; from there he set out on foot as a missionary, moving from place to place. The same practice was followed by other monks, notably Chad and Cedd, who later were instrumental in converting Mercia and Essex.

The Synod of Whitby

There were differences between the Roman and Celtic churches. A dispute arose because of conflicting ways of calculating the date of Easter – the most important festival in the Christian calendar. There was also the uncomfortable consequence of Oswsy's marriage to Enfleda, daughter of Edwin. When her father was killed, Enfleda escaped to Kent with Paulinus and her mother. There she observed the Roman tradition, which she retained when she became Oswy's wife and settled in Northumbria. The king and his spouse thus had different loyalties. It led to the awkwardness of one partner still fasting during Lent, while the other was celebrating with feasting after Easter.[23] To settle the matter a synod was held in 664 at the abbey at Whitby. Presiding at the synod were Oswy and Hilda, Abbess of Whitby. Colman, a monk from Lindisfarne, put the case for the Celtic Church. For Rome, there was Agilbert, latterly Bishop of Wessex, and Wilfrid. Putting the mathematical calculations to one side it seems that poor Colman was outmanoeuvred by Wilfrid, who dominated most of the discussions because of Agilbert's poor grasp of English. Wilfrid asserted that his mathematical tables were those used in Rome 'where the apostles St Peter and St Paul lived, taught, suffered and were buried'. Thus, given that 'St Peter holds the keys to the kingdom of heaven', Oswy, 'with a smile' (perhaps wry) came down on the side of Rome. From then onwards the Catholic Church predominated in Northumbria. It is certain that Oswy would have been influenced by the views of Wilfrid who argued fervently and forcibly for the Roman side, claiming the Celtic practice of calculating the date of Easter to be a sin. As for poor Colman, he abdicated as Bishop at Lindisfarne and returned with those in sympathy with him to Iona.

Northumbrian Saints

Wilfrid[24]

Wilfrid came from a noble Northumbrian family. He was born in 634, the same year as Cuthbert, who was perhaps the best loved of all Northumbrian saints. The contrast between the two men could not be greater; while Cuthbert lived a life of poverty, often as a recluse, Wilfrid was rich, argumentative and proud. He studied as a young man at Lindisfarne and then at the Kentish court. It was in Kent that he met the influential Benedict Biscop and came under the influence of the Roman church. In about 652 he set out on a pilgrimage to Rome, the first Englishman to go on a pilgrimage to the Holy See. While in Rome he met the Pope and became thoroughly inculcated in the Roman Church. On his return he remained for three years in Lyon before eventually returning to Northumbria as abbot of Ripon. Now firmly in the Roman camp he promptly expelled Abbot Eata and the saintly Cuthbert for their Celtic preferences.

After the Synod of Whitby, the powerful Wilfrid became Bishop of the Northumbrians. But who was to consecrate him? The Archbishop of Canterbury had recently died, and pride prevented Wilfrid from being consecrated by a humble local man. Accordingly, he travelled to Gaul to be consecrated by the Bishop of Paris. On his return, he found that another cleric, Chad, had been installed in his place and it took the intervention of Theodore of Tarsus, the new Archbishop of Canterbury, to overturn Chad's appointment and reinstall Wilfrid.

Part of Theodore's plan was to split the diocese of York into three separate parts. As Bishop of York, this would reduce Wilfrid's powers and he was furious, not least because all the new bishops had previously belonged to the Celtic Church. He also argued with King Ecgfrith who responded by expelling him. Determined to get redress, Wilfrid made another trip to Rome to appeal to the Pope, becoming the first Englishman to dispute royal authority by an appeal to the Holy See. And the support of the Pope he duly got. Wilfrid returned to Northumbria with a papal decree in his hand with instructions for his reinstatement as Bishop of York. Ecgfrith was not impressed and exiled Wilfrid once more, who then set sail for Sussex. Here, he founded a monastery at Selsey and began his conversion of the South Saxons, the last of the Germanic settlers to abandon their pagan beliefs. He remained in Sussex for five years until, in 686, on the death of Ecgfrith, and on the recommendation of Theodore – the pair having patched up their quarrel – he returned to York. But not for long, for no sooner was he was back in Northumbria than he fell out with Ecgfrith's successor, Aldfrith, forcing him to leave for the court of the king of Mercia and then for yet another journey to Rome to seek the Pope's support. He got it and returned as Bishop of Hexham. Wilfrid remained at Hexham for the rest of his life, dying a rich man in 709.

Cuthbert[25]

Although Wilfrid is perhaps a more interesting character, by far the best-loved Northumbrian saint was Cuthbert. He was born in 634, probably near Dunbar, and as a young man entered the monastery at Old Melrose. He accepted the verdict of the Synod of Whitby, came to Lindisfarne, adhered to the Roman customs and travelled throughout Northumbria, mainly on foot, to spread the Gospel. In 676, he retreated from the evils of the world and went to live as a hermit on one of the desolate Farne Islands, off the coast of Northumbria. Here, probably living in a cave, he was visited from time to time by those seeking the spiritual counsel of this holy man. Much against his inclinations – it would have meant him abandoning his solitary life – he was elected Bishop of Lindisfarne. He eventually agreed and, obeying the wishes of King Ecgfrith, was installed by Archbishop Theodore in 685. His calling for a hermit's life remained, however, and after only a short while he returned to the Farne Island, with only his beloved eider ducks as neighbours, and there he died. Cuthbert died on 20 March 687 and was buried at the Church of St Peter, Lindisfarne. But his story was far from over. Eleven years later his body was exhumed and found to be intact and in perfect condition – thereby giving him cult status.

In the late 8th century, Northumbria was attacked by the Vikings and by 875 the monks of Lindisfarne were so fearful that they abandoned their monastery, taking with them Cuthbert's coffin (and the Lindisfarne Gospels). Wandering as a travelling band of monks they were known as the 'Community of St Cuthbert'. The Vikings, under their leader, Halfdan, were firmly settled in Northumbria but Halfdan's son, Guthred, became a Christian and granted the monks a permanent settlement at Chester le Street. Here a cathedral was built, Cuthbert was laid to rest and the place became a centre of pilgrimage. In 995, Cuthbert was finally buried in Durham where his body remains to this day.

Cedd

Cedd was born in about 620, the eldest of four brothers, one of whom was Chad. He studied under Aidan at Lindisfarne and followed Aidan's example by leading a simple life free from the love of wealth or power. As we have seen, King Oswy married his daughter to Peada of Mercia on condition he became a Christian.[26] And it was Cedd, with a small company of priests, who made the journey to Mercia to begin the conversion of the pagan Mercians. He met with only limited success and so was sent instead on a mission to the East Saxons, eventually becoming their bishop.[27, 28]

Chad

Chad, like his brother Cedd, studied under Aidan at Lindisfarne. Early in his ministry he travelled to Ireland before succeeding Cedd as Bishop of the Northumbrians. So that he could install the fiery Wilfrid, Theodore of Tarsus asked Chad to step down, which he did 'with the greatest of humility'.[29] Theodore held Chad in the highest regard and therefore sent him, at the request of Wulfhere of Mercia, to complete the conversion of the Mercians begun by his brother Cedd. It was to Lichfield that Chad came and there he became bishop. Chad died in 672 and lies buried in Lichfield.[30]

Hilda[31]

Hilda was born in 614 and was brought up at the court of her great-uncle, King Edwin. She was baptised by Paulinus in 627 at the same time as Edwin but after his death at the Battle of Hatfield Chase, she left for East Anglia. She was invited back to Northumbria in 647 and one year later became Abbess of Hartlepool. By 657 she was abbess at the double monastery at Whitby where both Wilfrid and John of Beverley studied. It was Hilda who encouraged Caedmon, a cowherd at Whitby, famous now for his poetry. She also hosted the Synod of Whitby in 664.

Northumbrian Scholars

The Venerable Bede[32,33]

Bede is sometimes known as the 'Father of English History' and his *Ecclesiastical History of the English People*, completed in about 731, is without question the most important study of Anglo-Saxon England in the centuries following the departure of the Romans. At the age of seven, Bede entered the monastery of St Peter at Monkwearmouth under Benedict Biscop.

It was Biscop who founded the joint monasteries of Monkwearmouth (present-day Sunderland) and St Paul's at Jarrow. Biscop travelled to Rome on five occasions and returned with books and manuscripts to equip the library at Wearmouth, which became renowned throughout Christendom. It was here that Bede studied and produced all his sixty books.

He describes his life thus:

> I was born on the lands of this monastery (Monkwearmouth) and on reaching seven years of age I was entrusted by my family first to the most reverend Abbot Benedict and later to Abbot Ceolfrith for my

education. I have spent all the remainder of my life in this monastery and devoted myself entirely to the study of the Scriptures. And while I have observed the regular discipline and sung the choir offices daily in church, my chief delight has always been in study, teaching and writing. I was ordained deacon in my nineteenth year and priest in my thirtieth, receiving both these orders at the hands of the most reverend Bishop John at the direction of Abbot Ceolfrith. From the time of my receiving the priesthood until my fifty-ninth year, I have worked, both for my own benefit and that of my brethren, to compile short extracts from the works of the venerable Fathers on Holy Scripture and to comment on their meaning and interpretation.

Bede's best-known work is his *Ecclesiastical History of the English People*. In fact, it is a compilation of five books. The first describes the Church during the Roman occupation and the reconversion of the people of Kent by Augustine. The second details the consolidation of Christianity in Kent and its introduction to Northumbria. The third describes the growth of the Church in Northumbria and the Synod of Whitby. The fourth tells of Theodore as Archbishop of Canterbury and Wilfrid's mission to Sussex. The fifth book completes Bede's history. Bede died in 735. It is said that his body was stolen from Jarrow and in 1020 placed in Cuthbert's tomb in Durham Cathedral.

It was at the double monastery of Wearmouth and Jarrow that the *Codex Amiatinus* was produced and given to the Pope as a gift. It is the earliest surviving manuscript of St Jerome's translation of the Bible. Written at the time of Bede, this immense book of 1046 leaves of vellum is now in the Laurentian Library in Florence and has been described as the 'finest book in the world'.

Wood Carving of the Venerable Bede at St Paul's Church, Jarrow

Alcuin[34, 35]

Alcuin was a scholar of equal renown to Bede. He was born in Northumbria, probably in the 730s, and studied at York Minster for the first forty or fifty years of his life. It was while returning from a visit to Rome in the early 780s that he met the great European ruler Charlemagne, who invited him to join his court. Described as a 'man most learned in every field' Alcuin wrote textbooks on all manner of subjects – grammar, rhetoric, theology, astronomy and much more. He thrived at Charlemagne's court, taught Charlemagne himself and his sons as well as many eminent churchmen. In 794 he became Abbot of Tours and pupils were sent there from far and wide for instruction. Much of Alcuin's writings survive, including his exhortation to Archbishop Aethelheard of Canterbury (792–805), urging him to exert his authority over his bishops, writing that he 'must boldly raise the standard of the Holy Cross' and 'counsel your bishops carefully to work with all urgency for the word of life'. And 'to bring into the house of God the zeal for reading… and the study of books, that they may have among their number him whom they can elect as their pontiff'. He made two return visits to England but spent the rest of his life on the Continent, much distressed by Viking raids on Lindisfarne, observing that 'never before has so much terror appeared in Britain'. There can be no doubt that Alcuin's scholarship laid the foundation for teaching in the monasteries of northern Europe. He died in Tours in 804.

By the early 8th century, the power of Northumbria had declined, and it is to Mercia that we must now turn.

References

1. Bede, *The History of the English Church and People,* Book Two, Chapter 1
2. Ibid., Book Five, Chapter 24
3. Ibid., Book One, Chapter 34
4. Stenton, *Anglo-Saxon England, 3rd edition* (1971), p.78
5. Philip Holdsworth in Lapidge ed., *Blackwell Encyclopaedia of Anglo-Saxon England* (1999), p. 163
6. Bede, Book Two, Chapter 12
7. Ibid., Book Two, Chapter 9
8. Ibid., Book Two, Chapter 16

9. Leyser, *A Short History of the Anglo-Saxons* (2017), p. 29

10. Bede, Book Two, Chapter 20

11. Ibid., Book Three, Chapter 2

12. Venning, *The Anglo-Saxon Kings* (2011), p. 46

13. Bede, Book Three, Chapter 6

14. Ibid., Book Three, Chapter 11

15. Ibid., Book Three, Chapter 21

16. Ibid., Book Three, Chapter 24

17. Leyser, p. 42

18. Bede, Book Four, Chapter 21

19. Ibid., Book Four, Chapter 26

20. White, *St Patrick His Writings and Life* (1920) p. 31 and p. 54

21. Bede, Book Three, Chapter 1

22. Ibid., Book Three, Chapter 16

23. Wesley Stephens, in Lapidge ed. (1999), p. 155

24. Frodsham, *Cuthbert and the Northumbrian Saints* (2009) p. 83

25. Ibid., p. 57

26. Bede, Book Three, Chapter 21

27. Ibid., Book Three, Chapter 22

28. Ibid., Book Three, Chapter 23

29. Ibid., Book Four, Chapter 2

30. Ibid., Book Four, Chapter 3

31. Frodsham, p. 49

32. Dictionary of National Biography (2004), p.758

33. Patrick Wormald in Campbell, ed., *The Anglo-Saxons* (1982), p. 70

34. Mary Garrison in Lapidge, ed., (1999) p. 24

35. Leff, *Alcuin of York and the Foundation of Medieval Education* (1984)

Mercia

We have seen how Penda, who reigned from 626 to 655, was in frequent conflict with Northumbria. He is described by Bede 'as a most energetic member of the royal house of the Mercians,' and there is no doubt about his prowess as a military ruler. Penda was finally defeated and killed at the Battle of Winwaed (a river near Leeds) by King Oswy of Northumbria. Up until that time, however, he was a successful warrior and under him, Mercia became a power to be reckoned with. As well as Northumbria, he led successful campaigns against the West Saxons, and the Anglo-Saxon Chronicle and Bede record that he drove Cenwalh from his Wessex kingdom. This was in 645. Cenwalh had married Penda's sister but later rejected her and took another wife. Penda duly sought redress. Bede also tells us of Penda's attack on the East Angles. Their leader, Sigbert, mindful of his monastic vows and unwilling to fight himself, was dragged out of his monastery to motivate his men armed only with a stick. It was of little surprise that the East Angles were roundly defeated.[1]

Penda was Mercia's last pagan Anglo-Saxon king. But, he did tolerate Christian missionaries. As Bede records, 'King Penda did not forbid the preaching of the faith to any, even of his own Mercians who wished to listen.'[2] Christianity finally came to Mercia under Penda's son and successor, Peada. He wished for the hand of Aelflaed, daughter of Oswy of Northumbria, but Oswy would only grant permission if Peada and his Mercian people became Christian. Accordingly, Peada was baptised by Bishop Finan, and four priests, including the saintly Cedd, went to Mercia to convert his people.[2] It was at this time, while Peada was effectively Oswy's vassal, that the monastery at Medehamstede (later to become Peterborough) was founded. Peada's reign was short-lived. Bede informs us he was murdered 'through the treachery of his wife' in 656.[3] As for the details of this foul deed, we have none. For a short while afterwards, Oswy of Northumbria gained ascendancy in Mercian territory until three noblemen rebelled against Northumbrian rule and installed Wulfhere, Peada's younger brother, as king.[3]

Wulfhere was an altogether stronger leader. He embraced Christianity and was a friend and patron of Wilfrid of Northumbria. In Stephen of Ripon's biography of Wilfrid, he tells how Wulfhere 'invited Wilfrid with real affection to his territory' and rewarded him with 'many tracts of land (where Wilfrid) soon established minsters for the servants of God.'[4]

Wulfhere was to extend Mercian influence into Wessex. In 661, he attacked the West Saxons at Ashdown (Berkshire Downs) and in the same year raided the Isle of Wight and the Meon Valley. He gave land he had seized to his godson, Aethelwold, the king of the South Saxons, who had been converted by Wulfhere's friend, Wilfrid.[5] London also came under his influence when he transferred the bishopric of London to Wine, recently expelled from Winchester.[6] He also held sway in the east of England, for Bede describes the East Saxons as 'rulers… under Wulfhere, king of the Mercians.'[7] He married the daughter of the king of Kent and is likely to have had influence in that kingdom as well.[8]

Wulfhere exploited his power south of the Humber in 674 when he 'roused all the southern peoples' in a war against Ecgfrith of Northumbria. It was to no avail; although he survived the battle, Wulfhere's warriors were defeated and he died within a year to be succeeded by yet another son of Penda, Aethelred.[9]

The Tribal Hidage[10]

It is very likely that a document known as the Tribal Hidage originated in Mercia during Wulfhere's reign. It is a fascinating but also confusing document, an 11th century copy of which now resides in the British Library. No one knows precisely when it was compiled or for what purpose, but it lists assessments of land according to their hidage. A hide is an Anglo-Saxon term and means the amount of land sufficient to support a peasant and his family. Confusingly for 21st century readers, it cannot be related to a specific area of land, such as an acre, for it varied from one place to another and was dependent on the value of the land.

The Tribal Hidage could possibly be a compilation of tribute assessments which a powerful kingdom could extract from its subordinate kingdoms. It lists a total of thirty-four kingdoms south of the Humber. Mercia has 30,000 hides,

Wessex 100,000. But many smaller kingdoms were listed, some assessed at between 300 and 7000 hides. These, such as Hwicce at 7,000 hides, were mainly in Mercia, which is why the document is thought to originate there. However, there are other opinions; some say it was compiled later in the reign of Offa, or even in Northumbria. Despite all the uncertainty, it is still a very valuable document if only because it demonstrates that the concept of an Anglo-Saxon heptarchy is far too simple an interpretation. Within each major territory of the heptarchy there were many smaller kingdoms, some of which over time came to prominence but then declined.

The Domination of Mercia

Aethelred began his reign in 676 with a campaign against Kent. Bede, revealing his Northumbrian loyalty, records that Aethelred's 'wicked soldiers' destroyed the city of Rochester.[11] In 679, Aethelred turned his attention towards his northern neighbour when Mercia and Northumbria faced each other in battle again. Aethelred avenged his brother (Wulfhere) by defeating Ecgfrith at the Battle of the river Trent. It was at this point that the saintly Archbishop of Canterbury, Theodore, stepped in and 'smothered the flames of this awful peril by his wholesome advice' and thereby brought a lasting peace to the two warring nations.[12] By so doing, any residual claims Northumbria might have to supremacy ended. But Mercian control of the south of England had still to be won. It was hampered by the strong kings, Caedwalla and Ine, who were both rulers of Wessex.

It was during Aethelred's reign that the vast see of Lichfield was split into dioceses at Leicester, Worcester, Lichfield, Dorchester and Hereford – all part of Archbishop Theodore's reorganisation of the church. Aethelred, a pious man and friend of Wilfrid, abdicated as ruler in 704 and entered the monastery at Bardney, where he died. There followed the short reigns of Cenred (Wulfhere's son) and Ceolred (Aethelred's son). It was Ceolred who, according to St Boniface, died of a fit brought on 'while feasting in splendour with his companions.' There followed the reign of Aethelbald, a cousin of Ceolred, and so began, in 716, a period of Mercian dominance, continued by Offa, which was to last for eighty years.

Aethelbald spent his early years in exile, banished by his cousin Ceolred to the desolate and damp low-lying eastern Fens.[13] Here he met the saintly Guthlac (see Lincolnshire, Crowland) living as a hermit who – maybe in Aethelbald's dream world – prophesised that one day he would be king. In 716, two years after Guthlac died, Aethelbald did become king and in thanksgiving founded Crowland Abbey on St Bartholomew's Day. He was to continue as king until 757, the longest reign of any Anglo-Saxon monarch.

By 731, according to Bede, 'all England south of the Humber was under his control'.[14] He also held London, which Bede describes as 'an emporium of many nations who came to it by land and sea'.[15] The Ishmere Charter, which granted land near the river Stour (Worcestershire) in 736, describes Aethelbald as a 'king not only of the Mercians but also of all provinces which are called by the general name of South English'. The same document names him 'King of Britain'.[16] Aethelbald's overriding influence is further attested by the fact that three consecutive Archbishops of Canterbury came from Mercia – Tatwine, Norhelm and Cuthbert.

Aethelbald held control of Wessex, but his rule was fragile. The Anglo-Saxon Chronicle records that he captured the manor of Somerton (Somerset) in 733. Four years later he ravaged Northumbria.[17] But the men of Wessex did not submit without a fight and 'fought strongly against King Aethelbert' in 740 and even 'put Aethelbald to flight at Beorhford' (Burford) in 752.

As for his character, Aethelbald fell victim to the wrath of St Boniface who railed against his sins: stealing money belonging to the Church, imposing forced labour on clergy, fornicating with nuns and violating Church principles. In fairness, Boniface also praises Aethelbald for his almsgiving, peaceful rule and endowment of monasteries.[18] Despite all his success, Aethelbald came to an unfortunate end – murdered by his bodyguards at Seckington, near Tamworth. He lies buried at Repton.[19]

Aethelbald was succeeded by Beornred, but a stronger man was waiting. His name was Offa, a descendent of Penda's brother. Offa soon 'put Beornred to flight and attempted to conquer the Mercian kingdom with sword and bloodshed.'[20] He then set about consolidating Mercian authority and by 765 his overlordship of Kent was secured.[21] This is not to say Offa had it all his own way and that his rule was never challenged. The Anglo-Saxon Chronicle tells us that, in 776, 'the Mercians and the people of Kent fought at Otford' (near Sevenoaks). The outcome of the battle is uncertain and there is no record of Offa prevailing. That Mercia and Offa may have been on the losing side is suggested by the fact that the Kentish sub-king lived on for a number of years and that Offa's name is absent from charters during this period.[22] Regardless of what happened, however, as confirmed by later charters, by 785 Offa regarded Kent as a province of the Mercian kingdom and the same went for Sussex.[23] It is also clear that Offa was active in East Anglia, the Anglo-Saxon Chronicle recording that in 794 he had Aethelbert, a local king, beheaded. This was a most barbarous act. Aethelbert wanted to marry Offa's daughter and for this was brutally beheaded near to Hereford. Some say Offa's queen, Cwenthryth, was behind the foul deed, but whatever the case, it had in its cruelty no precedence. It was the only execution of a king by a fellow sovereign in Anglo-Saxon history.[24]

Offa had control of London and its environs and minted coins there. A charter of 767 records that 'I, Offa, by the divine controlling grace, king of the Mercians, will concede and grant most willingly to Stithberht, a venerable man possessed of an abbot's charge, land of thirty hides in Middlesex (Harrow on the Hill)'. The charter was witnessed by Offa himself and Jaenberht, Archbishop of Canterbury.[25]

There were further hostile encounters in Wessex and in 779 'Cynnewulf of Wessex and Offa fought around Bensington' (Benson). Mercian influence in Wessex was further confirmed when Beorhtric (Cynewulf's successor) married Offa's daughter, Eadburh. The Chronicle records that Beorhtric helped Offa because 'he had his daughter as his queen.' Eadburh seems to have been a formidable lady who had 'power throughout almost the entire kingdom' and that 'she began to behave like a tyrant after the manner of her father'.[26]

King Offa of Mercia is forever remembered for the earthwork, Offa's Dyke, which Asser (Alfred the Great's biographer) tells us 'ran from sea to sea'. Recent research has established that only sixty-four miles of the bank dates from one specific period. This section runs from Rushock Hill in Herefordshire to Llanfynydd in Clwyd. The dyke is made up of a ditch, six feet deep, and to the east a rampart of about twenty-five feet in height. The whole structure is sixty feet across. Evidence suggests that it was built to give protection against assaults from the Welsh. This is based on the fact that its route is sited so as to give a clear view to the west, so giving early warning of an advancing enemy. To the north is Wat's Dyke, running from the river Vrnwy to the Dee estuary, a total of forty-nine miles.[27] It has been estimated that at least 5,000 and perhaps as many as 125,000 men were employed in its construction. Such numbers pay testament to Offa's organising ability.

In 786, Pope Adrian sent George, Bishop of Ostia, and Theophylact, Bishop of Todi, to England – the first mission to England since St Augustine – to guide the king's nobles and clergy. The legates would have met Offa as well as

Offa's Dyke, near Forden, Powys

Jaenberht, Archbishop of Canterbury. Jaenberht was at odds with Offa, probably because of his intervention in Kent and possibly because of Jaenberht's refusal to officiate at Offa's son's coronation. In response, Offa persuaded the pope of the need for a third archbishopric and that it should be in his own kingdom. Offa is therefore renowned for establishing an Archbishopric at Lichfield, where in 787, Archbishop Hygeberht (Bishop of Lichfield at the time) received the pallium from Rome. The great scholar Alcuin later wrote of this remarkable event that the archbishopric at Lichfield had been founded 'not, as it seems, by reasonable consideration, but by a certain desire for power.' But Alcuin also had praise for Offa, writing of his efforts to 'instruct in the precepts of God' and for founding many churches and monasteries, including St Alban's Abbey.[28] Predictably, the archbishopric came to an end in 803, soon after Offa's death in 796.

Attempts were made for Offa's daughter to marry Charles, the son of the great European ruler, Charlemagne. Foolishly, Offa demanded a like-for-like reciprocation whereby his son, Eigfrith, would marry Charlemagne's daughter. This would have put Offa on an equal footing with Charlemagne, who would have none of it. The fall-out led for a while to both countries barring each other's merchants from trading in their respective countries.[29] An alternative explanation could be that Charlemagne was harbouring Egbert of Wessex, a rival for paramountcy in Wessex and exiled in Francia by Offa and his son-in-law, Beorhtric.

Much is made of letters between Offa and Charlemagne and on them Offa's prestige rests. A letter from Charlemagne, written in 796, clearly shows that the previous dispute had been patched up. Charlemagne writes that 'between royal dignitaries and exalted personages of the world, the keeping of the laws of friendship… is wont to be of profit to many.' He then refers to 'securing the links of love' and addresses Offa as 'most beloved brother.' The letter also guarantees safe passage for pilgrims and protection for merchants. It also mentions, mysteriously, black stones that Offa had requested Charlemagne to send to him.[30] These rare stones have since been identified as black porphyry columns sent from Ravenna to adorn Charlemagne's chapel at Aachen.[31] The reference to merchants reminds us that it was at this time that there was a marked increase in trade and the growth of emporia such as Lundenwic, Ipswich and Southampton.

Offa died in 796 and with him died Mercia's domination of the Anglo-Saxon world. What are we to make of him? Opinions differ. Some compare his achievements with those of Alfred the Great. Others are more reserved and emphasise his love of power rather than any desire he may have had for English unity.

References

1. Bede, Book Three, Chapter 18
2. Ibid., Book Three, Chapter 21
3. Ibid., Book Three, Chapter 24
4. Blair, *The Church in Anglo-Saxon Society* (2005), p. 92
5. Anglo-Saxon Chronicle, 661
6. Bede, Book Three, Chapter 7
7. Bede, Book Three, Chapter 30
8. Venning, *The Anglo-Saxon Kings* (2011), p. 80
9. Simon Keynes, in Lapidge ed., *Blackwell Encyclopaedia of Anglo-Saxon England* (1999), p. 490
10. John Blair, in Lapidge ed. (1999), p. 455
11. Bede, Book Four, Chapter 12
12. Ibid., Book Four, Chapter 21
13. Kirby, *The Earliest English Kings* (1990), p. 110
14. Bede, Book Five, Chapter 23

15. Ibid., Book Two, Chapter 3
16. Patrick Wormald, in Campbell, ed., *The Anglo-Saxons* (1982), p. 95–7
17. Anglo-Saxon Chronicle, 737
18. Fletcher, *Who's Who in Roman and Anglo-Saxon England*, (1989), p. 98–100
19. Anglo-Saxon Chronicle, 757
20. Simon Keynes, in Lapidge, ed. (1999), p. 340
21. Stenton, *Anglo-Saxon England* (1971), p. 207
22. Venning, *The Anglo-Saxon Kings* (2011), p. 113
23. Stenton, p. 208
24. Venning, p. 115
25. Whitelock (ed), *English Historical Documents 500–1042* (1979), p. 500
26. Keynes and Lapidge eds., *Alfred the Great, Asser's Life of King Alfred and other Contemporary Sources* (1983), p. 71
27. Margaret Worthington, in Lapidge, ed. (1999), p. 341
28. Yorke, *King and Kingdoms of Early Anglo-Saxon England* (1990), p. 116–8
29. Stenton, p. 220
30. Whitelock, ed. (1979), p. 848
31. Leyser, *The Anglo-Saxons* (2017), p. 83

Wessex

For much of the 7th century Wessex came under repeated military assaults from Mercia. But after the death of Wulfhere of Mercia in 674, there was a period of relative peace. From about 686, Wessex was ruled by Caedwalla, described by Bede as 'a daring young man of the royal house of the West Saxons'.[1] Caedwalla conducted campaigns against Surrey and Kent and soon brought Sussex and the Isle of Wight under his control. In thanks for his conquest of the Isle of Wight he gave a large swathe of land to his friend, Wilfrid of Northumbria, who brought Christianity to the people of Sussex, the last Anglo-Saxon kingdom to be converted.[2] Although nominally a Christian, Caedwalla had never been baptised. He is often portrayed as a particularly brutal man who '[wasted] the province [of Sussex] with slaughtering and plunder' and 'strove to exterminate all the natives [of the Isle of Wight] and replace them with settlers from his own province.' Caedwalla was wounded while fighting on the Isle of Wight and in 688, he abdicated. He left Wessex and travelled to Rome, perhaps acting on the advice of Wilfrid, to be baptised by Pope Sergius who gave him the name Peter. He died shortly afterwards and lies buried in St Peter's Church, described as 'King of the Saxons'. Caedwalla was succeeded by Ine, who reigned for thirty-seven years, from about 689 to 727.[3] Ine acquired land in the west in the British kingdom of Dumnonia (Devon and Cornwall) and extended Wessex control to the river Tamar, but his hold on Surrey, Sussex and Kent was weakened.[4]

Ine is remembered for his law codes of 694. They survive only because they were added as supplements to the law codes of Alfred the Great and, if Alfred was selective in their incorporation, may not be complete. Ine was a Christian and his laws promoted Christianity. For instance: a child is to be baptised within thirty days; if not, thirty shillings' compensation is to be paid. And, if a slave works on a Sunday at his master's command he is to be freed and his master to pay a thirty-shillings fine. If a slave works without his master's knowledge he is to be flogged.[5] The laws of Aethelbert of Kent first introduced the concept of wergild and an excellent example of its use is found early in the reign of Ine. Caedwalla had installed his brother, Mul, as a sub-king of Kent but Mul was 'burned' in a Kentish revolt.[6] In payment, the Anglo-Saxon Chronicle records that in 694 'the people of Kent made terms with Ine and paid him 30,000 pence because they had burnt Mul'.[7]

Ine's laws have the earliest references to shires, and it is possible that he may have subdivided Wessex into the present-day counties of Hampshire, Wiltshire, Dorset, Somerset and Devon.[8] They also confirm the existence of an open field system of farming and according to Stenton 'the beginnings of a manorial economy'.[9]

Ine was to follow in the footsteps of Caedwalla and in 726 abdicated and travelled to Rome to die – evidently a move to ease his passage to heaven. Wessex was then ruled by a series of kings, but throughout this period Mercia was dominant. Wessex asserted its ascendency once more in the reign of Egbert, who came to the throne in 802. But first we must consider St Boniface, 'Apostle of the Germans.'

St Boniface[10]

Boniface, born Winfrid, stands alongside Alcuin in his influence on continental Europe and is perhaps the best known of the Anglo-Saxon missionaries. It is thought he was born in Crediton in 672 and studied first at a Benedictine monastery at Adescancastre (near Exeter) and later at Nursling near Southampton. It was always his wish to convert the Frisians and in 716 he travelled there as a missionary. He was unsuccessful and was forced to return to Nursling. In 723 he was in Fritzlar in Northern Hesse where he came upon a 'holy tree' dedicated to the Germanic god Thor. The story goes that, in defiance, Boniface promptly set about chopping the tree down and challenged Thor to strike him dead. Instead a great wind descended and blew the tree to the ground. So amazed were the onlookers that they immediately discarded all belief in Thor and converted to Christianity. Fritzlar Cathedral stands on the site today. In 732, Boniface was in Rome where Pope Gregory II appointed him Archbishop of Germany. At the time he was under the care of Charles Martel, the Frankish king, who established four dioceses in Boniface's see of Mainz.

In 747, Boniface wrote to Cuthbert, Archbishop of Canterbury, urging reform of the Anglo-Saxon church. The result was the Council of Clovesho at which secular practices in monasteries were condemned. (The location of Clovesho is unknown but Keynes has suggested it may have been at Brixworth).[11]

But Boniface had still to convert the Frisians. Accordingly, he travelled there in 754 but, together with his compatriots, was killed in the town of Dokkum, in the Netherlands. He is buried at the abbey at Fulda.[11]

Egbert

Egbert was born in about 770 and spent his early years in exile in Francia, forced there by Offa and the then king of Wessex, Beorhtric, who was married to Offa's daughter. When Beorhtric died, Egbert became king of Wessex in 802, probably supported by the Frankish king, Charlemagne.

Wessex's star soon began to rise. The Anglo-Saxon Chronicle tells us that 'the people of Wiltshire had a victory' over an incursion from Mercia.[12] Some years later, in 815, Egbert 'ravaged Cornwall from east to west'.[13] In 825 he won a decisive battle against Mercian forces under Beornwulf at the Battle of Ellandun, thought to be at Wroughton, near Swindon. Egbert capitalised on his victory at Ellandun by sending an army to Kent under his son, Aethelwulf (father of Alfred the Great). Meanwhile East Anglia sought Egbert's help against Mercia. All these conflicts were decisive in ending Mercian dominance of Southern England.[14] Four years later Egbert drove Wiglaf out of Mercia and forced Northumbria to submit. As it turned out, Wiglaf may have restored Mercian independence in 830,[15] but by then a much greater threat faced Egbert and, for that matter, all the Anglo-Saxon kingdoms: invaders from Scandinavia had arrived.

In 836 Egbert suffered a crushing defeat at the hands of the Vikings. The Anglo-Saxon Chronicle records that 'King Egbert fought against a crew of thirty-five ships at Carhampton (Somerset) and a great slaughter was made there, and the Danes had possession of the battlefield.'[16] Two years later the invading Vikings combined with the Britons of Cornwall and met Egbert at Hingston Down (Cornwall). He succeeded in putting the 'Danes to flight'[17] but more Danish raids were to follow. Egbert did not see them. He died in 839 and was succeeded by his son Aethelwulf.

King Alfred and the Danes

The first record of a Viking (a general term for invaders from Norway, Sweden or Denmark) raid was in the year 789 when the Anglo-Saxon Chronicle records that 'for the first time three ships of Northmen (came)' and landed at Portland.

The king's men went out to meet them, thinking they were traders. They were sadly misguided; the Danes promptly slaughtered them.[18] Later, the Chronicle records that in 793:[19]

> Dire portents appeared over Northumbria and sorely frightened the people. They consisted of immense whirlwinds and flames of lightning and fiery dragons were seen flying in the air. A great famine immediately followed these signs and a little after that in the same year, on 8th January, the ravages of heathen men miserably destroyed God's church on Lindisfarne with plunder and slaughter.

Alcuin responded to the events with similar sentiments: 'never before had such an atrocity been seen.'

Other sporadic raids followed – on Iona in 794 and Ireland one year later. To begin with, the Northmen came only as raiders looking for treasure, but in 851 the Danes wintered for the first time in England on the Isle of Thanet. The Chronicle records that '350 ships came into the mouth of the Thames and stormed Canterbury and London… and went south across the Thames into Surrey'.[20] Raids got ever more frequent and ever bloodier. By the 860s the Viking leaders Ivor the Boneless, Halfdon and Ubbe Ragnarsson had subjugated all of East Anglia and Northumbria. Their army was often referred to as the Great Heathen Army and it was during this time that King Edmund of East Anglia was defeated; by tradition tied to a tree and shot with arrows.

Continuing with the story of the kingdom of Wessex, King Aethelwulf had five sons. In 855 he visited Rome but died soon after his return. At first Wessex was ruled jointly by two of his elder sons but by 868 Aethelwulf's fourth son, Aethelred, ruled alone. The youngest son was Alfred, who has gone down in history as the only English king to be called 'Great'. Alfred first saw conflict in 868 when he accompanied his brother, King Aethelred, to besiege the Vikings at Nottingham.[21] There followed a series of battles in Wessex, first in late December 870 at Englefield, near the River Kennet, about six miles west of Reading.[22] The Saxons were victorious, but their victory was short-lived for they soon succumbed to the Danes at Reading who 'like wolves burst out of all the gates and joined battle with all their might'.[23]

The men of Wessex were forced to retreat to Ashdown on the Berkshire Downs. Here, legend tells us that Alfred summoned his followers by blowing into a large sarsen stone with holes in it. It issued a mighty booming sound so

Statue of King Alfred the Great at his birthplace of Wantage

loud that it could be heard for many miles around. The stone can still be seen today at Kingston Lisle (324871). Kingstanding Hill, west of Streatley, has been suggested as the site of the ensuing battle.[24] Despite the ferocity of the Danes (led by Halfdon and Bagsecg), Alfred was triumphant and Bagsecg was killed. Further skirmishes followed but Alfred, now king, was forced to pay off the Danes with money. The Danes then withdrew to London. Hoards of coins dating from this time have been found in excavations in London and the surrounding area, confirming Alfred's cash payment.[25]

By 876, the Danes were led by Guthrum and his rule prevailed in Mercia and Northumbria. But his sights were set on Wessex and in 876 he sailed into Poole Harbour to meet Alfred at Wareham. The outcome was inconclusive. The Danish fleet sailed west but 'encountered a great storm at sea and 120 ships were lost at Swanage'.[26] Despite promising to leave in peace, the Danish army advanced on Exeter before returning to Mercia. The following winter (878) the Danes advanced again to Chippenham where the Chronicle records that 'they occupied the land of the West Saxons and settled there and drove a great part of the people across the sea and conquered most of the others and the people submitted to them except King Alfred.'[27]

After this setback, Alfred stood alone. He took refuge in the lonely Somerset marshes at Athelney. It was here in the home of the wife of a swineherd, so the legend tells us, that he was asked to keep an eye on some cakes, baking in the woman's stove. So preoccupied was he in his thoughts on how to regain his kingdom, that he let the cakes burn. The Anglo-Saxon Chronicle takes up the story:

> Then in the seventh week after Easter he [Alfred] rode to 'Egbert's Stone' east of Selwood, and there came to meet him all the people of Somerset and of Wiltshire and of that part of Hampshire which was on

this side of the sea, and they rejoiced to see him. And then after one night he went from that encampment to Iley and after another night to Eddington and there fought against the whole army, put it to flight, and pursued it as far as the fortress and stayed there a fortnight. And then the enemy gave him preliminary hostages and great oaths that they would leave his kingdom and promised that their king would receive baptism and they kept their promise. Three weeks later, King Guthrum, with thirty of the men who were the most important in the army came (to him) at Aller, which is near Athelney, and the king stood sponsor to him at his baptism.[27]

Such was Alfred's great triumph and upon these events his fame rests. They were underpinned, as we shall see, by his religious faith and love of learning.

The Peace of Wedmore (as it became known) was sealed and Alfred entertained Guthrum (now renamed Aethelstan) for twelve days and nights and 'freely bestowed many excellent treasures on him and his men'.[28] The treaty that Alfred and Guthrum agreed is preserved at Corpus Christi College, Cambridge, and by its terms, Mercia was split in two. Alfred ceded what became known as the Danelaw, the boundary of which with Wessex ran from the Thames, along the River Lea and then along Watling Street to Chester and the north-west. All to the east now lay under Danish control. Significantly, Alfred was able to restore the city of London 'and made it habitable again'[29] and entrusted it to the care of Aethelred, ruler of Mercia. That Mercia was now under Alfred's control was confirmed by Aethelred's marriage to Aethelfleda, Alfred's daughter.

After his victory at Eddington, Alfred lost no time in reorganising his military defences. He reformed the fyrd (army) into a standing army, enlarged the navy and built a series of garrisons (fortified towns) known as burhs. Burhs were vast earthen walls surrounded by ditches; the one at Wareham in Hampshire is a good example and is readily visible today. A document was produced, probably in Alfred's reign, but if not, in that of his son, Edward the Elder, called the Burghal Hidage. It lists the burhs and specifies that each 5½ yards of wall had to be secured by four men. One man would be provided from each hide of land and thus the number of hides indicates the number of men needed to secure the fortress.[30] Alfred's defensive system of burhs was a remarkable achievement. They were strategically placed; nowhere in his kingdom was more than twenty miles from one, or to put it another way, within one day's march of his army. They were either fortifications salvaged from abandoned Roman towns, e.g.

Winchester, iron age forts, e.g. Porchester, or new sites altogether such as Wallingford, Wareham and Cricklade.[31] The expense, both to build and then to maintain them, must have presented astonishing demands on his nobles. And the mere fact that they complied – albeit sometimes reluctantly – confirms the power and influence that Alfred wielded.

While it is incorrect to say that Alfred founded the English navy, he certainly strengthened it. The Anglo-Saxon Chronicle in 896 reports that King Alfred had:

> long ships built to oppose the Danish warships. They were almost twice as long as the others. Some had sixty oars, some more. They were both swifter and steadier and also higher than the others. They were built neither on the Frisian nor the Danish pattern, but as it seemed to him himself that they could be most useful.[32]

Alfred's accomplishments in Wessex cannot be underestimated. However, Viking raids in England continued. Many were from Francia by Vikings who had previously settled there. For the most part they were put down, including by Alfred's son-in-law, Aethelred, for those directed on Mercia. But military conquests were just one part of Alfred's achievements. He was a learned man and built on the laws of his predecessors, Aethelbert of Kent and Ine. He had his own series of laws and significantly he likened them to those of Moses and thus implied an unbroken continuum from Moses to Christ and to his own day.[33]

Much can be garnered of Alfred's love of learning from the preface to his translation of Gregory the Great's *Pastoral Care* – a work which outlines the qualities required of a man who rules over others. In the preface, Alfred laments how in times gone by there were:

> men of learning… throughout England, both in religious and secular orders; and how there were happy times then throughout England. [And then] how people from abroad sought wisdom and instruction in this country; and how nowadays, if we wished to acquire these things we would have to seek them outside. [Also], remember what punishments befell us in this world when we ourselves did not cherish learning nor transmit it to other men.

Alfred also makes an excellent case for books to be translated into English:

I recalled how the Law was first composed in the Hebrew language, and thereafter, when the Greeks learned it, they translated it into their own language and all other books as well. The Romans, after they had mastered them, translated them all through learned interpreters into their own language. Similarly, all the other Christian peoples turned some part of them into their own language. Therefore, it seems to me better – if it seems to you – that we too should turn into the language that we all can understand certain books which are the most necessary for all men to know.[34]

A copy of Alfred's translation of *Pastoral Care* was sent to each bishopric in his realm. He also translated Boethius's *Consolation of Philosophy* and the *Soliloquies* of St Augustine of Hippo.

Alfred died in 899. He was buried at Old Minster in Winchester, his remains later translated to New Minster and finally to Hyde Abbey. He was succeeded by his son, Edward the Elder.

Edward the Elder and the Danelaw

Edward the Elder deserves greater recognition; his victories over the Danes were significant and paved the way for a united England. It could be well argued that he also should be styled 'Great'. But it was not without difficulty that he inherited his father's kingdom. There was a rival who had a legitimate claim to the throne and he was Aethelwold, the son of Aethelred (King Alfred's predecessor). Aethelwold was quick to rebel. In 900, the Chronicle relates how 'the Atheling, Aethelwold, Edward's father's brother's son, rode and seized the residences at Wimborne [where his father was buried] and at Twineham' [present-day Christchurch]. 'Then the king [Edward] rode with the army to the encampment at Badbury, near Wimborne.' Aethelwold refused to give battle with Edward and under cover of darkness defected to Northumbria and the Danish army. Edward was then immediately crowned king at Kingston upon Thames.[35]

But Aethelwold was still at large and now allied to the Danes. In 901, he landed in Essex and rallied the Danish army in East Anglia to move against Mercia and Wessex. Aethelwold and his Danish allies were successful in reaching the Thames at Cricklade, but Edward was quick to retaliate and ravaged the land in Cambridgeshire between the Devil's Dyke, the Fleam Dyke and the river Ouse.[36] Edward then retreated but the Kentish warriors, fighting alongside him, although ordered to disband, refused to do so and were ambushed by the Danes, with Aethelwold amongst their company. Significantly for Edward, now safely back in Wessex, Aethelwold was killed at the ensuing Battle of Holme (perhaps Holme in Huntingdonshire), his death thus establishing Edward as king without rival.[37] Edward promptly fought back and sacked East Anglia before retreating to the south.

After the defeat of Aethelwold there was a period of relative peace but war began again in 909 when the Danes went on the offensive once more. After harrowing the south-west, they moved up the River Severn before they were overcome at the so-called Battle of Tettenhall, near Wolverhampton.[38] (In fact the battle was fought at nearby Wednesfield.)

The Danes had settled in the area east of Watling Street (the Danelaw) for the best part of twenty-five years. Place names in Yorkshire, Lincolnshire and Leicestershire – names ending in '–by' and '–thorpe' – identify their settlements, for example, Grimsby and Scunthorpe. Having settled and begun to till the land, their chief concern was to retain their own customs. They were subject to their own laws and divided their land into wapentakes rather than the hundreds of Anglo-Saxon custom. (A wapentake means taking of weapons and refers to an agreement at an assembly demonstrated by brandishing weapons.)[39] For the most part a wapentake can be taken to be equivalent to a hundred.

But Edward's ambition was to retake the Danelaw. In the following years, he moved against the Danes, helped in no small way by his sister, Aethelflaed, 'Lady of the Mercians'. Aethelflaed was a formidable woman. Her husband, Aethelred, died in 911 and for the following eight years she ruled Mercia alone and led military campaigns against the Danes. Burhs were built by her at Bridgnorth, Tamworth, Stafford and elsewhere. That she held sway in Mercia enabled Edward to concentrate his attacks on the Danes in the South. Bedford submitted to Edward in 914/5, Northampton, Huntingdon, Colchester and Cambridge in 917, followed by Stamford and Nottingham in 918. Meanwhile, the 'Lady of the Mercians' took Derby and Leicester; York alone remaining in Danish hands.[40]

Aethelflaed died in 918 and was succeeded in Mercia by her brother, King Edward the Elder, who thus ruled over both kingdoms of Wessex and Mercia. It was a personal triumph for Edward, but he still faced difficulties from the Vikings in Northumbria. In 902, Viking settlers in Ireland were expelled from

Dublin. Ragnal, their leader, immediately turned his attention to England, and via the Isle of Man and Cumbria, settled in Northumbria. In response, the Northumbrian leader, Eadwulf, sought help from King Constantine of Scotland. The issue was settled in 918 at the Battle of Corbridge. Ragnal prevailed and Northumbria and York fell to the Vikings.[41] A controversial entry in the Anglo-Saxon Chronicle for 920 informs us that at Bakewell, in the Peak District, Edward met a grand company of men – the king of the Scots, the Viking Ragnal, and the sons of Eadwulf, all who dwelled in Northumbria, plus the king of the Strathclyde Welsh. Supposedly, they all submitted to Edward and accepted him as their lord.[42] Recently, scholars have questioned the authenticity of the Bakewell meeting, asserting that Edward was in no position to proclaim his authority in such a way and pointing out that there is no other written confirmation of such a meeting. But whether the Chronicle's report is accurate or not, Edward's reputation stands firm. Edward died in 924, engaged in fighting the Welsh at Farndon-Upon-Dee. He was buried at New Minster, Winchester, and then at Hyde Abbey. Edward was succeeded in Mercia by his eldest son Aethelstan and in Wessex by Aelfweard, his second son. But Aelfweard died within days and accordingly Aethelstan took control over both kingdoms.

References

1. Bede, Book Four, Chapter 15
2. Ibid., Book Four, Chapter 16
3. Ibid., Book Five, Chapter 7
4. Stenton, *Anglo-Saxon England* (1971), p. 73
5. Whitelock ed., *English Historical Documents* (1979), p. 398
6. Stenton, p. 70
7. Anglo-Saxon Chronicle, 694
8. B.A.E. Yorke in Lapidge, ed., *Blackwell Encyclopaedia of Anglo Saxon England* (1999), p. 251
9. Stenton, p. 313–4
10. Andy Orchard in Lapidge, ed., p. 69
11. Keynes (1993)
12. Anglo-Saxon Chronicle, 802
13. Ibid., 815
14. Stenton, p. 231

15. Ibid., p. 232–3
16. Anglo-Saxon Chronicle, 836
17. Ibid., 838
18. Ibid., 789
19. Ibid., 793
20. Ibid., 851
21. Stenton, p. 248
22. Abels, *Alfred the Great* (1998), p. 127
23. Keynes and Lapidge, eds., *Alfred the Great, Asser's Life of King Alfred* (1983), p. 78
24. Peddie, *Alfred the Good Soldier* (1989), p. 81
25. Abels, p. 140
26. Anglo-Saxon Chronicle, 876–7
27. Ibid., 878
28. Keynes and Lapidge, eds., p. 85
29. Ibid., p. 98
30. Simon Keynes in Lapidge, ed. (1999), p. 76
31. P. Wormald in Campbell, ed., *The Anglo-Saxons* (1982), p. 152
32. Anglo-Saxon Chronicle, 896
33. P. Wormald in Campbell, ed., p. 157
34. Keynes and Lapidge, eds. (1983), p. 125
35. Anglo-Saxon Chronicle, 900
36. Ibid., 903
37. Stenton, p. 322
38. Ibid., p. 323
39. Sean Miller in Lapidge, ed., p. 467
40. Lesley Abrams in Higham and Hill, eds., *Edward the Elder* (2001), p. 138
41. Leyser, *The Anglo-Saxons* (2017), p. 109
42. Anglo-Saxon Chronicle, 920

Anglo-Saxon England

Edward the Elder was succeeded by his son, Aethelstan, who was brought up in Mercia at the court of his aunt, Aethelflaed, Lady of the Mercians. It is more than likely that he accompanied his aunt in her many military campaigns.[1] As a child, Aethelstan got off to an excellent start in life when his grandfather, Alfred the Great, presented the young boy with a scarlet cloak, a belt with gems and a sword with a gilded scabbard. He was crowned king at Kingston-upon-Thames, the traditional boundary between Mercia and Wessex.[2] Although his father had secured all the country south of the Humber, Northumbria and its capital at York remained in Norse hands under the Northumbrian Viking king Sihtric Caech, Ragnal's successor. Aethelstan duly turned his attention in that direction. His first move was to marry his sister to Sihtric Caech at the Mercian capital of Tamworth.[3] But within the year Sihtric was dead. He left a son, Olaf, from a previous marriage, as his successor, who was supported by the boy's uncle, Guthfrith, king of the Vikings in Ireland. Aethelstan lost no time in attacking Northumbria and Guthfrith and Olaf were expelled. There followed the Treaty of Eamont (near Penrith) on 27 July 927. But Guthfrith was still at large. He attacked York but was forced to surrender to Athelstan who promptly despatched him back to Ireland.[4, 5]

The Treaty of Eamont was particularly comprehensive. The Anglo-Saxon Chronicle records that Hywel, king of the West Welsh, Constantine, king of the Scots and Owain, king of Gwent, all acknowledged Aethelstan as their overlord. Before long other Welsh princes submitted to him at Hereford. He also expelled the Britons from Exeter to beyond the river Tamar. In 934, Aethelstan moved to attack Scotland. A large land force advanced north as far as Kincardineshire, supported by a naval fleet which reached Caithness.[6] It was on his journey to Scotland that Aethelstan stopped off at Chester-le-Street to worship at the place where St Cuthbert now lay. Wishing to be identified with Northumbria's foremost saint, Aethelstan lavished gifts on the exiled monks and presented them with a painting of himself offering a copy of Bede's *Life of St Cuthbert* to the saint.[7] Aethelstan can thereby lay claim to be the first English king to be depicted in a painting.

But his greatest achievement was yet to come. The Danish Olaf III Guthfrithson, king of Dublin and successor of Guthfrith, Constantine, king of Scots and Owen I, king of Strathclyde allied together and met the forces of Aethelstan and his brother Edmund at the Battle of Brunanburh.[8] The site of the battle was probably Bromborough on the Wirral peninsula and Aethelstan's famous victory of 937 has been commemorated in a poem:

> In this year King Aethelstan, Lord of warriors,
> ring-giver to men, and his brother also,
> Prince Eadmund, won eternal glory
> in battle with sword edges
> around Brunanburh…
>
> The enemy perished,
> Scots men and seamen,
> fated they fell. The field flowed
> with blood of warriors, from sun up
> in the morning, when the glorious star
> glided over the earth, God's bright candle,
> eternal lord, till that noble creation
> sank to its seat. There lay many a warrior
> by spears destroyed; Northern men
> shot over shield, likewise Scottish as well,
> weary, war sated on the dusky flood-tide, he saved his life…
>
> Likewise, there also the old campaigner through flight came
> to his own region in the north – Constantine –
> hoary warrior. He had no reason to exult
> the great meeting; he was of his kinsmen bereft,
> friends fell on the battle-field,
> killed at strife: even his son, young in battle, he left
> in the place of slaughter, ground to pieces with wounds…

Never was there more slaughter
on this island, never yet as many
people killed before this
with sword's edge: never according to those who tell us
from books, old wisemen,
since from the east Angles and Saxons came up
over the broad sea. Britain they sought,
Proud war-smiths who overcame the Welsh,
glorious warriors they took hold of the land.

Because of the defeat of all his enemies, Aethelstan can thus lay claim to be the first king of a united England. He minted coins and they depict him as 'King of the Whole of Britain'. His new status was also recorded by Peter, a monk at Winchester, who described him as ruling 'this England now made whole'. He had dealings with mainland Europe and his sisters married into noble families. But Aethelstan's victory at Brunanburh was short-lived: a united England was brief in the extreme. He was dead within two years and the Danes came back. Aethelstan lies buried at Malmesbury and was succeeded by his eighteen-year-old half-brother, Edmund in 939,[9] whose mother, Eadgifu, was Edward the Elder's third wife.

Traditional Tomb of King Aethelstan at Malmesbury Abbey

The Danes Return

Edmund was present with Aethelstan at the Battle of Brunanburh. They fought and defeated Olaf Guthfrithson who was forced to take refuge in Ireland. But Olaf was to return to England and by 940 was in possession of York and the Midlands, a serious reversal of fortune for the English king. Battle between Olaf and Edmund was averted by the intervention of the Archbishops of Canterbury and York, and the English and Danish leaders agreed that, once more, Watling Street should be the border between Olaf's territory to the east and Edmund's to the west.[10]

Olaf Guthfrithson was soon to die and was succeeded first by Olaf Sihtricson, a far weaker leader and then by Raegnald, Olaf Guthfrithson's brother. Edmund was able to take advantage of the ensuing confusion and reasserted himself by taking Northumbria and then the five Danish boroughs of Leicester, Nottingham, Derby, Stamford, Lincoln and their surrounding territories.[11]

Edmund then moved north-west. The Anglo-Saxon Chronicle records that, helped by his Welsh allies, 'he ravaged all [of] Cumberland and gave it all to Malcolm, king of Scots, on condition that he be his ally, both at sea and on land.'[12] Edmund met his end in 946 while celebrating St Augustine's Day in Pucklechurch (Gloucestershire). There was a brawl and Edmund was murdered by a thief called Leofa.[13]

Edmund was succeeded by his brother Eadred who was crowned, as was now the custom, at Kingston-upon-Thames. His reign was concerned with events in Northumbria. The Anglo-Saxon Chronicle records that in 946 he 'reduced all Northumbria to his rule'.[14] Later at Tanshelf (present-day Pontefract) all Northumbria pledged their loyalty to him.[15] The agreement was short-lived; the Northumbrians went back on their word and within the year 'Northumbria had accepted the Norse leader, Eric Bloodaxe, as their king'.[16]

Eric 'Bloodaxe' was aptly named. He had a fearsome reputation and had succeeded his father, Harold Fairhair, as king of Norway. So violent was his reign that he was forced out of Norway by a popular revolt in favour of his brother, Haken. 'Bloodaxe' then set sail for Northumbria.[17]

Eadred was forced to deal with this new development and promptly marched north and ravaged all of Northumbria, including Ripon Abbey. He promised the Northumbrians an even worse fate unless they deserted Eric 'Bloodaxe'. At this point the course of events in Northumbria is unclear. We know that Olaf Sihtricson made another appearance, only to be driven out by 'Bloodaxe', who was eventually expelled himself, leaving Eadred to prevail. Eadred, though, suffered from ill health and died at Frome in 955. He was buried at Old Minster, Winchester and was succeeded by Eadwig, the son of Edmund.[18]

Eadwig's reign got off to an unfortunate start. On the day of his consecration, Dunstan, later to be Archbishop of Canterbury, found him 'cavorting with a noble woman'. We will have more to say about Dunstan later; suffice it now to record that he was not impressed and urged the sixteen-year-old Eadwig to denounce the lady, Aelfgifu, as a strumpet. Eadwig was later to marry Aelfgifu, his third cousin, but consanguinity was frowned upon by the church and the marriage was annulled by Odo, Archbishop of Canterbury, 'because they were too closely related'. Dunstan's disapproval of Eadwig's behaviour resulted in Dunstan's exile from the country. But it must not be assumed that Eadwig was hostile to the church. In his short reign he gave the church many gifts, including land at Southwell in Nottinghamshire, enabling the Archbishop of York to found a minster there.[19]

More difficulties came Eadwig's way in 957 when the nobles of Northumbria decided that, rather than Eadwig, they wanted his brother, Edgar, as their king. The matter was resolved by dividing the kingdom in two – Edgar ruled north of the Thames, and Eadwig to the south. Eadwig reigned for the next four years. He died in 959, at which time Edgar took control over the whole country.[20]

King Edgar the Peaceful

Then began the rule of Edgar I. England was now united under Edgar and his reign saw Anglo-Saxon England at its most accomplished. Edgar is known to us as Edgar the Peaceful and, compared with kings before and after, there is a scarcity of information about his time in power, a sure sign of peace and order. Edgar at once recalled Dunstan from exile and appointed him Archbishop of Worcester. Throughout his reign he gave every encouragement to Dunstan and the monastic revival movement.[21]

How was Edgar's England administered? Edgar would obviously have had advisors and would have wished to consult with people. These would have been the great men of the day, the king's council or Witan, a term meaning wise men. It was in no sense a representative assembly but would be called as and when required and typically consisted of the two archbishops, ealdormen and perhaps abbots and thegns. At its meetings grants of land would be confirmed, new laws proposed, particularly concerning law and order, where punishment of wrongdoers would be harsh.[22] The principal administrative area of the country was the shire. Each shire had an ealdorman and later a reeve – hence 'shire-reeve' or sheriff, the king's representative in that shire.[23] The shire court met twice per year. Within each shire was a series of hundreds, each served by the hundred court. A document known as the Hundred Ordinance decreed that the hundred court should meet every four weeks. Thegns were the most powerful men at local level. They would typically hold land and be expected to give military service. Many would have ambitions to be appointed shire-reeves or ealdormen.[24] In what was an agricultural society, the great bulk of the population were peasants (not a derogatory expression) made up of individual families running a farm supported by their slaves. Slavery was common and persisted well beyond the Norman Conquest; the Domesday Book estimated that 10% of the population were slaves.[25]

The culmination of Edgar's reign was his coronation at Bath. The ceremony was orchestrated by Dunstan and there are elements of it in the present-day ceremony. It took place in 973, when Edgar was thirty years of age, a full fourteen years after he succeeded Eadwig. The coronation included – most importantly – anointing with holy oil, a ritual which was intended to place it alongside the consecration of a priest. There followed a famous ceremony on the river Dee, where his sub-kings came to pay homage. Florence of Worcester records that:

> His eight sub kings, namely Kenneth, king of Scots, Malcolm, king of the Cumbrians, Maccus, king of many islands, and five others, Dufnal, Siferth, Hywel, Jacob and Juchil, met him, as he commanded, and swore that they would be faithful to him and be his allies by land and sea. And on a certain day he went on board a boat with them and with them at the oars and himself seizing the helm, he steered it skilfully on the course of the river Dee, proceeding from the palace to the monastery of St John the Baptist, attended by all the crowd of ealdormen and nobles also by boat.

Two years later, in 975, Edgar was dead, the Anglo-Saxon Chronicle recording that 'in this year Edgar, king of the English, reached the end of his earthly joys, chose for him the other light, beautiful and happy, and left this wretched and fleeting life'.

Dunstan, Aethelwold, Oswald and the Monastic Revival

The movement of monastic reform began in Europe at Cluny where a monastery was founded in 910. Cluny kept strictly to the Rule of St Benedict and became the leader of Western monasticism. In 930, Fleury on the Loire was reformed, taking its influence from Cluny. Dunstan is best remembered as leader in England of the great monastic revival. He was born in about the year 910, the son of a Somerset thegn, and spent his early life as a pupil at the abbey of Glastonbury. Dunstan was the nephew of Athelm, Archbishop of Canterbury, and it was this connection that brought him to the Royal Court.[26] But it was an unhappy time. Dunstan made himself extremely unpopular with his contemporaries, so much so that they set about him and plunged him into a stinking cesspool. Unwilling to accept this sort of treatment, Dunstan made his way to Winchester where his kinsman, Bishop Aelfheah, ordained him priest and monk. He came into the service of Eadgifu, who installed him as adviser to her son King Edmund. Once more, however, Dunstan fell out of favour and was on the point of banishment. Edmund, the story is told, was riding his horse near to Cheddar Gorge when the horse took fright and bolted. It was at this moment that the king realised that Dunstan had been improperly treated at court. Edmund must have escaped his equestrian ordeal without mishap, for he is then recorded as patching things up with Dunstan, riding with him and installing him as abbot of Glastonbury.[26] It was while at Glastonbury that Dunstan was confronted by the Devil. A well-known rhyme tells of the legend:

> St Dunstan, as the story goes
> Once pull'd the devil by the nose
> With red hot tongs, which made him roar
> That was heard three miles or more.

It was during Dunstan's fifteen years as Abbott of Glastonbury that the monastic revival took root in England. It had become common practice for leading magnates to appoint their own men as abbots of the monasteries they had endowed and for clerics to favour relatives as their successors. Simony (the selling of ecclesiastical offices for money) was also far from infrequent. The reformers were determined that the Rule of St Benedict should be strictly obeyed, that monks should lead a spiritual life of self-sacrifice and that simony should be forbidden.

Aethelwold was a contemporary of Dunstan at Glastonbury. Aethelwold was appointed abbot at Abingdon by King Eadred in 954 and then under King Edgar he became Bishop of Winchester in 963. A learned scholar but also an uncompromising leader, Aethelwold expelled the secular canons from Winchester and replaced them with Benedictine monks from Abingdon. An ambitious building programme was put in place at Winchester which, in 971, included the translation of the relics of St Swithun into the cathedral. (It must be said that this was against the saint's wishes. During his lifetime Swithun had insisted that he should be buried outside, so all could walk on his grave and raindrops fall upon it). Aethelwold translated the Rule of Benedict into English and was with all likelihood responsible for the Regularis Concordia, a document stipulating the way the Rule of St Benedict should be observed throughout all monasteries.[27] It was to Fleury that Oswald, another reformer and nephew of Oda, Archbishop of Canterbury, went for instruction. He was later appointed to the see of Worcester.[28]

We have already seen how Dunstan upset King Eadwig and during his reign he was forced into exile at Ghent. The monastic revival benefitted from a huge boost in the reign of King Edgar. When Edgar became king, Dunstan was recalled and appointed bishop at Worcester and London. In 960 he became Archbishop of Canterbury.[29] All these men were fervent reformers.

A Disputed Succession

Edgar's peaceful reign ended when he died prematurely at the age of thirty-two. It was unfortunate that he failed to nominate a successor, for a dispute arose between those who supported Edward, his eldest son, and those who favoured Aethelred (later known to us as the Unready), his son by Aelfthryth, his second wife. A complication was that there was uncertainty about the identity of Edward's mother. Some say his mother was the nun, Wulfthryth, whom Edgar may or may not have married. Others assert that he was the son of Aethelflaed, who was Edgar's queen when he was king of Mercia.[30] Dunstan and Oswald both supported Edward and they anointed him king at Kingston.[31] But matters were far from settled. The reign got off to a bad start when a comet, always seen as a bad omen, was seen in the sky. As the Anglo-Saxon Chronicle records: 'Then was also revealed up in the skies a star in the firmament which men call Comet by name. The vengeance of the Ruler was manifested widely throughout the people [and] in this year great famine occurred in England.'

To add to the country's troubles a reaction to the monastic revival set in. Many leading nobles resented land taken from them and given to monasteries. The great magnates of the day were split into two camps. Aethelwine, Ealdorman of East Anglia, supported Edward, as did Dunstan and Oswald. Aelfhere, Ealdorman of Mercia, with Bishop Aethelwold and the Queen Dowager, Aelfthryth, came down for Aethelred.[32] Matters were settled beyond doubt, however, when on 18 March 979, Edward arrived at Corfe to visit his stepmother, Aelfthryth, and his half-brother, Aethelred. He was brutally murdered. But by whom? Some say by nobles loyal to Aethelred, others by Aelfthryth or by Aelfhere.[33]

Although it was said of Edward, 'that his outbursts of rage had alarmed all who knew him and especially members of his own household,' he came to be recognised as a saint.[34] Edward the Martyr (as he became known) was buried first at Wareham and then reburied at Shaftesbury. Aethelred, only ten years of age, now became king.

Aethelred the Unready

Although, as far as we can tell, he had no hand in it, the brutal death of his brother, Edward, was hardly the ideal start to Aethelred's reign. He is known to us as the 'unready' and it has always been assumed, with very good reason, that this term referred to the fact that in his reign England fell to the Vikings. But recently historians have examined how the term 'unready' was derived and what it meant in Edward's day and have concluded that a more truthful meaning is 'ill advised' or, in other words, Aethelred had poor counsellors.[35, 36] It is likely, for instance, that early in his reign he played second fiddle to his mother, also to Bishop Aethelwold and Aelfhere.

Aethelred, still only a child, was consecrated king at Kingston on 4 May 979 and despite previous reservations there was 'much rejoicing by the councillors of the English people'.[37] But the happy event was soon tempered when sporadic Viking raids began again. The Vikings were now more organised and posed a much greater threat since Norway and Denmark were both united under King Harold Bluetooth. The adventurers began the practice of using ports in Normandy as staging posts, taking advantage of the fact that Normans – who arrived in northern France from Scandinavia only two generations before – were of the same stock as themselves. Tensions consequently arose between England and Normandy, only alleviated by the intervention of Pope John XV, who brokered a treaty between Aethelred and Duke Richard of Normandy to discourage the Vikings from getting safe haven in Normandy.[38]

In 991, the invaders returned in earnest. A large force occupied a small island (Northey Island) in the Blackwater Estuary, near Maldon in Essex. It was linked to the mainland by a causeway and waiting there was Byrhtnoth, ealdorman of Essex, and his army. The Danes' request for tribute was refused, and in a brave (or perhaps foolhardy) gesture, Byrhtnoth invited the invaders across the causeway so that battle could commence on equal terms. The Battle of Maldon was decisive. The Danes, under Olaf Tryggvason (son of Harold Fairhair), defeated the English and Byrhtnoth was killed.[39]

Following this crushing setback, a treaty was agreed between the two parties and so began a period when England once again began paying the invaders tribute, gold or silver, in a vain attempt to keep them at bay. In another fruitless ploy, Aethelred took to employing Vikings as quasi mercenaries. The vast sum of twenty-two thousand pounds of gold and silver was paid after the defeat at Maldon. It had little effect, for in 994 a vast army of ninety-four ships descended on London, led by Olaf Tryggvason and Sweyn Forkbeard, son of King Harold Bluetooth. London survived but the fleet then ravaged Kent, Sussex and Hampshire before being bought off by payment of 16,000 pounds of gold and silver. Even though Olaf returned to Norway to become its king, other groups were still at large. There continued raid after raid until 24,000 pounds of tribute was paid in 1002 for the supposed benefit of a truce![40]

Despite the ravages of war, religious life continued and, in some sense, thrived, with two important reformers: Aelfric of Eynsham and Wulfstan of York. Aelfric came out of Aethelwold's monastery at Winchester. He wrote a series of 'Catholic Homilies' whilst resident at Cerne Abbas before becoming abbot at Eynsham in Oxfordshire. Wulfstan – influential as a counsellor of Aethelred – was Bishop of London and then Archbishop of York and Bishop of Worcester. Apart from sermons he was responsible for compiling law codes in Aethelred's reign, and his work continued under the later rule of Cnut.[41]

Hoping to secure an alliance with Duke Richard of Normandy, in 1002, Aethelred married Emma, the duke's sister. But he was still beset with troubles lamenting that the Danes were 'sprouting like cockle amongst the wheat.' In a fit of anguish, Aethelred ordered all Danish men in England to be killed. The Chronicle reads: 'In this year [1002] the king ordered slain all the Danish men who were in England, this was done on St Brice's Day, because the king was told that they would faithlessly take his life and then all his councillors and possess his kingdom afterwards.'[42] How far this decree was acted upon, if at all, is unclear but in a well-known incident a group of Danes took refuge by boarding themselves up in the church of St Frideswide Priory in Oxford (now Oxford Cathedral), whereupon the mob 'set fire to the planks and burnt the church with its ornaments and books.'[43] To what extent this was an isolated incident is difficult to determine. Suffice to say that Sweyn Forkbeard's sister, Gunhilde, was killed in the slaughter and Sweyn was soon to visit England, intent on revenge.

Despite Aethelred gathering a large fleet of ships in the hope of warding off imminent Viking raids, one of its commanders, a Sussex thegn named Wulfnoth, was accused of treason. Wulfnoth, with twenty ships under his command, turned to piracy. He was pursued by eighty ships but a storm drove both fleets ashore. The unhappy episode ended with the majority of ships destroyed by fire.[44] The way was thus left free for the Viking, Thorkell the Tall, in August 1009, to land with a large army at Sandwich.[45] Within a year Wessex was subjugated. Viking assaults were now relentless.

Thorkell's army brutally murdered Aelfheah (Alphege), the Archbishop of Canterbury, at Greenwich after he had refused to pay tribute. (Nicholas Hawksmoor's St Alphege church at Greenwich is a present-day reminder.) In despair and complying with an edict of Wulfstan, Aethelred ordered the entire nation to fast and pray for three days as penance for Thorkell's raids. On pain of flogging, all were to obey, walk barefoot to church and survive on bread and water alone.[46] Then, against all expectations, Thorkell went over to Aethelred's side, a gesture that may have induced Sweyn Forkbeard to invade.

Sweyn and Cnut

After the death of his father (Harold Bluetooth), Sweyn Forkbeard, in 987, became king of Denmark and then ruler of Norway in 1000. After a series of raids in the early part of the new millennium the Chronicle records events that changed the course of English history.

And in the same year [1013] before the month of August, King Sweyn came with his fleet to Sandwich, and then went very quickly around East Anglia into the mouth of the Humber, and so up along the Trent until he reached Gainsborough. And then at once Earl Uhrtred and all the Northumbrians submitted to him... When he perceived that all the people had submitted to him... he turned southwards with his full forces and left the ships and hostages in the charge of his son, Cnut. When he had crossed the Watling Street, they did the greatest damage that any army could do. He then turned to Oxford, and the citizens at once submitted and gave hostages; and from there to Winchester, where they did the same.[47]

Meanwhile, Aethelred was in London with the Viking, Thorkell the Tall, newly recruited to the English. Sweyn attacked but London held out forcing the invading Danes to head for Winchester where they received the submission of the men of Wessex. It was but a brief respite for Aethelred. London soon fell and Aethelred, his queen Emma and their young sons Alfred and Edward (later Edward the Confessor) took refuge in Normandy with Richard, the queen's brother, 'and were there with him until the happy event of Sweyn's death.'[47]

The 'happy event' was soon to come. Sweyn was king of England for just a few weeks. He died at his base at Gainsborough on 3 February 1014. His son, Cnut, present also at Gainsborough, was then immediately recognised as king by all his followers. The English councillors, however, immediately sent for Aethelred (exiled in Normandy) and urged him to return and be their king if (according to the Chronicle and significantly) 'he would govern them more justly than he did before'.[48] The appropriate assurances were given and 'during the spring [he] came home to his own people and was gladly received by them.'[48] Stenton notes the constitutional interest of the agreement as being the first recorded pact between an English king and his subjects.[49] Aethelred then advanced against Cnut in Lincolnshire but Cnut was unwilling to engage. He left for Denmark but not before offloading hostages at Sandwich, all with their hands, eyes and noses removed![49] For harbouring Cnut, Aethelred took his revenge against the people of Lincolnshire. Despite being 'gladly received', serious tensions still plagued Aethelred's court, due in no small way to the murderous Eadric Streona of Mercia.

Cnut's retreat from England damaged his reputation. But he was soon to return, assisted in his plans for a reinvasion by Eric of Hlathir, the most esteemed nobleman in Scandinavia. He was also joined by Thorkell the Tall who had defected from Aethelred's service. Cnut finally landed in England in the summer of 1015. The Chronicle records that he arrived first at Sandwich with a vast fleet and then sailed round the south coast to enter the river Frome and gain the submission of Wessex. Aethelred was too ill to fight and all resistance to the Danes was left to Edmund Ironside, Aethelred's son by his first wife, Aelfgifu.[50]

In defiance of his father and indicative of the discontent at Aethelred's court, Edmund Ironside married Ealdgyth, the widow of a Danelaw thegn who had been brutally murdered on the orders of Eadric Streona, ealdorman of Mercia. In so doing, Edmund was able to take the Five Boroughs of Derby, Lincoln, Nottingham, Stamford and Leicester. He then raised an army in Lincolnshire only to learn that Eadric Streona, and presumably Mercia, had deserted to Cnut. Ironside then joined with Earl Uhtred of Northumbria and moved on Mercia. But Cnut was now in Northumbria forcing Uhtred to return, where he submitted. The defence of London was vital and Edmund joined his father there, but on 23 April 1016 Aethelred died and Edmund Ironside was immediately proclaimed king.[51]

Edmund Ironside immediately set out to regain the loyalty of the men of Wessex who had previously come down in favour of Cnut. Cnut, meanwhile, saw his chance to take London and sailed up the Thames. His progress was impeded by London Bridge and, according to legend, he dug a canal, south of the river, to gain access upstream. (No remains of such canal have ever been found.) Further battles took place and to his credit, Edmund won a famous victory at Otford in Kent, forcing Cnut to take refuge on the Isle of Sheppey. It was after this victory that the duplicitous Eadric Streona left the service of Cnut and joined Edmund.[52] Eventually, Cnut won a decisive battle at Ashingdon in south-east Essex, assisted by the treacherous Eadric, who had changed sides once more. Cnut realised that it would be wise to make peace with Edmund. An agreement was therefore sealed at Deerhurst in Gloucestershire, under the terms of which Edmund ruled Wessex and Cnut the rest of the country beyond the Thames. But Edmund Ironside's reign was no more than six months. He died on 30 November 1016 and all England accepted Cnut as king.[53]

References

1. Martin J. Ryan, in Higham and Ryan, eds., *The Anglo-Saxon World* (2013), p. 301
2. Foot, *Athelstan, the First King of England* (2011), p. 31–3
3. Anglo-Saxon Chronicle, 926
4. Stenton, *Anglo-Saxon England* (1971), p. 340
5. Anglo-Saxon Chronicle, 927

6. Stenton, p. 341–2

7. Foot, p. 88

8. Stenton, p. 343

9. Sean Miller, in Lapidge, ed., *Blackwell Encyclopaedia of Anglo-Saxon England* (1999), p. 16

10. Ibid., p. 159

11. Stenton, p. 358

12. Anglo-Saxon Chronicle, 945

13. Sean Miller, in Lapidge, ed. (1999), p. 159

14. Anglo-Saxon Chronicle, 946

15. Ibid., 947

16. Ibid., 948

17. Stenton, p. 360

18. Sean Miller, in Lapidge, ed. (1999), p. 150

19. Stenton, p. 365

20. Sean Miller, in Lapidge, ed. (1999), p. 151

21. Stenton, p. 367

22. B.A.E. Yorke, in Lapidge, ed. (1999), p. 124

23. Simon Keynes, in Lapidge, ed. (1999), p. 421

24. Ibid., p. 443

25. Faith, *English Peasantry and the Growth of Lordship* (1997)

26. Stenton, p. 446

27. Michael Lapidge, in Lapidge, ed. (1999), p. 19

28. Ibid., p. 348

29. Ibid., p. 146

30. Higham, *The Death of Anglo-Saxon England* (1997), p. 6

31. Williams, *Aethelred the Unready* (2003), p. 10

32. Sean Miller, in Lapidge, ed. (1999), p. 163

33. Higham, (1997), p. 12–14

34. Stenton, p. 372

35. Sean Miller, in Lapidge, ed. (1999), p. 15

36. Simon Keynes, *The Declining Reputation of King Aethelred the Unready*, in Hill, ed., *Ethelred the Unready* (1978), p. 227

37. Simon Keynes in *Dictionary of National Biography* (2004), Vol. 1, p. 410

38. Stenton, p. 375–6

39. Ibid., p. 376–7

40. Ibid., p. 378

41. Ibid., p. 459
42. Anglo-Saxon Chronicle, 1002
43. Lavelle, *Aethelred II* (2008), p. 104
44. Stenton, p. 382
45. Anglo-Saxon Chronicle, 1009
46. Leyser, *The Anglo-Saxons* (2017), p. 147
47. Anglo-Saxon Chronicle, 1013
48. Ibid., 1014
49. Stenton, p. 386
50. Anglo-Saxon Chronicle, 1015
51. Stenton, p. 388–90
52. M.K. Lawson, in *Dictionary of National Biography*, Vol. 17 (2004), p. 769
53. Stenton, p. 393

The End of
Anglo-Saxon England

Cnut

The Anglo-Saxon Chronicle tells us that Cnut succeeded to the throne of England in 1017. His appearance is described by Trow, who takes his information from a Nordic Saga:

> Cnut was exceptionally tall and strong, and the handsomest of men, all except for his nose, that was thin, high set and rather hooked. He had a fair complexion none-the-less, and a fine, thick head of hair. His eyes were better than those of other men, both the handsomer and keener of their sight.[1]

There were other contenders for the crown of England but one way or another they caused Cnut little difficulty: Eadwig was Aethelred's son, but the Chronicle records that he was outlawed.[2] Edmund Ironside had two sons – Edward and Edmund. They both fled abroad, Edward well out of the way in Hungary.[3] Aethelred had sons by his wife, Emma – Alfred the Atheling and Edward (later the Confessor). They were both in exile in Normandy.[4]

In 1017, Cnut married Aethelred's widow, Emma. Much to her displeasure (and also that of the Church), he was also married to Aelfgifu of Northampton. For her part, Emma insisted that Cnut, on oath, would never set up the son of any wife other than herself to rule after him. These marital unions were to lead to much confusion when Cnut died. He nominated Harthacnut, his son by Emma, as his successor but he also had sons by Aelfgifu. They were Swein Knutson and Harold Harefoot and they were to demand consideration as well.[5]

It was at Southampton that Cnut pledged to be a good lord and in return received a promise of fidelity from his leading English nobles. He may then have been crowned in London at St Paul's Cathedral by Archbishop Lyfing.[5] Immediately after his succession, Cnut divided his kingdom into four parts. Wessex was placed under his own control, Erik Hlathir was granted Northumbria, Eadric Streona had Mercia and Thorkell the Tall held East Anglia.[6] And tribute continued to be paid. The Chronicle records that in 1018, England paid 72,000 pounds and that did not include the 10,500 pounds paid by London.[7]

Much of what we know of the reign of Cnut comes from a work, written in praise of Queen Emma in 1041, by a Flemish monk, probably from St Omer. It is known as the *Encomium of Queen Emma*. It records that the duplicitous Eadric Streona was killed to discourage others from disloyalty 'so that retainers may learn from this example to be faithful, not faithless to their king.' Florence of Worcester writes that Eadric Streona was 'rightly killed' at London and his corpse thrown over the city wall and left unburied. It is likely that Eadric's execution would have been encouraged by Aelfgifu of Northampton (Cnut's first wife) given that he had overthrown her father.[8] And Cnut's purge did not end there. Others to fall were Northman of Mercia and Aethelweard and Brihtric of Wessex. Eadric Streona was replaced by Leofric, husband of Lady Godifu (Lady Godiva). Later, Cnut fell out with Thorkell. He was expelled in 1021 and in Northumbria, Erik Hlathir died, to be replaced by Siward.

Cnut became king of Denmark in 1018 and in 1028, king of Norway. He was in England in 1020 and attended a council at Cirencester and later that year consecrated a church at Assundun (either Ashdon or Ashingdon, both in Essex) in memory of his victory over Edmund Ironside.[9] But Cnut was spending more and more time away from England. Accordingly, control of Wessex was given to Godwin, the son of a Sussex thegn. Cnut found him 'the most cautious in council and the most active in war.'[10] Godwin married Cnut's sister-in-law and fought alongside Cnut in Scandinavia. His appointment as Earl of Wessex had lasting consequences – Godwin was a man on the rise. As time went by, particularly because of Cnut's continuing absence in Scandinavia, caused by threats to his power there, Earl Godwin became ever more powerful.

Cnut died in 1035 at the Abbey of Shaftesbury and was buried at Winchester. As for his reign, he ruled in a way that gave England an extended period of peace. Early in his rule at a meeting at Oxford, Wulfstan, Archbishop of York, records that 'Cnut, with the advice of his councillors, fully established peace and friendship between the Danes and the English and put an end to all their former enmity.'

Despite having two wives, he was a Christian and gave generously to the church. He was present in Rome at the accession of Conrad II as Holy Roman Emperor and met the pope. While in Rome he took the opportunity of negotiating with the pope and emperor measures to ease the passage of pilgrims to Rome by making possible freedom from tolls on their journey.[11] He also attended when the body of St Alphege, who had been brutally murdered some years before at Greenwich by drunken Vikings, was translated from St Paul's Cathedral to Canterbury.[12] He freed the canons of St Milburg, Much Wenlock, from taxes they would otherwise have to pay and gave land to the monks of Durham. He provided money for the abbey at Ramsey to build a church, gave Archbishop Lyfing of Canterbury land in Sussex and was a benefactor of New Minster, Winchester.[13] And there is, of course, the famous story of the waves. According to Henry of Huntingdon, Cnut's throne was placed beside the sea (at either Bosham or Southampton.) Whereupon he ordered the tide to halt:

> Yet, continuing to rise as usual [the tide] dashed over his feet and legs without respect for his royal person. Then the king leapt backwards saying let all men know how empty and worthless is the power of kings, for there is none more worthy of the name but He whom heaven and earth and sea obey by eternal laws.

Harthacnut and Harold Harefoot

The succession in England after Cnut's death was complicated by the situation in Scandinavia. Following his conquest of Norway, Cnut installed Earl Hakon, son of Eric Hlathir, as regent.[14] But Hakon was to lose his life at sea and so Cnut's first wife, Aelfgifu, with their son, Swein, set out from England with every intention of ruling the Norwegians. It was a disastrous episode: the Norwegians rallied round Magnus, their own man. Aelfgifu soon abandoned the idea and left matters in Scandinavia in the hands of Harthacnut, Cnut's son by Emma.[15] This turn of events meant, although Harthacnut was nominated by his father as successor in England, he was too preoccupied by Magnus and the Norwegians to come to England and claim his throne. England was therefore left in the unenviable position of being without a king.[16]

Apart from Harthacnut, who was backed by his mother Emma, Earl Godwin and the Archbishop of Canterbury, there were two other potential contenders for the kingship. The northern faction of Leofric and Siward wanted Harold Harefoot, son of Cnut by Aelfgifu. To complicate matters further, the Norman chronicler, William of Jumièges, informs us that Robert, Duke of Normandy, wanted Edward (later the Confessor), who was Emma's son by Aethelred, and even attempted a raid to bring this about. In the event, Robert's ships were blown off course, he soon died and that, for the moment, was that.[17] It is interesting to speculate whether Robert had advance plans for his infant son, William, later the Conqueror.

The Archbishop of Canterbury, Emma and Godwin favoured waiting for Harthacnut. But Harthacnut was still unable to leave Scandinavia and so there was little choice but to accept Harold Harefoot. For a while he acted as regent but, in the continuing absence of Harthacnut, was recognised as king.[18]

Within the *Encomium of Queen Emma*, it is recorded that Emma wrote a letter inviting her two sons by Aethelred (Alfred and Edward) to visit her in Winchester. But the biography informs us that the letter was a forgery, penned by Harold Harefoot. There seems no reason to suspect that Harold wrote such a letter – it was, after all, not in his interests for a rival to his throne to leave exile in Normandy. As it turned out, in 1036, it was Alfred who came. His journey ended in his murder. The Anglo-Saxon Chronicle takes up the story:

As Alfred and his men approached the town of Guildford in Surrey, thirty miles south-west of London, they were met by the powerful Earl Godwin of Wessex, who professed loyalty to the young prince and procured lodgings for him and his men in the town. The next morning Godwin said to Alfred: 'I will safely and securely conduct you to London, where the great men of the kingdom are awaiting your coming, that they may raise you to the throne.' This he said in spite of the fact that the throne was already occupied by the son of Cnut, Harold Harefoot, and he was actually in league with King Harold to lure the young king to his death. Then the Earl led the prince and his men over the hill of Guildown, which is to the west of Guildford, on the road to Winchester, not London... Godwin repeated his tempting offer; showing the prince the magnificent panorama from the hill both to the north and south, he said: 'Look around on the right hand and on the left and behold what a realm will be subject to your dominion.'

(Those familiar with the area will recognise this as the view from the Hog's Back, the road (A31) from Guildford to Farnham and thence to Winchester).

Continuing with the Chronicle's account:

> Alfred then gave thanks to God and promised if ever he should be crowned king, he would institute such laws as would be pleasing and acceptable to God and men. At that moment, however, he was seized and bound together with all his men. Nine-tenths of them were murdered, and since the remaining tenth was still so numerous, they too were decimated. Alfred was tied to a horse and then conveyed by boat to Ely. As the boat reached land his eyes were put out. For a while he was looked after by the monks, but soon after he died, probably on February 5, 1036.[19]

Meanwhile, Harthacnut's position had improved in Scandinavia. With every intention of claiming the English throne he sailed to meet his mother, Emma, who had fled to Bruges. News reached him that Harold Harefoot was unwell and not expected to live. Harthacnut accordingly waited for Harefoot's death before landing in 1040 with a large force of sixty-two warships at Sandwich.[20, 21]

Harold Harefoot was buried at Westminster Abbey, and according to the Chronicle, Harthacnut, outraged by the murder of Alfred and blaming Harold, ordered the body to be dug up and 'thrown into the fen', presumably the bog that was Thorney Island.[22] Florence of Worcester adds that the body was recovered and 'buried by the Danes at St Clement Danes, their cemetery in London'. Godwin also had to face the music. Harthacnut accused him of complicity in the murder of Alfred. To save his skin, Godwin gave Harthacnut a 'richly decorated ship' and in his defence asserted he had little choice but to obey Harold Harefoot because he was required to be loyal to his king.[23]

Then came the unexpected appearance from Normandy of Edward, Emma's son by Aethelred, seemingly invited by Godwin and the Bishop of Winchester. (Unexpected because Harthacnut was still alive.) A meeting took place on the Hampshire coast in 1041 at a place called Hursteshevet (later identified as Hurst Beach), where Edward, in the company of the 'thegns of England', was promised the kingdom provided he upheld the laws of Cnut and his sons, that is, those laws laid down by Archbishop Wulfstan. Edward was then, it seems, received at Harthacnut's court,[24] but not for long. Within the year, while at a wedding in Lambeth and drinking the health of the bride, Harthacnut collapsed and died.

The Chronicle reported: 'and all the people then received Edward as king as was his natural right.'[25] The question remains, why was Edward invited from exile while Harthacnut was still alive?

Edward the Confessor and the Godwins

Edward, known to us as the Confessor, was born in Islip in Oxfordshire in about 1005 and was consecrated king at Winchester in 1042. His only possible rival for the crown was Swein Estrithson, grandson of Sweyn Forkbeard. But Harthacnut had sent Swein to Denmark to deal with the ambitions of Magnus of Norway and moreover Edward had the support of all the leading English magnates: Earl Godwin, Leofric of Mercia and Siward of Northumbria. Interestingly, Edward is reported to have made a treaty with Swein Estrithson, promising him the kingdom on his death.[26]

In the same year as his accession, it is recorded that Edward fell out with his mother, Emma, and sought redress by seizing her lands.[27] Edward's resentment stemmed from the time of her marriage with Cnut, when she promised preference to any son she may have with Cnut rather than favouring Edward. Harthacnut was her favourite and Edward resented this. And there was even the suggestion that she favoured Magnus of Norway over Edward. There was certainly a threat from Magnus, prompting Edward, in 1045, to take command of a large fleet of ships at Sandwich in readiness for an attack. In the event, no attack came, Magnus being occupied with war in Scandinavia.[28]

In 1045, Edward, despite Godwin's involvement in the death of his brother Alfred, married Earl Godwin's daughter, Edith. The marriage produced no children, which of course led to a succession problem. *Vita Aedwardi Regis* (the Life of King Edward – a manuscript commissioned by Queen Edith in 1067, written shortly after Edward's death) records that 'he preserved the dignity of his consecration with holy chastity and lived his whole life dedicated to God in true innocence'. In contrast, Barlow asserts that 'the theory that Edward's childlessness was due to deliberate abstention from sexual relations lacks authority, plausibility and diagnostic value.'[29] Barlow's position is strengthened by the record that prayers were said 'for the king to be given fertility and an heir'.[30]

Early in his reign, Edward was faced with an ecclesiastical crisis. It came in 1051 after the death of Eadsige, Archbishop of Canterbury, and soon afterwards of Aelfric Puttoc, Archbishop of York. The monks at Canterbury wanted their own man, Aelric, as the new archbishop. He was also favoured by Godwin. Edward took exception and insisted on the Norman, Robert of Jumièges, who at the time was Bishop of London. Robert of Jumièges was no friend of Godwin. He accused him of seizing church lands and planted in Edwards's mind a rumour that, not satisfied with murdering Alfred, he was intent on murdering Edward himself.[31]

Then came an important council. It was held in London and, if we are to believe the Norman chronicler, William of Poitiers, writing after the Norman Conquest, a treaty was formulated with Normandy whereby on Edward's death William, Duke of Normandy (later the Conqueror) would be appointed as his heir. The reasons given were (1) that Edward was indebted to William and his family for helping him obtain the throne, (2) they were kinsmen and (3) because William was most suited to help Edward during his reign and succeed afterwards. Apparently, the treaty was endorsed on oath by Godwin, Leofric and Siward.[32]

The same chronicler reported that Robert of Jumièges, while on his way to Rome to collect his pallium, stopped off in Normandy to inform Duke William that he had the right of succession in England when the childless Edward died.[33] Although this information comes from a Norman chronicler, it has the ring of credibility, given that Edward himself was half Norman.

Edward's uneasy relationship with the Godwins was further damaged by an incident in 1051, involving Edward's brother-in-law, Eustace, Count of Boulogne. While on a visit to England to meet with Edward, Eustace became involved in a skirmish at Dover. Dover was in Earl Godwin's sphere of influence and many were killed. Edward was furious at what had happened and ordered Godwin to punish the people of Dover. He refused, so defying his king.[34] In a show of force, Edward immediately summoned his followers to Gloucester. Godwin and his two sons, Harold and Swein, did likewise and summoned their army to Beverstone, fifteen miles to the south. War between the two camps seemed inevitable, but Edward's nobles cautioned against conflict, the Anglo-Saxon Chronicle recording:

> They were all so much in agreement with the king that they were willing to attack the army of Godwin if the king had wished them to do so. Then some of them thought it would be a great piece of folly if they joined battle, for in the two hosts there was most of what was noblest in England, and they considered that they would be opening a way for our enemies to enter the country and to cause ruin among ourselves.[35]

The outcome was a council called in London to which Godwin was summoned to give an account of himself. He declined to attend unless guaranteed safe conduct and the exchange of hostages. Edward was unwilling to comply and sent Bishop Stigand of Winchester with a message for Godwin informing him that he could have a pardon if he restored Edward's dead brother, Alfred. Godwin knew the game was up! He fled to Bosham on the Sussex coast with his wife, Gytha, and his sons, Swein and Tostig. Robert of Jumièges at once set off in hot pursuit, intent on their capture. All Godwin's party embarked for Bruges to the court of Baldwin, Count of Flanders. Meanwhile Godwin's other sons, Harold and Leofwine, made haste for Bristol and boarded a ship for Ireland. Poor Queen Edith (Godwin's daughter) came out of it badly. Encouraged by Robert of Jumièges, Edward despatched her to a nunnery, with, according to one source, the services of only one maid.[36]

It was at this time, according to the D version of the Anglo-Saxon Chronicle, that Duke William of Normandy visited England with a great force of Frenchmen and met with Edward. What was the purpose of the visit? Did Edward confirm William as his heir?

But the Godwins were soon back from exile with armed forces. In anticipation, Edward instructed earls Ralf of Mantes and Odda of Deerhurst to command a fleet of ships based at Sandwich. Harold and Leofwine sailed from Ireland and landed at Porlock in Somerset. They were driven off by forces loyal to Edward and then made their way via Land's End to the English Channel. Meanwhile, Godwin sailed from Bruges, gave Ralf and Odda the slip, and landed at Dungeness in Kent where he received a warm welcome from his followers. Ralf and Odda were quick to respond with both land and naval forces and, helped by gale force winds, drove Godwin back to Bruges. But he was soon back and met up with Harold's and Leofwine's fleet off the Isle of Wight. The combined fleet then sailed eastwards, gathering reinforcements all the way, and entered the Thames, unmolested, to reach Godwin's manor at Southwark in September 1052. The two armies faced each other across the river, the King's on the north and Godwin's on the south. Despite the king having fifty ships at his disposal, Godwin had the upper hand. Archbishop Robert of Jumièges – always Godwin's mortal enemy – could see the way things were going and with other Frenchmen made good their escape, Robert to a ship at the Essex coast and then to Normandy. Next day, Godwin met with the king's council and declared his innocence of all charges. His lands and those of his sons were promptly restored.[37] It was a personal triumph.

Earl Godwin, presumably reconciled with Edward, died in 1052. He suffered a stroke while feasting with the king at Winchester.[38] For reasons that are not entirely clear, Edward now retreated into the background and left matters of state in the hands of Godwin's sons. Wessex passed to Godwin's son, Harold. Two years later, Siward of Northumbria died to be replaced by Tostig, Harold's brother. Earl Aelfgar of East Anglia was outlawed, and his land given to Gyrth, another son of Godwin and finally, his youngest son, Leofwine, gained land in the Midlands.[39] The Godwins had thus secured their position as the most powerful family in the land.[40] What was Edward's reaction to all this? Baxter writes that according to the *Vita Edwardi Regis*, he spent all his time out hunting!

> And so with the kingdom made safe on all sides by these nobles (the sons of Godwin) the most kindly King Edward passed his life in security and peace, and spent much of his time in the glades and woods in the pleasures of hunting. After divine service, which he gladly and devoutly attended every day, he took much pleasure in hawks and birds of that kind which were brought before him and was really delighted by the baying and scrambling of the hounds. In these and such activities he sometimes spent the day, and it was in these alone that he seemed naturally inclined to snatch some worldly pleasure.[40]

Final Years

As for the succession, we have already seen that Edward promised it to Swein Estrithson of Denmark, grandson of Sweyn Forkbeard. He later promised it to William of Normandy and then, on his death bed, according to the Anglo-Saxon Chronicle, granted the realm to Earl Harold, 'as he had been chosen to the position.' But there was always the son of Edmund Ironside, Edward the Aetheling, far away in Hungary. In 1054, Bishop Ealdred of Worcester made steps to bring him home. He returned in 1058 but died shortly afterwards.[41] The Aetheling had a son, Edgar, but he was a mere child of five years.[42] Then came the voyage Harold is alleged to have taken to Normandy. The Bayeux Tapestry depicts him leaving Bosham harbour in 1064. It seems he was blown off course and landed in Ponthieu where he was captured and handed over to Duke William.[43] Harold then apparently went on campaign with William against the Duke of Brittany and in the process swore allegiance to William over holy relics.

What are we to make of Edward's wishes for the succession? Baxter's view is that Edward's choice of successor changed with the political climate at the time.[44] It is a compelling argument. Perhaps the last word should go to William of Malmsbury, who wrote in the 1120s that 'it is these differences of opinion (between English and Norman sources) that puts my narrative at risk since I cannot decide what precisely is the truth'.[44]

Back in England events unfolded which led to a rift between Harold and his brother Tostig – a rift which, one year later, would have disastrous consequences for the survival of Anglo-Saxon England. Tostig was having difficulties in Northumbria. His policy of heavy taxation and overbearing rule prompted the Northumbrians to rebel and replace him with Morcar, brother of Edwin of Mercia. In the autumn of 1065 the rebels stormed York, killing as many of Tostig's followers as they could find. But they didn't stop there; they continued south as far as Oxford to petition the king and demand that unless Edward expelled Tostig they would make war. Tostig expected help from his brother but help was not forthcoming; Tostig even accused Harold of fomenting the trouble. Neither was help forthcoming from his other brothers, Gyrth of East Anglia or Leofwine. Tostig – by now Harold's enemy – was forced to flee to Flanders.[45] Events came to a head when Edward died on 5 January 1066, only a few days after perhaps his greatest achievement, the consecration of his great abbey at Westminster.

Following the decision of the Witenagemot and on a cold day in January 1066, Harold Godwinson was crowned King of England. Duke William of Normandy immediately prepared to invade, supporting his claim to England by Harold's oath on holy relics. Harold and his army were waiting for William's invasion, only to be overtaken by events elsewhere. His brother Tostig was intent on revenge. Tostig gathered a fleet in Flanders and harried the Sussex coast before landing at Sandwich to meet up with reinforcements from the Orkney Isles. Tostig then sailed northwards but was prevented from taking Northumbria by Morcar and the Northumbrians. He then sought refuge with Malcolm III of Scotland.[46] Tostig then allied himself with Harold Hardrada, king of Norway, who to press his own claim to the kingdom landed with an army of warriors in the north-east and made his base at Riccall on the river Ouse. The Norwegians lost no time in burning Scarborough and then advanced on York. There, just outside the city at Fulford, they met and defeated the combined forces of Edwin and Morcar.[47]

On learning of Edwin and Morcar's defeat, Harold Godwinson marched north. It took him a mere four days to reach York. Meanwhile, Harold Hardrada and Tostig were a few miles away to the east at Stamford Bridge, totally unaware of Harold's imminent arrival. Taken by surprise the Norwegians were completely overcome and both Harold Hardrada and Tostig were killed.

The Battle of Stamford Bridge took place on 25 September 1066; three days later Duke William landed at Pevensey in Sussex. Harold then began the long march south. He arrived to give battle with William, north of Hastings, at the famous Senlac Hill. The outcome is well known! William was crowned King of England on Christmas Day 1066.

References

1. Trow, *Cnut, the Emperor of the North* (2005), p. 92
2. Anglo-Saxon Chronicle, 1017
3. Stenton, *Anglo-Saxon England* (1971), p. 397–8
4. Ibid., p. 408
5. Lawson, *Cnut, England's Viking King*, (2004), p. 82
6. Stenton, p. 398
7. Anglo-Saxon Chronicle, 1018
8. Lawson, p. 83
9. Ibid., p. 90
10. Williams, in *Oxford Dictionary of National Biography*, Vol. 22, p. 626
11. Trow, p. 193
12. Howard, *Harthacnut, The Last Danish King of England* (2008), p. 21
13. Lawson, p. 140–2
14. Ibid., p. 98
15. Eric John, in Campbell ed., *The Anglo-Saxons* (1982), p. 214
16. Ibid., p. 215
17. Ibid., p. 216
18. Stenton, p. 420
19. Anglo-Saxon Chronicle, 1036
20. Eric John, in Campbell ed. (1982), p. 221
21. Stenton, p. 422
22. Anglo-Saxon Chronicle, 1040
23. Howard, p. 112
24. Leyser, *The Anglo-Saxons* (2017), p. 161–3
25. Anglo-Saxon Chronicle, 1042

26. Barlow, *Edward the Confessor* (1989), p. 54–7

27. Anglo-Saxon Chronicle, 1043

28. Barlow, p. 92

29. Ibid., p. 82

30. Stephen David Baxter, in Mortimer ed., *Edward the Confessor: The Man and the Legend* (2009), p. 85, n36

31. Barlow, p. 104–6

32. Ibid., p. 107

33. Eric John, in Campbell, ed. (1982), 224–5

34. Rex, *King and Saint: The Life of Edward the Confessor* (2008), p. 121

35. Anglo-Saxon Chronicle (D), 1051

36. Barlow, p. 113–5

37. Ibid., p. 120–4

38. Ibid., p. 127

39. Ibid., p. 193

40. Stephen Baxter, *Edward the Confessor and the Succession Question*, in Mortimer ed., (2009), p. 104

41. Ibid., p. 96–8

42. Ibid., p. 98–103

43. Howarth, *1066, the Year of the Conquest* (1977), p. 71–2

44. Stephen Baxter in Mortimer ed. (2009), p. 77

45. Barlow, p. 233–9

46. Stenton, p. 587

47. Howarth, p. 133

Anglo-Saxon Art

Anglo-Saxon art evolved over a period of many hundreds of years. It had its beginnings in its Germanic and pagan past but was open to influence from many places. Inspiration was taken from Roman, Byzantian, Carolingian, Irish sources and more, all of which merged, coalesced and focussed to give a unique Anglo-Saxon style, typically full of plant and animal images.

After the Anglo-Saxons converted to Christianity in the late 6th century, specifically religious imagery predominated, such as the inhabited vine scroll representing the 'true vine' as in John's Gospel, John 15, 1–7. Other images widely found are acanthus sprays, interlace patterns, animals and hybrid creatures.

Early influences were taken from Rome. A style known as 'Saxon Relief' began in the area of northern Europe, west of present-day Hamburg, from where Saxon migrations to Britain began. It is an adaptation of the animal and geometric patterns found on Roman metalwork and examples have been excavated in 5th and early 6th century Anglo-Saxon burials in this country

A style originating in Norway and Denmark in the 5th century was named 'Animal Style I' by the Swedish scholar, Bernard Salin (1861–1931), in 1904. Here, human and animal forms are more stylised. In his standard work, Kendrick characterised Style I as 'a discordant mosaic of little bits and pieces without regard to the natural rhythm of the animal.' Conversely, Leslie Webster asserts that, rather than being haphazard, 'artists worked to a carefully constructed artistic vocabulary and grammar.' In other words, to a set of rules. A good example is the brooch found at Chessel Down in the Isle of Wight and now housed in the British Museum. 'Animal Style II' developed, also from Scandinavia, about 50 to 100 years later. Decoration is less heavy than Style I. There are long-bodied animals, intertwined with other beasts and often curling back and biting their own bodies.

One of the earliest Anglo-Saxon settlements in England was at Mucking, an abandoned Romano-British site in south Essex. It was excavated between 1965 and 1978. Many sunken buildings were revealed as well as larger structures. Finds included brooches and pottery and, significantly, a 5th century buckle cast in bronze. It was inlaid with silver and its design anticipated finds at Sutton Hoo. Later, a site at Prittlewell, near Southend, was excavated. As many as 110 objects were uncovered including a lyre and a body in a wooden coffin. It has been speculated that he is Saeberht, king of Essex, who died in 616.

Most important of all and the supreme example of Anglo-Saxon art of the early 7th century is the wealth of finds excavated at Sutton Hoo (see Suffolk). There is metalwork of the highest quality, a ceremonial helmet and shield, silver plate of Byzantine origin, shoulder clasps hinged together with a removable pin, the lid of a purse and much more. A gold buckle from the find (British Museum) has Style II ornamentation. In the circular disc at the top a snake-like creature is clearly seen biting its own body and in the complicated web of interlacing in the main body of the buckle thirteen different animals have been identified. Both Style I and Style II can be difficult to decipher and the reader is referred to the excellent British Museum blog by Rosie Weetch and Craig Williams where the authors illustrate how to unravel the complex and hidden designs.

The largest hoard of Anglo-Saxon metalwork ever discovered, the Staffordshire Hoard, only recently came to light (see Staffordshire). In all, a staggering 1,662 objects were discovered including eighty-six sword pommel caps and seventy-one sword hilt collars, many inlaid with garnet. The hoard contained only military material, including a helmet in Style II with animals biting their own bodies, but with no domestic or female items. A fascinating find was a gold strip with a biblical inscription from the Book of Numbers 10:35 in Latin and translated as 'Rise up, O Lord, and may thy enemies be dispersed and those who hate thee be driven from thy face.' One theory as to the nature of the treasure is that it was a trophy hoard captured by the Mercian kings – for instance, Penda – in their warlike raids into Northumbria.

Style II lasted for about 100 years but then Christianity came to the Anglo-Saxons. There is a tradition that when St Augustine reconverted the English in 597, Gospels were sent to him by Pope Gregory, the so-called St Augustine Gospels. They date from the 6th century and were made in Italy. For many years they resided at Canterbury and, following the dissolution of the monasteries in the 16th century, Matthew Parker (Master of Corpus Christi College, Cambridge and Archbishop of Canterbury) was allowed to transfer them – along with other illuminated manuscripts – to Corpus Christi College. They are housed there today and are used at the installation of every Archbishop of Canterbury. Their decorative work was an influence on the development of Anglo-Saxon illuminated manuscripts.

As we have seen, Benedict Biscop travelled many times from his monastery at Monkwearmouth and Jarrow to Rome, bringing back skilled masons, glaziers, craftsmen and, most importantly, books. These masons and glaziers were instrumental in building Biscop's monastery at Monkwearmouth and Jarrow. It was one monastery in two places and would have been colourfully decorated. Bede records that 'Wearmouth and Jarrow were founded on the Roman model,' Wearmouth in 675 and Jarrow in 681. But significantly at Wearmouth there is sculpture in the native insular tradition (art of the post-Roman era in the British Isles) in the jambs of the entrance door. Each has a serpent with interlocking beaks and intertwined tails both coming together as crosses in X and T shapes. Also to Rome, looked the fiery Wilfrid, who founded the monastery at Hexham – like his character – with grandeur. His biographer, Stephen, wrote: 'our holy bishop, being taught by the spirit of God, thought out how to construct these buildings nor have we heard of any other house on this side of the Alps built on such a scale.' William of Malmesbury later commented: 'those who have visited Italy allege that at Hexham they see the glories of Rome once again.' Of this church, the crypt survives.

Benedict Biscop was succeeded at Monkwearmouth/Jarrow by Abbot Ceolfrith. In 692 he commissioned the astonishing Codex Amiatinus, a Vulgate version of the Bible consisting of 1,040 leaves of vellum. Ceolfrith intended to gift it to the pope and set off for Rome in person. He died on his journey in 716 and the Bible was eventually discovered at the Abbey of San Salvatore in Tuscany. It is now at the Laurentian Library in Florence. The work is of such high quality that it was only in the 19th century that it was finally acknowledged that the superbly decorated bible came from supposedly backward Northumbria and not Italy.

From Northumbria came very beautiful illuminated Gospels. Apart from a fragment of a Gospel book at Durham Cathedral Library, the earliest surviving illuminated Gospel in the insular style is the Book of Durrow. Whether it was produced at Durrow Abbey in Ireland, at Lindisfarne or Iona is open to debate. It is now at Trinity College, Dublin and dates from about 680.

Cuthbert is probably Northumbria's best-loved saint and Bishop Eadfrith produced in his honour, in about the year 700, the Lindisfarne Gospels. The

Vikings forced the monks to leave Lindisfarne in the late 9th century and they settled at Chester-le-Street, taking Cuthbert's body and the Lindisfarne Gospels with them. It was here that the priest Aldred inserted an Old English version of the Bible between the lines of the original Latin text, the first translation of the Gospels into English. The Gospels reflect the Anglo-Saxon love of colour and are still beautifully preserved. A masterpiece of Anglo-Saxon art, with elements of Style II, they are full of interlace patterns, knotwork, animals and birds. They are now housed in the British Library.

And from Northumbria came the whalebone Franks Casket (British Museum). The Christian 'Adoration of the Magi' is depicted as well as scenes from Roman and Germanic mythology. It was eventually found in an antique shop in Paris, where Sir Augustus Wollaston Franks, curator at the British Museum, purchased it and donated it to the museum.

With the coming of Christianity, human figures became more prominent in Anglo-Saxon art, often associated with stories from the Bible. There were also elaborate vine scrolls to represent Christ as the true vine (John 15, 1–7). And it is in Northumbria again that we can see splendid examples of sculpture. There are many, but the supreme ones are the crosses at Ruthwell (in Scotland but then in Northumbria) and Bewcastle. The Easby Cross, also from Northumbria, is another excellent example. It was found incorporated as three separate pieces in Easby parish church in North Yorkshire. A fourth was found in a nearby field. All sections have been combined and are now on display in the Victoria and Albert Museum. Christ in Majesty is shown above and below are the heads of the apostles. The other faces have vine scrolls and interlace richly inhabited by animals.

Those who wish to delve deeply into Anglo-Saxon stone sculpture can do no better than to consult the *Corpus of Anglo-Saxon Stone Sculpture.* This mighty project identifies, records and publishes English sculpture dating from the 7th to the 11th centuries. It describes all sculpture within this period, including that introduced by Viking invaders, from freestanding carved crosses to grave markers. The project was born in 1977 at the University of Durham under the direction of Professor Dame Rosemary Cramp and has expanded throughout the country supported by more than thirty researchers. A series of bound and fully illustrated volumes is the result, covering every Anglo-Saxon sculpture in England, thus far covering some thirty-three historic English counties. It is intended that the whole country should be covered. Certain volumes are now online and it is the aim that all should be.

In 1991, Cramp published *Grammar of Anglo-Saxon Ornament* as a general introduction to the Corpus, where she classified Anglo-Saxon stone sculpture in a consistent format. Crosses, tombs and grave markers were considered, typically decorated with plant scrolls often inhabited by leaves, fruit or creatures. Most ubiquitous of all is interlace ornamentation. It developed in the 7th century and has many different forms, which Cramp has categorised. Significantly, she emphasised that dating can raise difficulties. Unless the sculpture contains an inscription which can point to a date, it can be imprecise.

Political ascendency passed from Northumbria to Mercia in the 7th century. Its capital was Tamworth and nearby is Lichfield where the Northumbrian monk, Chad, founded a monastery in 669. Angels feature frequently in Anglo-Saxon stone sculpture. The 8th century painted sculpture of the archangel Gabriel discovered in 2003 during excavations at Lichfield Cathedral is a supreme example. It is work of the highest quality and is thought to be part of a chest containing the remains of St Chad. It conveys a sense of motion, as does the angel at Breedon on the Hill. Also housed at Lichfield are the St Chad Gospels, similar in style to the Lindisfarne Gospels.

A synod was held at Chelsea in 816 and from it came a decree that all churches should display an image of the saint to which they were dedicated. There are excellent examples at Deerhurst (Gloucestershire) and Breedon on the Hill (Leicestershire). There are other fine sculptures at Breedon. Here, the animal ornamentation of the frieze at Breedon is strikingly different from earlier Anglo-Saxon art. All the creatures are vibrant, energised and full of movement.

In the 9th century, power passed to Wessex and with it came a new style, the so-called Trewhiddle style, named after a place in Cornwall, where a hoard of silver and copper was discovered by tin miners in 1774. (It became the custom to name a particular style after the place where it was first discovered.) Leslie Webster describes it as having 'small fields or cartouches, usually with beaded frames, containing lively, often speckled animals, foliage and geometric motifs, the background often inlaid with niello.'

The 9th century saw the ascendancy of King Alfred the Great and the most celebrated works of this period are the 'Alfred Jewel' and the 'Fuller Brooch'. The 'Alfred Jewel' (Ashmolean Museum, Oxford) is exquisitely beautiful. It consists of an enamel image of a man set within a rock crystal. There is much debate about its purpose but it seems likely to be a pointer, used to highlight Biblical text. The 'Fuller Brooch' (British Museum) is late 9th century, inlaid with niello, and depicts the five senses. In the centre a man stares out at us; around him are four male figures, the first smells a leaf, the second rubs his hands together, the third places his hand at his ear and the fourth puts his hand into his mouth, hence the five senses – sight, smell, touch, hearing and taste.

Richard Bailey makes the point that Anglo-Saxon sculpture is there for us all to see today in churches the length and breadth of the country. It would have been appreciated by the local people for whom it was intended. It is therefore very much a local art made close to where it was sited.

At the same time as Wessex came to prominence amongst the Anglo-Saxon kingdoms, England came under attack from pagan and marauding Vikings. Their first assaults were raids for loot but by the late 9th century many had settled and converted to Christianity. The famous 'Jellinge Stone' in Denmark (there is a replica at the Danish church in London's Regent's Park) records that Harold Bluetooth had 'made the Danes Christian'. Their artistic style came, of course from the same root as Anglo-Saxon art. It has much animal ornamentation and their legendary long boats, which heralded such havoc, were decorated in this manner.

Viking settlements in Northumbria were predominantly in Yorkshire with far fewer north of the Tyne; in Cumbria, Scandinavians came from Ireland and in both areas often settled in pre-existing Anglo-Saxon villages. The most distinctive feature of Viking sculpture is the ringed headed cross. Once again various styles are named after finding places. The Borre style, named after finds at Borre in Norway, has, as Richard Bailey explains, a ribbon plait bounded by hollow-sided lozenges. The plait splits in two and then reunites, as can be seen in the Gosforth Cross (see Cumberland). The Jellinge style, prevalent in England, has animals typically in the shape of a double-lined ribbon – see for instance, Middleton in North Yorkshire. The Ringerike style, from a site near Oslo, has animals with contoured and curving bodies with curling tendrils – see Otley and the sarcophagus from St Paul's Cathedral, now in the Museum of London. Interestingly, the Scandinavians did not make monuments in stone until the Jellinge Stone. Accordingly, they borrowed heavily from the native Anglo-Saxon sculpture they found in their new settlements. For instance, the Giant's Thumb at Penrith has a typical Viking-age ringed head but Anglian vine scrolls. The Vikings brought their ancient Norse myths with them and often – for example the Sigurd saga and the story of Wayland the Smith – they are found incorporated within monuments containing Christian symbols.

There are many examples of Viking-age hogback monuments in the north of England. These are gravestones shaped like a boat or long house with creatures resembling bears at each end. There are excellent examples at Penrith and Brompton-in-Allertonshire. But why bears? Nobody seems to know. Bailey commented that it is 'one of the great puzzles of Viking art.'

Alfred the Great is best known to us for halting the advance of the Vikings and his efforts were continued by his successors, Edward the Elder and Aethelstan. Because of the new emphasis on learning and the contacts these Wessex kings had with the Continent, many important Carolingian manuscripts came to England and influenced the 'Winchester School'. Anglo-Saxon art thrived in the 10th century during the monastic reform movement of Dunstan, Aethelwold and Oswald, in particular devotional images with continental influence and images of kingship. But surviving Anglo-Saxon wall paintings are rare. There are, however, excellent examples at Nether Wallop in Hampshire and Winchester Museum.

Further Reading/Sources

1. Richard N. Bailey, *Viking Age Sculpture* (Collins, 1980)
2. Rosemary Cramp, *Grammar of Anglo-Saxon Ornament: A General Introduction to the Corpus of Anglo-Saxon Stone Sculpture* (Oxford University Press, 1991)
3. Rosemary Cramp, ed., *Corpus of Anglo-Saxon Stone Sculpture*, Series of Volumes Published for British Academy by Oxford University Press
4. Nicholas J. Higham and Martin J. Ryan, *The Anglo-Saxon World* (Yale University Press, 2013)
5. Catherine E. Karkov, *The Art of Anglo-Saxon England* (Boydell Press, 2011)
6. Sir Thomas Kendrick, *Anglo-Saxon Art to AD 900* (Methuen, 1938)
7. Sir Thomas Kendrick, *Late Saxon and Viking Art* (Methuen, 1949)
8. James Lang, *Anglo-Saxon Sculpture* (Shire Publications, 1988)
9. Leslie Webster, *Anglo-Saxon Art* (British Museum, 2012)
10. Rosie Weetch and Craig Williams, blog.britishmuseum.org/2014/05/28decoding-anglo-saxon-art
11. David Wilson, *Anglo-Saxon Art* (Thames & Hudson, 1984)

Part Two

A County-by-County Exploration

Bedfordshire

Bedford

The church of St Peter de Merton stands in the centre of the town and is far older than at first it appears. It was originally entered from a porch in the west. The porch was then raised to a tower. The tower is Saxon, with typical long-and-short work at its quoins, except for the top, which is a 19th century restoration. The chancel of the present church would, therefore, have been the nave of the original Saxon church.

Clapham

Clapham lies a couple of miles outside Bedford on the Kettering road. It was held by the Abbot of Ramsey in the 10th century. There is an excellent Anglo-Saxon tower at the church of St Thomas of Canterbury (TL034526). It is constructed of rubble, has three stages and like so many it was probably used as a lookout over the river Ouse to its west. Inside, the tower has characteristic Saxon double splayed windows and a triangular door giving access to the first floor. Pevsner concludes that the top stage is Norman, but the church guide writes that following restoration work in the 1980s, the top of the structure was revealed as all of one piece with the lower stages and probably built by Saxon masons to a Norman design in the 1060s, under the direction of Miles Crispin or Robert Doyley, who held the manor at that time.

Reference

1. Anon., *Clapham Parish Church*, Church Guide

Stevington

The church of St Mary (SP990536) stands to the north of the village, not far from the River Great Ouse and dates from before the Norman Conquest. It has a west tower, the lower part of which is Anglo-Saxon, with typical long-and-short work at the quoins. Inside, and seen from the west end of the south aisle, there is a narrow arch to the tower, also with long-and-short work. This was the original entrance to the tower or perhaps to a porticus. Above is a double splayed window, with another to the north.

Reference

1. Anon., *A Guide to Stevington Church*, Church Guide

Thurleigh

Thurleigh lies about five miles due north of Bedford in quiet countryside. Its church of St Peter (TL051585) has a splendid Anglo-Saxon tower and an equally fine south door giving access to it. Above the doorway is a tympanum showing Adam and Eve, the serpent and the tree.

Turvey

Turvey is situated on the main road from Bedford to Northampton. Evidence that the church of All Saints (SP940526) dates from Saxon times can be seen above the south arcade. Exposed are double splayed windows. They mark out the wall of the original nave, dating from about 980 AD. In the 13th century the nave wall was pierced by the present 13th century arcade.

Reference

1. www.allsaintsturvey.org.uk

Berkshire

Abingdon

Before boundary changes, Abingdon was in Berkshire. There are no visible Saxon remains of the famous abbey at Abingdon. The abbey was founded in 675 and Pevsner tells us (taking information from the Abingdon Chronicle) that it had twelve cells and twelve chapels, one for each monk. It was destroyed by the Danes and re-founded by Aethelwold. He was Abingdon's most famous abbot and was prominent – together with Dunstan – in the great monastic revival of the 10th century. Aethelwold later became Bishop of Winchester in 963. He was vehement and ruthless in his opposition to secular clergy (as opposed to those who followed the Rule of St Benedict). On his appointment as Bishop of Winchester he replaced its clerics with monks from Abingdon, making many enemies in the process. Abingdon was also the burial place of Aelfric, former abbot at Abingdon and later Archbishop of Canterbury between 995 and 1005. His body was later transferred to Canterbury.

Aston Tirrold

Aston Tirrold lies at the foot of the Berkshire Downs, about two miles south-east of Didcot. There is a square-headed doorway in the church of St Michael (SU557861) which gives access to the vestry. In all probability it is Saxon. Aston Tirrold is a contender for the site of the Battle of Ashdown. It was at this battle, on 8 January 871, that Prince Alfred defeated the Danes, albeit temporarily. The men of Wessex were under the command of Alfred's brother, King Aethelred. He prayed for victory at a nearby church (could this have been Aston Tirrold?) and refused to give battle before the priest had finished. Meanwhile, Prince Alfred (soon to become King Alfred the Great) took matters into his own hands and, impatient for the fight to begin, ordered his men to charge the Danes. Alfred and his men were victorious.

Reference

1. Stephen Whitwell, Aston Tirrold and Aston Upthorne, Notes on the Churches, Church Guide

Boxford

Boxford is about three miles north-west of Newbury. Boxford Parish Church (SU429716) sits on the bank of the river Lambourn and church restorers recently discovered a real gem. A perfect example of an Anglo-Saxon shutter-window was brought to light. The frame, complete with a hinged wooden panel, was found by architect Andrew Plumridge during repairs to St Andrew's Church. Andrew, of Peter Scott and Partners, was working on an area badly affected by damp. He removed sections of cement and the window was found, embedded in the wall. Andrew consulted diocesan archaeologist Julian Munby and Reading University medieval specialist Professor Roberta Gilchrist. They both confirmed that the window predates the Norman Conquest.

Wickham

Wickham is a couple of miles west of Boxford and – apart from the proximity of the motorway – is in peaceful countryside. There is a fine Anglo-Saxon tower at the church of St Swithun (SU395716). Wickham was given to the monks of Abingdon in 686 by Caedwalla, king of Wessex. It lies on the Roman road which linked Newbury with Cirencester, thus explaining the use of so many Roman tiles in the tower. As was the custom, it was used as a watchtower from which an approaching enemy could be seen. The now blocked door above ground level was where the watchman would have placed his ladder to gain access, pulling it up once inside. He could also light a beacon to give warning. The tower is of flint with the usual long-and-short work quoins, splayed windows and bell opening with baluster shafts. The top is a Victorian addition.

Reference

1.   Anon., St Swithun's Church, Wickham, Church Guide

Other Places of Interest

- Pevsner speculates that St Mary's Church (SU584870) **Cholsey** may have a Saxon core, on the evidence of long-and-short work quoins in the crossing tower.
- In a barn at Strattenborough Castle Farm (SU237922), **Coleshill**, according to Pevsner, there is an 11th century tympanum in the Viking style. It shows a lamb in a circle. The property is in private hands.
- According to Pevsner, the church of St Mary (SU668641), **Stratfield Mortimer**, has an Anglo-Saxon coffin lid inscribed to Aegelwardus, which he describes as an eminently important piece.

Buckinghamshire

Little Missenden

Little Missenden lies about three miles west of Amersham, just off the road to Wendover, with the tiny river Misbourne running through it. The main attraction of the church of St John the Baptist (SU922990) is its early wall paintings, particularly that of St Christopher. It is also a fine Saxon church. The Saxon nave, according to the guidebook, dates from between 950 and 1000. It was cut through in the 12th century by the present arcades, but traces of Saxon work remain near the St Christopher wall painting. The Saxon Bishop of Dorchester instructed the monks of Bicester to enlarge the church; Roman materials were used and are seen incorporated into the imposts of the Saxon chancel arch. There is a splayed window in the south wall and another in the south wall of the north aisle. There may have been a room over the nave of the original church. Access to it would have been gained by a ladder to a door, high up above the east side of chancel arch. The font is Norman, but it rests on what is thought to be the upturned capital of a Roman column.

Reference

1. Tom Higham, A Guide to the Church and Parish of St John the Baptist, Little Missenden, PCC, 2006

Taplow

Taplow lies on the banks of the River Thames, opposite Maidenhead. It takes its name from Taeppa's Barrow, an immense 6th century burial mound. The mound

(SU906822) lies within the grounds of Taplow Court, more specifically in the churchyard of the former parish church, which was demolished in 1830. It can be reached via a public footpath from the main road. The mound was excavated in the 19ᵗʰ century but unfortunately not very well, a dig described by Lesley Webster as 'catastrophic'. This was unfortunate because the finds were the finest Anglo-Saxon hoard ever discovered, until those from Sutton Hoo. Excavation revealed an adult male – obviously of high status, given the quality of the grave goods – facing towards the west and lying on a feather mattress within an oak chamber. He was wearing a gold embellished tunic secured by a large gold buckle and accompanied by many grave goods including over nineteen vessels, comprising drinking horns, cups and cooking vessels. Also found was a lyre and a gaming board. All are now housed in the British Museum. Lesley Webster speculates that the male may have been a sub-king of Kent on the basis that many of the objects are Kentish in origin.

Reference

1. Leslie Webster, *Anglo-Saxon Art*, British Museum Press (2012), p. 62–4
2. Ibid., 'The Rise, Fall and Resuscitation of the Taplow Burial', Lecture, 28 October 2001

Wing

Set in pleasant countryside on the road from Leighton Buzzard to Aylesbury, the church of All Saints (SP881225) is one of the finest Anglo-Saxon buildings in the country. As one enters the churchyard, the magnificent polygonal Anglo-Saxon apse, which the church is so famous for, comes into full view. It shows great similarity to the apse at Deerhurst in Gloucestershire.

The name Wing means 'the settlement of Withun's people' and the place was originally in the Anglo-Saxon kingdom of Mercia. After the Viking invasions it became part of Wessex. All Saints was a minster church with its clergy preaching and taking confessions over a wide area. The first mention of Wing comes in a late 10ᵗʰ century will of Lady Aelfgifu who held land here. She was a member of the Wessex royal family. For a short while she was married to King Eadwig, until the marriage was annulled as they were too closely related. When a young girl, her behaviour with Eadwig (apparently cavorting with him when his mind should

| *All Saints' Church, Wing*

have been on other matters) displeased the reforming monk, Dunstan, so much that he urged Eadwig to denounce her as a strumpet. It ended up with Dunstan being exiled from the country. Her will recorded that she left sacred relics to the church at Wing. These would have been displayed in the crypt and viewed through a squint. At the time of the Norman Conquest, the parish priest was Goldric.

The church was built during two periods. First was the crypt, which is entered from the church via two staircases to the north and south. It is lit by the three semi-circular openings in the apse, seen from outside at ground level; the opening on the south side of the apse leads to a staircase to give access to the crypt from outside. Thought to be 8th century, the crypt has an inner chamber defined by four huge piers of masonry that support the vault. An ambulatory surrounds this central spine.

The upper part of the apse came later. It is seven-sided and has pilaster strips linked by semi-circular blank arches; above that there are blank, straight-sided, triangular-headed arches. Between two of these arches on the south are round-headed windows.

The nave at Wing has been compared to the Saxon church at Brixworth in Northamptonshire and may be of the same date. It is Saxon and ninety feet long, with walls rising to thirty-five feet. The original unmoulded chancel arch has a twin window above, with Roman tiles in the arches and a baluster shaft

The Crypt at All Saints' Church, Wing

between. There are three semi-circular arches, bulky in character, giving access from nave to aisles.

Two doorways were revealed during a restoration in 1954. They are high up at the west end of the church, on both north and south, and probably gave entrance to a gallery.

Reference

1.   Richard Gem, All Saint's Church, Wing, R.J.L. Smith, Much Wenlock, 2003

Other Places of Interest

- St Botolph's Church (SU828972) **Bradenham** has a south doorway from the Anglo-Saxon/Norman overlap period.
- St Mary's church (SP806190) **Hardwicke** has a double splayed Anglo-Saxon window above the north doorway.
- St Michael's Church (916536) **Lavendon** dates from before the conquest. The lower stage of the tower is early 11th century and has Saxon windows on three sides.

Cambridgeshire

Cambridge

The Church of St Bene't's was founded in the Anglo-Saxon era and dates from about 1020. It is the oldest building in Cambridge and stands in Bene't Street, opposite to the Eagle pub, where, incidentally, James Watson and Francis Crick first informed the world that they had discovered the structure of DNA. The tower of three stages – separated by string courses – is clearly Saxon and has characteristic long-and-short quoins of Barnack stone at all four angles. It has circular holes, high up, which are said to have been deliberately put in to encourage owls to nest and hence catch mice. There are twin openings at the bell-stage with baluster shafts and pilaster strips above. Taylor and Taylor postulate that these could have risen to a gable on each face, and above that a Rhenish helm similar to that at Sompting in Sussex. The adjacent round-headed windows were installed in the 16th century. Inside, the tower arch is Anglo-Saxon and of majestic proportions with carvings of beasts on the capitals. Unusually, the jambs of the arch have long-and-short work. The original Saxon walling of the tower is also exposed inside. Above the tower arch is a Saxon window or doorway; its more recent stained glass depicts St Benedict. St Bene't's is the chapel of Corpus Christi College, which is situated next door to the south.

Reference

1. Anon., St Bene't's Church – History and Architecture, Church Guide

The Devil's Dyke, Cambridgeshire

Devil's Dyke and Fleam Dyke

There are a number of linear earthworks in Cambridgeshire. **Devil's Dyke** – in some sections up to nine metres in height and thirty-five metres across – is the largest and runs from the village of Reach (TL567661) in a south-easterly direction to Pickmore Wood, west of Woodditton (TL652583). It was constructed in the 6th or 7th century and served as a barrier between the swamps of fenland to the north and wooded territory to the south and by so doing blocked passage along the ancient Icknield Way. It has been surmised that it was a defensive barrier, built by the people of East Anglia against the raiding Mercians. It can be inspected conveniently between Swaffham Bulbeck and Swaffham Priory at TL582648 on the B1102. The dyke is mentioned in the Anglo-Saxon Chronicle in 905. It was then that Edward the Elder seized territory from the Danes when he 'laid waste their land between the dyke and the Ouse and as far northwards as the Fens'.

Fleam Dyke runs from east of Fulbourn (TL537556) in a south-easterly direction towards Balsham and fulfilled a similar purpose. There are other smaller earthworks – Bran Ditch and Brent Ditch. Other theories are that the earthworks were defensive barriers built by the Romano-British against Anglo-Saxon incursions. Whatever their date, there were certainly ferocious battles here – many mutilated skeletons have been unearthed nearby.

Ely

Ely Cathedral is forever associated with St Aetheldreda. Sometimes known as Aethelthryth, she was the daughter of King Anna of the East Angles and had been married to Tonbert, a local prince, but shortly after the marriage, he died. Aetheldreda then married King Ecgfrith of Northumbria but even so, wished to remain a virgin. Unhappy about this, Ecgfrith bribed Bishop Wilfrid with the gift of much land if he could persuade her to change her mind. It was to no effect and in 673, Aetheldreda eventually retired from worldly affairs, to found a double monastery at Ely, for both men and women.

Legend has it that Ecgfrith pursued her, but she managed to evade him. The story is related on the carvings of the pillars of the octagon in the cathedral. Aetheldreda died

St Aetheldreda, Ely Cathedral

seven years later and was succeeded by Seaxburga. Aetheldreda's tomb was opened by Seaxburga and according to her physician, Cynifrid, the tumour on her neck which had caused her death had been healed and 'her linen clothes looked fresh and new, and touching them had the effect of casting out devils and the wood of her coffin cured blindness'.

In 869, the Vikings destroyed the monastery and it lay in a ruinous state until re-founded as a Benedictine abbey by Bishop Aethelwold of Winchester in 970. In the south aisle of the cathedral is a Saxon cross shaft. It is inscribed in Latin: 'Give, O God, to Ovin, your light and rest, amen'. Ovin was steward to Aetheldreda.

References

1. Bede, A History of the English Church and People, Book Four, Chapter 19
2. Peter Sills, Ely Cathedral Souvenir Guide, Scala Publishers, 2011

Other Places of Interest

- Within the tower at Holy Trinity Church (TL588508) **Balsham**, there is a Saxon coffin lid with cross and interlace decoration.
- There are rows of Saxon carved stones set into the south wall of the chancel (outside) at All Saints' Church (TL455516), **Little Shelford**. Others are on both sides of the south porch, also outside.
- All Saints' Church (TL428681) **Rampton** has Saxon tombstones, decorated with interlace, set in the chancel east wall.
- There is a Saxon interlaced carved stone at the west end of the south aisle of St Andrew's Church (TL471521), **Stapleford**.

Cheshire

The highlight in Cheshire are the two splendid Anglo-Saxon crosses at Sandbach.

Macclesfield

In a children's playground in Macclesfield's West Park are three Anglo-Danish cross shafts. They are similar to others in North Staffordshire and Cumberland – square above but circular at the bottom. As at Wincle (see below), they have

Anglo-Danish Cross Shafts, West Park, Macclesfield

circular bands towards the top. There are panels at the top of two of the crosses and interlace on the other. They were placed in West Park in 1858. Before then they were used as posts for two gates at Ridge Hall Farm, Sutton, a local farm, and were known as the Mere stones.

The Cleulow Cross at Wincle stands on a mound within a clump of trees at SJ952674. It is tapered at the top and has two circular bands towards the top.

Neston

Neston lies in flat countryside, on the west of the Wirral. The church of St Mary and St Helen (SJ292774) was rebuilt in 1874. At the same time, various Anglo-Scandinavian stones were rescued from the foundations of the former church, and one, which was employed as a lintel, from its tower. They are now on display inside the church in an exhibition which includes an interpretation. On the stone used as the lintel there are the lower halves of two figures, a man in a tunic and a woman in a long-sleeved gown. Below them is a hunting scene where a stag, held by a dog, is speared by a huntsman. On the other side, two mounted men fight with spears. Another stone shows an angel and, on the rear, two men fighting each other – they could be Cain and Abel. Other stones have the usual interlace patterns. An interesting project at the church has been to reconstruct the possible original appearance of the stones when they were used as grave markers. Thus a replica has been made, full of colour.

Reference

1.   David Morris, *The Neston Stones Project*, Burton and Neston History Society

Prestbury

Prestbury is about three miles north of Macclesfield on the main road to Wilmslow. The small river Bollin flows nearby. In the churchyard of St Peter's Church (SJ901769) is part of an Anglo-Danish cross with spiral scroll and knotwork. The west face has an animal with four legs and its head at the bottom.

Sandbach

Sandbach is famous for its two Anglo-Saxon crosses. They stand in the marketplace and have been dated to about 850. Their original site is unknown and they were probably brought here in the late Middle Ages. The crosses were desecrated, either after the Reformation or during the Civil War, and the parts dispersed. In 1816 they were recovered as far as was possible and re-erected.

Anglo-Saxon Crosses, Sandbach

The one on the north (nearest the pub) has at the top of its east face (nearest the betting shop) a representation of the Three Wise Men visiting Jesus who is held in Mary's arms on the left. On the right are the Magi, above one another in alcoves.

Next down is the Crucifixion scene. Jesus's arms are surrounded by symbols of the Apostles – St Matthew holds a book, there is an ox (St Luke), eagle (St John) and lion (St Mark). The two figures at the foot of the cross are St John on the left and Mary on the right. On the same slab, below, is a Nativity scene – an ass and an ox look on the manger with an angel above.

The next one down is the Transfiguration. Elijah stands on the right, holding a scroll. Moses is on the left with tablets of stone.

The circle at the bottom shows Christ in the centre, with St Peter on the right, holding a key and St Paul on the left with a book.

The west face, towards the top, shows Christ on the way to Calvary. He is within an arch at the top right, being led by a figure on the left. Below right is Simon of Cyrene carrying the cross with a soldier with a spear to the left. Below is a rather worn representation of the Annunciation.

On the north face there is a winged serpent and below a series of eleven figures on what could be the Ladder to Heaven. The south face has vine scrolls and knotwork decoration; at its bottom is a man and animals.

The south cross is smaller and has figures within diamond shapes on its east face and figures within alcoves on its west face. The north face has figures within rectangular panels and the south face fourteen figures set in niches.

Other Places of Interest

- The fine church of St Mary (SJ846615) **Astbury** has a fragment of an Anglo-Danish cross shaft with cable moulding in the west bay of the north aisle. It was found in the late 19th century.

East Face of North Cross, Crucifixion Scene, Sandbach

- A sandstone Anglo-Saxon cross stands outside the church of St Barnabas (SJ349814), **Bromborough**.
- There is a small fragment of Anglo-Saxon sculpture in the south wall of the tower (inside) of St Laurence Church (SJ521773) **Frodsham**.
- The church of St Chad at Church Hill, Over, **Winsford** (SJ650651) has, according to Pevsner, a small piece of Anglo-Saxon interlace in the chancel.

Cumberland and the Ruthwell Cross

Cumberland takes its name from the Welsh kingdom of Cumbri. It later became part of the kingdom of Strathclyde, which extended from Glasgow to Chester. By the late 7th century it was under the control of King Ecgfrith of Northumbria. In the late 9th century the Vikings began to settle, probably from Ireland, as witnessed by the many Norse names – for example those ending in '–thwaite'. The glory of Anglo-Saxon art in Cumberland is the justly famous Bewcastle Cross.

Aspatria

Aspatria lies on the main Carlisle-to-Maryport road, midway between Wigton and Maryport. Inside the Church of St Kentigern (NY147419) and to the west of the nave is part of an Anglo-Danish cross shaft with intricate carving. Above the somewhat weathered cross is a modern banner, showing the original appearance of the cross.

Reference

1.   Anon., 'A Guide to St Kentigern's, the Parish Church of Aspatria', Church Guide

Bewcastle

The Bewcastle Cross (NY565745) is justly famous and comparable only with the cross at Ruthwell, across the Scottish border. Church and cross stand in remote and idyllic countryside about ten miles north of Brampton with the Border Forest Park to the east. The cross is work of the highest quality and stands to the south of the diminutive church of St Cuthbert. The church's guidebook ponders how such outstanding craftsmanship was available in Bewcastle in the 7th or 8th century and concludes that the cross is the work of stone carvers (or their apprentices) imported from the Mediterranean to the monasteries at Monkwearmouth and Jarrow. Pevsner concurs, stating that they are, 'together with Ruthwell in Dumfriesshire, the greatest achievement of their date in the whole of Europe. The technical

Bewcastle Cross, Cumberland

mastery is amazing. How can it have been possible in stone at such an early date?'

Pevsner has dated the cross to the late 7th century on the basis of the inscription in Runes, which is said to commemorate someone called Hwaetred and perhaps Alchfrith, son of King Oswy of Northumbria.

The west face is weathered but has been interpreted, from the top, as John the Baptist holding the Agnus Dei. There is a runic inscription below and a figure of Jesus stepping on a serpent and a lion. He holds a scroll in one hand and gives a blessing with the other. Beneath is another runic inscription, and at the bottom, a man, perhaps St John the Evangelist, holding a staff in his right hand with a bird on his left hand.

The east face has a vine scroll along its entire length with animals within scrolls, squirrels, birds and a horse standing on its rear legs.

The south face has knotwork at the top, then a vine scroll with fruit, acorns, flowers and a sundial within. Below is more interlaced knotwork, then more vine scroll and at the bottom, interlace work. A sundial is also worked into the design.

The north face has vine scroll with fruit, then a section of interlaced knotwork. Next down is a chequered pattern, then interlaced knotwork and at the bottom, vine scroll.

Pevsner has concluded that there is Coptic and Mediterranean influence in the stone carver's work.

Reference

1. Anon., Bewcastle, A Brief Historical Sketch, Church Guide

Dacre

Dacre takes its name from the small beck that runs nearby. It lies in splendid countryside, about four miles south-west of Penrith and north-east of Ullswater. It is first mentioned by Bede who records that miracles were performed in the name of St Cuthbert 'at the monastery which, being built near the river Dacore, took its name from it.' Apparently, the monastery possessed a lock of Cuthbert's hair which, when placed on a young monk's tumour, immediately effected a cure. According to William of Malmesbury, writing in the 12th century, Dacre was the scene of the 'Peace of Dacre'. (This is obviously the same as the Treaty of Eamont of 927.) King Constantine of Scotland and Owen of Cumbria arrived to pay homage to King Aethelstan of England. At the same time Constantine's son was baptised with Aethelstan as godfather. The peace did not last and in 937 Aethelstan was forced to come back with an army to defeat the allied forces of the Cumbrians and Scots.

The Church of St Andrew (NY460266) has in its chancel two parts of Viking crosses. According to the excellent church guidebook, the smaller one dates to the 9th century. It was found in 1900 and has two pairs of feet above a winged lion and serpent. The larger stone has two figures holding hands below a four-legged beast. Rachel Newman says this may be Abraham and Isaac – the four-legged beast being the sacrificial ram. Below is the figure of an animal with another on its back. It could be the 'Hart and Hound' symbol used by Bede and others to represent the soul pursued by the forces of evil. At the bottom is a Fall scene. Adam (naked) and Eve (clothed) are picking fruit. It dates from the 10th century. The whole is decorated with leaves and flowers.

Reference

1. Rachel Newman, *A Brief History of the Church and Village of Dacre*, Dacre PCC, 2008
2. Richard N. Bailey, *Viking Age Sculpture*, Collins, 1980, p. 172–4

Penrith

There are two Norse monuments in St Andrew's Churchyard (516302), popularly known as the Giant's Thumb and the Giant's Grave. To the west is the Giant's Thumb, a Norse cross speculated to have been erected in about 920 by Owen Caesarius, a Cumbrian king, in memory of his father. The cross, re-erected in 1887, has interlace and a wheel head.

Further to the east is the Giant's Grave, said by some to be the grave of Owen Caesarius himself. It was opened in 1675 and 'ther found the great long shank bones of a man and a broad sword besides found ther by the churchwardens'. There are two crosses, both of which are taller than the Giant's Thumb. The one on the west is 11 ft tall with interlace and the one on the east, six inches shorter, again with interlace but with what could be two figures, a man and a

The Giant's Graves, Penrith

woman with serpents above. As at Gosforth, the crosses are round at their bases, becoming square above. They are both badly weathered. In between are four hogback tombstones of red sandstone.

Reference

1. Anon., *A Guided Tour of St Andrew's Church*, Penrith, Church Guide

Plumbland

Plumbland is about eight miles north east of Cockermouth, north of the main Cockermouth-to-Carlisle Road. The Church of St Cuthbert (NY142393) has a hogback tombstone dated to about 980. Designed to represent a hall, its roof shingles are clearly evident. It was split in two in the early 13th century. One part was used as a corbel to support a figure, the other as a springer for a window arch. Also, if you can make it out, there is a fragment of a cross shaft incorporated into the first floor of the tower.

Reference

1. Anon., *The Parish Church of St Cuthbert, Plumbland*, Church Guide

The Viking Trail

There is an excellent selection of Anglo-Norse crosses towards the west coast of Cumberland. Chris Jones has published a guide to many of them in *The Viking Trail* and much of the following is taken from his booklet. There is much to see, so beginning in the south and working north there is first Waberthwaite.

Reference

1. Chris Jones, *The Viking Trail*, Lakeland Heritage, 2002

Waberthwaite

The tiny Church of St John (SD100951) lies in idyllic countryside at the mouth of the River Esk. There are two carved preaching crosses in the churchyard, now well covered by lichen. They were previously part of the porch – the larger upright one served as the lintel and the smaller one as the entrance slab and now, by the wear of many worshippers' feet, badly worn. They were rescued in the 19th century by Lord Muncaster. On the lower panel of the east face of the upright one is knotwork, above is a horse and on the top panel a bird, both difficult to discern.

Reference

1.   Anon., *St John Church Waberthwaite*, Church Guide

Muncaster

The Church of St Michael (SD104965) stands on the main road half a mile north of the river Esk. It has a red sandstone cross shaft, the west face of which displays a ring chain pattern in the Borre style. Chris Jones surmises that it represents the sacred tree, Yggdrasil, which connected earth to heaven. There is a plaiting pattern on the east face and below, a cross head, which was found set into a garden wall at nearby Irton.

Irton

The Victorian Church of St Paul at Irton (NY092005) is set in heavenly countryside with the Wasdale fells as a backdrop. In the churchyard is an Anglian cross, complete with its cross head. The cross is ten feet in height. The head of the west face has a circle containing five pellets in the shape of a cross. The pellets very likely represent the five wounds of Christ – the five piercing wounds Christ received on the cross. The shaft has two panels of interlace between which is a square panel which may contain runes. The head of the east face has a raised circle enclosing a boss and surrounded by pellets. The vertical arm of the head contains badly worn figures. The shaft has five sections. The upper two are worn, the third has a richly decorated cross, the fourth a key pattern and the fifth resembles the third.

Gosforth

The village of Gosforth lies just east of the main Barrow-to-Whitehaven Road. The cross at St Mary's Church (NY073036) is one of the finest in the country. It is 10th century, fifteen feet high, round at the bottom and tapering to a square at the top. It is decorated on one face with a Borre-style ring chain. Chris Jones identifies the cross with the sacred ash tree Yggdrasil of Norse myth. The bottom of the east face shows Christ with his arms spread out but not on the cross. A moulding on Christ's right shows a stream of blood running down to the spear below, held by Longinus (the Roman soldier who pierced Jesus's side). To the right of Longinus is a female, said to be Mary Magdalene. Below this are beasts tied together. Above, there is plaiting and above that the heads of beasts to top and bottom, the lower one in combat with a man with a spear. Bailey has compared this scene with the Norse myth, Ragnarök. In the story, Vioarr takes revenge for the killing of his father Odin by slaying the wolf. Good therefore triumphs over evil – a parallel with the crucifixion.

The Fishing Stone, Gosforth, Cumberland

There are two scenes at the bottom of the west face. The upper one shows a man repelling a monster with his spear. In his other hand he has a horn. Bailey has identified the figure as Heimdallr, the watchman god, whose horn alerts the gods for the final battle. Below is a figure upside down on a horse. He has been identified as Loki, the Norse trickster god who is being punished by having the venom of a snake dripped on his head. Below, his wife, Sigyn, tries to collect the venom in a bowl.

The south face shows a horned creature, probably a stag; below is a wolf or a dog entangled in interlace and below this a man on a horse. There are two horsemen on the north face, one upside down.

Inside, the church has two hogback tombs dating from the early 11th century, discovered during a late 19th century restoration. The 'Saint's Tomb' (the east end of the roof is broken) is said to show the story of Ragnarök, the battle between good and evil with Vioarr, Odin's son, killing the Fenrir-wolf.

At its end is a Crucifixion scene. The 'Warrior's Tomb' has on its south face a battle – men with shields and spears – which in legend celebrates the victory of the Norse leader Grice over the English army of King Aethelred at Hardknott Pass in 1000.

There are other Viking-age fragments at the end of the north aisle – in particular the 'Fishing Stone'. Here, in the upper panel, a hart treads on a serpent and below, in the lower panel, there are two men in a boat with fishes. The stone is said to represent Christianity triumphing over paganism. Quoting from Chris Jones's booklet, the upper panel depicts a hart (a Christian symbol) trampling on the monster serpent, Jörmungand. Below, Thor is out fishing for the world serpent with the giant Hymir. Thor does catch the serpent Jörmungand, but Hymir panics and cuts the line. In frustration Thor hurls his hammer out at the vanishing serpent. According to Bailey, Thor has cut off the head of an ox belonging to Hymir and used it as bait. Hymir catches whales, whereas Thor hooks the world serpent. The stone is thus symbolic of good triumphing over evil.

Reference

1. Richard Bailey, *Viking Age Sculpture*, Collins, 1980, p. 125–132
2. Ella Tyson, *A Short History of St Mary's Church, Gosforth*

Beckermet

There are two churches at Beckermet. Standing alone and isolated, half a mile south-west of the village, near to a disused railway line, is St Bridget's (NY016061), sometimes referred to as the Old Church. There are two cross shafts in the churchyard, one of which has an inscription which has been variously translated as recording the burial place of Bishop Tuda, who died of plague in 664; or a memorial to Abbot Adulf from Iona; or a prayer in Manx Gaelic for Iuan mac Cairbre.

In the village is St John's Church (NY019067) with, it is claimed, fragments from eleven crosses. They are all inside. In the porch is a Norse cross head with a central boss surrounded by pellets and a separate shaft with spirals. Beneath the windows of the north aisle are fragments of Norse cross shafts, all of high quality.

Reference

1. Norman Roberts, *St John's Church, Beckermet, Built on a Strong Foundation*, Church Guide, 1979

St Bees

There is a legend that St Bees takes its name from a saintly Irish girl, Bega, who fled here in about 900 and lived the life of a hermit. When Norse settlers arrived they called the place Kirkeby Beghoc, i.e. a village near Bega's church. The church (NX969121) is three miles south of Whitehaven and was originally a Benedictine nunnery; it is Norman but has part of a splendid Anglo-Danish cross shaft in the south aisle with intricate carving.

Reference

1. Anon., *St Bees Priory, A Short Guide*, PCC, 1978

The Ruthwell Cross

The cross is in Scotland at Ruthwell in Dumfriesshire (NY099674), but in the 8th century Ruthwell was part of Northumbria and too important to omit.

It dates from the 8th century but was desecrated by iconoclasts in 1642 and all but abandoned. In 1823 it was rescued by Henry Duncan (famous for opening the world's first commercial savings bank) and set up in the manse garden. Then in 1867 it was taken inside Ruthwell church and placed in a specially built apse where it can be viewed today.

The main lower section of the shaft, on its north side, has Christ standing on beasts surrounded by a Latin inscription translating as 'Jesus Christ: the judge of righteousness: the beasts and dragons recognised in the desert the saviour of the world.' Below, St Paul and St Anthony break bread in the desert, also surrounded by a descriptive Latin inscription. Then comes the Flight into Egypt and at the bottom a badly worn panel, which could be a Nativity.

The south side has Mary Magdalene washing Christ's feet – see Luke, Chapter 7, Verse 37–8. Below, Christ heals a man born blind – see John 9:1

and below that the Annunciation; the angel Gabriel is entering on the right and approaching Mary.

The upper part of the cross shows a break between it and the lower panels. On the south side are Martha and Mary and above, an archer. On the north side, John the Baptist holds the lamb.

The remaining two sides have vine scrolls inhabited by a variety of creatures. As well as the Latin inscriptions the cross has, at its surrounds, runes from the poem the 'Dream of the Rood.'

Other Places of Interest

- With expansive views of the Firth of Solway, St John the Evangelist (NY069390) at **Cross Canonby** has, according to Pevsner, a 10th century cross shaft.
- The Church of St Mungo (NY073364) **Dearham**, also according to Pevsner, has a large collection of Anglo-Danish sculpture.
- Part of a Norse cross shaft with scroll is incorporated as a quoin in the south-east wall of the nave of **Haile** church (NY031088), set in a quiet valley with the Kirkbeck stream running nearby.

Derbyshire

Bakewell

Bakewell is an ancient place as confirmed in the Anglo-Saxon Chronicles, which record that Edward the Elder visited in the 920s and ordered a burgh to be built. There followed a meeting with Scots, Northumbrians and Strathclyde Welsh which 'chose Edward as father and lord'. The event has, however, been disputed by some historians. The church of All Saints, Bakewell (SK216685), has a fine collection of Saxon sculptures. There are two well-preserved Saxon crosses in the churchyard. The larger, by the south transept, was under a protective covering and surrounded by scaffolding when I visited. However, Pevsner tells us it has vine scrolls, animals and the defaced figure of a man. It has been dated to the 9th century. There is a display board in the church which gives a possible interpretation of it having a pagan side and a Christian side from which the following is taken:

Pagan Side of cross: From the top, Woden rides his horse, Sleipnir. Below, Ratasosk, the squirrel, communicates between gods and humans, eating the fruit of the vine, which is the fruit of Christ. (In Viking mythology humans lived out in the branches of a great ash tree called Yggdrasil while the gods lived at the top.) At the bottom is part of a figure with a bow and arrow.

Christian Side of cross: Pagans are taught Christ's quality of self-sacrifice, in contrast to Woden's aggression. In the Annunciation, an angel is the new messenger to Mary, the mother of Christ. Below, St Peter has the keys to heaven, rather than the 'world tree' route to Valhalla. At the bottom is probably King David, with lap harp, who wrote the psalm likening God's word to 'arrows of love'.

The smaller cross was originally at nearby Beeley and came via Darley Dale to the church at Bakewell. Once more, a display panel offers a possible interpretation. Thus:

South Face: At the top is a Norse mask. The pellets below this perhaps represent grapes, the fruits of the vine, a Christian image. There are two crosses with loose and unconnected rings, suggesting separate tribes or peoples. Below the horizontals the lower rings are connected, suggesting the joining up of separate groups of peoples, by the unifying influence of Christ.

West Face: The top spiral is an abstract form of vine, as on the larger cross shaft, representing Christ who said, 'I am the vine'. Then there is the figure-of-eight interlace. The lower panel has two spirals in an S shape. The second S looks incomplete. One view is that it is deliberate, so that human work should not be so perfect as to rival that of God.

North Face: Above and below the horizontals are angular figures of eight interlacements (as on the west and south faces) suggesting the joining up of separate groups of people.

East Face: At the bottom of the upper panel is a three cornered interlace or triquetra. This represents God as the Father, Son and Holy Spirit. The random interlace above may represent clouds. The eye by the horizontal may be the Trinity looking down on us. The lower panel shows a guilloche, a loop twisted so the cords cross and re-cross, suggesting a perfectly plaited and united community of separate peoples.

In the south porch more Saxon pieces line the walls.

Reference

1. Many Authors, *All Saints' Church, Bakewell*, Jarrold, 2002
2. D. Whitlock, *English Historical Documents*, 1955, p. 199.

Brailsford

Brailsford is midway between Derby and Ashbourne. All Saints' Church (SK245413) lies at the end of a lane west of the village proper, near to the tiny Brailsford Brook. In the churchyard there is a shaft of a mid-11th century Anglo-Saxon cross. It was discovered beneath a medieval cross in 1919. As at Norbury, there is a carving of a man on one side holding a sword. Before the Conquest, Brailsford was held by the Saxon, Elfin.

Eyam

Eyam lies in the idyllic Derbyshire Dales, just north of the main Chesterfield to Chapel-en-le-Frith road. It is famous for the outbreak of plague in 1665. Selflessly, the villagers opted to keep themselves isolated to prevent the disease

Anglo-Saxon Cross, Eyam

spreading. There is an excellent cross at the Church of St Lawrence (SK217765) dating from the 8th century and important because of its intact cross head. The cross stands in the south-east of the churchyard.

On the east face of the shaft are plant scrolls and leaves. The intact cross head (east) is decorated with angels who appear to be blowing trumpets. In the cross head of the west face are angels. Below, in the shaft (west) are two figures. The upper is cut off above the shoulders but shows a figure holding a child – presumably it is the Virgin and Child – below is a male figure, facing forward.

Reference

1.   John Clifford, *The Church of St Lawrence, Eyam*, Church Guide, 2004

Hope

Hope is situated on the main Sheffield to Chapel-en-le-Frith road with the High Peak to its north. In the churchyard at St Peter's (SK172834) is a Saxon cross shaft with well-preserved pattern work.

On one of the faces are two figures separated by what could be a cross. On the other face are two figures which appear to clasp each other, with possibly a further figure above.

Anglo-Saxon Cross, Hope

Norbury

Norbury is about five miles south-west of Ashbourne. The church has, as neighbours, the River Dove and the dismantled Uttoxeter-to-Ashbourne railway line. There are two Anglo-Saxon cross shafts at the church of St Mary and St Barlok (SK125424). They were discovered during a restoration of the church in 1899. Both have well-preserved interlace patterns, with one showing a figure of a man who holds a sword.

Before the Conquest, the manor was held by the Saxon, Sweyn. He was a follower of Hereward the Wake and his resistance to William the Conqueror landed him in prison.

Reference

1. Various, *The Church of St Mary & St Barlok*, Norbury, 2005
2. Bowyer, L.J. Rev., *The Ancient Parish of Norbury, Ashbourne*, J.B. Henstock, 1953

Repton

Repton is in the south of the county, in the Trent Valley between Burton and Derby. By the late 7th century there was an important monastery at Repton (Hreopedune) in the Anglo-Saxon kingdom of Mercia, remains of which survive today at the church of St Wystan (SK303272). We know that St Guthlac (see Crowland, Lincolnshire) studied and received his monastic tonsure from Abbess Aelfthryth at Repton and that three Mercian kings were buried here. First, the sub-king Merewalh in 686, then Aethelbald, who was murdered in 757 at nearby Seckington, and finally Wiglaf in 839. The church is dedicated to St Wystan. He was the grandson and successor to King Wiglaf. But Wystan had no ambition to rule and nominated his mother instead. She received a proposal of marriage from Wystan's cousin, Berhtferht, doubtless wishing for the crown himself. Wystan opposed the marriage and as a result was murdered by Berhtferht. Wystan was originally buried at Repton but later, during the reign of King Cnut, his remains were removed to the abbey at Evesham. It is said that because of the martyrdom of Wystan 'miracles were not wanting… for columns of light shot to heaven from the place where he was murdered and remained visible for thirty days.' There is also the story, endorsed in the 12th century by the Archbishop of Canterbury, of hair growing on Wystan's feast day at the place where he was murdered.

Anglo-Saxon Crypt, Repton

The glory of Repton is its crypt, only discovered in 1779, when a workman who was digging a grave fell into it. Pilgrims would have processed through the crypt, entering through one passage and leaving by the other.

The original church at Repton was in the shape of a cross, with a central crossing. Today, the chancel, the angles of the crossing and a small section of the north transept survive, best appreciated from the outside. The oldest part of the church is the crypt. Its walls can be seen as the lower parts of the chancel, below ground level in a trench. The next stage of the chancel ends in a string course and above that is a later section with pilaster strips. The walls of the crypt are seen from the outside at floor level as four steps, each one recessed from the one below. The crypt has two entrances inside the church in each transept. It has nine square bays, a vaulted roof and four columns with spiral fillets which run upwards around them. Extensive details are given in Dr Taylor's guide.

Repton lies on the river Trent, which gave the Vikings easy access to the hinterland of the country. They came to Repton in 873. Excavations have revealed a Viking enclosure of some three and a half acres, a Viking burial mound and the remains of a Viking warrior with sword by his side.

Reference

1. H.M. Taylor, *St Wystan's Church Repton*, Church Guide, 1989

Wirksworth

Wirksworth, about six miles south of Matlock, was a lead mining centre and there is a reference to this long-gone industry in the church. There is much Saxon sculpture to excite at St Mary's Church (SK287539). When the Mercian King Peada married Alchfled of Northumbria, Christianity came to Derbyshire. She was accompanied by four priests, based originally at Repton. There is a legend that one of them, Betti, founded the church at Wirksworth and that the famous Wirksworth Stone is Betti's gravestone.

The stone was found buried beneath the altar of St Mary's in 1820. It covered a grave containing a well-preserved skeleton – perhaps Betti's. It has been interpreted by R.W.P. Cockerton. Upper row: Christ washing the feet of his disciples. A Crucifixion with a lamb in its centre and the symbols of the four evangelists, with books, at the corners. The burial of the Virgin Mary. St John carries the sacred palm

| Anglo-Saxon Coffin Lid, Wirksworth

| The Derbyshire Lead Miner, T'owd Man, Wirksworth

and other apostles carry the body on a stretcher. The scene is the earliest known portrayal of this event in western art. The Presentation in the Temple. Simeon holds the Christ-Child with Mary to the right. Lower row: The Descent into Hell. Christ lifts up a baby – to represent the release of souls, but, according to Bartholomew the Apostle, with the exception of Herod, Cain and Judas Iscariot. The Ascension of Christ into heaven. The Annunciation – Mary is greeted by an angel with a scroll in his left hand. Mission – St Peter receives a scroll from the Virgin and Child.

There are many other sculptural fragments in both the north transept and south transept, including a splendid carving of a Derbyshire lead miner – 'T'owd Man', with his pick and kibble. Is it Saxon?

It was found at Bonsall and was transferred to the church in 1876. The carving reminds us of the lead mining that was centred around Wirksworth. As long ago as 714 AD, Wirksworth lead was used to make a coffin for St Guthlac of Croyland in Lincolnshire. (See Croyland, Lincolnshire.)

Reference

1.   M.R. Handley, *St Mary the Virgin Wirksworth, A Guide and History*, Church Guide
2.   R.W.P. Cockerton, *Archaeological Journal*, CXVIII, 1961, p. 230

Devon

Colyton

The small river Coly runs through the village of Colyton in East Devon. It is about four miles north of Seaton. There was a fire at St Andrew's Church (SY246942) in 1933 which, although causing much damage, revealed the remains of a Saxon cross incorporated into the west wall of the tower. It now stands in the south transept and is an outstanding work of art. On one side it has acanthus scrollwork at its base; above are three volutes of inhabited plant scrolls. First, what could be a lion, then a bird and foliage at the top. It has been dated to the late 10th century.

Reference

1.   Anon., *The Parish Church of St Andrew, Colyton*, Church Guide

Copplestone

In the middle of the street at Copplestone (SS771026), where the main Exeter-to-Barnstable road has a junction to Oakhampton, is a Saxon cross shaft. It is decorated with a variety of plait and knot patterns, rather badly weathered. On one side there is an opening, presumably for an image. Also on this side are two panels with crosses.

Crediton

Legend has it that St Boniface, Apostle of the Germans, was born at Crediton, which is about nine miles north-west of Exeter. Boniface was born with the name of Wynfrith between 672 and 675 and came from a well-to-do family. In spite of his father's objections, he was determined on a monastic life and joined the monastery at Exeter and later at Nursling, near Southampton. On the death of the abbot at Nursling it was expected that he would assume the role of abbot himself but instead, in 716, he left for Germany with the intention of converting the Frisians. The story goes that in

St Boniface, Crediton

northern Hesse he confronted the traditional pagan beliefs of the people by chopping down a tree dedicated to the pagan god Thor and challenged Thor to strike him dead. Then, a mighty wind descended on the oak and felled it to the ground. Boniface (of course) was not struck down and the crowd were so amazed by what they had witnessed that they all converted to Christianity.

Boniface was helped in his missionary work by the protection of the Frankish leader, Charles Martel. He was given jurisdiction over Germany as archbishop by Pope Gregory III. But Frisia was still to be converted and in 754 Boniface renewed his mission there. He was set upon and killed by a group of armed men between Franeker and Groningen. Boniface lies buried at the abbey of Fulda, now Fulda Cathedral.

In a park at Crediton is a statue of Boniface, unveiled by Princess Margaret in 1960. In 739, King Aethelheard of Wessex (King Ine's successor) gave land at Creedie (Crediton) to the Bishop of Sherborne and a monastery was founded. In 909, Crediton became the seat of the first bishop of Devon and Cornwall. It was not until 1050 that Bishop Leofric moved the see to Exeter – probably because Exeter's town walls offered better protection against invaders.

Reference

1.   Anon., Crediton Town Trail, Crediton Festival Organising Committee, 2009

Dolton

Dolton lies in splendid, undulating North Devon countryside. The Anglo-Saxon font at St Edmund's Church (SS570120) is a splendid piece. It is two parts of a cross shaft, placed one above the other, the uppermost block inverted to provide a larger area at the top. Interestingly the stone does not come from Devon and there have even been suggestions that it comes from Como, in Italy. It was carefully restored by Sian Pybus, a sculpture conservator, in 1997. The upper part (upside down) shows on the south side a face with moustaches emanating from its nostrils and ending in a dragon shape. On the west, are two winged dragons twisting together. There are dragons to the east and typical knot patterns to the north. On the lower part, the font has columns of knotwork figures of eight on two sides. On the other sides are knotwork patterns separated by upright bands, the centre one made up of twisted serpents. One of the latter is a reconstruction.

Reference

Shane Wadland, *St Edmund's Church*, Church Guide, 2004

Sidbury

The East Devon village of Sidbury is about four miles north of Sidmouth, on the road to Honiton. The tiny river Sid runs through the village before flowing into the sea at Sidmouth. The unique thing about the church of St Giles (SY141917) is its Saxon crypt. Regrettably, it is only open to view at certain times. Garwood, in his excellent guide, tells us that the people of Sidbury were converted to Christianity by Irish monks and that the crypt of the original church dates to about 680. It was originally accessed from steps leading down from the north side of the Saxon nave. Its dimensions are 2.83m east to west and 3.2m north to south and it would have been a place for the preservation of relics. It is likely that the crypt would have had a wooden roof, supported on wooden pillars. There are also the remains of a Saxon cross. Garwood informs us that local stone was used for the church's construction: Chert for the walls, steps and floor, while the quoins are of Beer stone.

Reference

Peter Garwood, *Sidbury Church and its 7ᵗʰ Century Crypt*, PCC, 1998

Dorset

Canford Magna

Canford Magna is separated from Wimborne Minster by the small River Stour. The interesting thing about the church (at SZ032988) is that its chancel was the nave of an ancient Saxon church, the chancel of which is now long gone. Inside, the chancel (present day) has two simple arches at its far east, leading north and south into what were originally porticus. The church guide speculates that the church at Canford Magna could have been founded by St Aldhelm, who became Bishop of Sherborne in 705, and that it was possibly burnt by King Cnut when he landed at nearby Wareham.

References

1. Anon., *Canford Magna Parish Church*, Church Guide
2. www.canfordparish.org

Melbury Bubb

Melbury Bubb lies in peaceful countryside, east of the main Roman road between Yeovil and Dorchester. It is not approached directly from the main road but from further east, south of Chetnole and then west along a small lane and across the railway line. All Anglo-Saxon enthusiasts come to Melbury Bubb to admire the famous upside-down font at the church of St Mary the Virgin (ST596065). Melbury Bubb takes its name from the Saxon Bubba, who presumably held land here. It is suggested that the font was once the base of an 11th century Saxon sculptured cross and that the Normans hollowed it out to use as their font. There is a lot of detail, difficult to make out because the font is inverted. There are four large creatures, arranged so that pairs face each other. A lion faces up to a stag, which turns its head away. The lion's mane and the stag's antlers are clearly defined. The lion has a quadruped in its mouth and the stag connects with a biped. The other facing pair is a four-legged cat-like creature with a long, interlaced tail. It faces a quadruped with a smaller quadruped in between.

Reference

1.   Anon., *Melbury Bubb*, Church Guide

Sherborne

Sherborne, about six miles east of Yeovil, (ST638165) takes its name from Scireburne, Saxon for a clear stream. It was in all probability a local centre of Christianity before 705, when King Ine of Wessex split the Diocese of Winchester in two and created the see of Sherborne. Aldhelm of Malmesbury was Sherborne's first bishop, a position he held concurrently as abbot of Malmesbury. St Aldhelm was born in about 640, travelled widely, including to Rome, and was one of the most eminent scholars of his day. He is renowned as the first Anglo-Saxon to write Latin verse, including amongst them, 101 riddles.

In 909, the see of Sherborne was sub-divided when bishoprics were founded at Wells and Crediton. Then, in 1075, after the Norman Conquest, the see was moved to Old Sarum (later Salisbury). In all, there were twenty-six Saxon bishops at Sherborne.

The Saxon cathedral of Aldhem was sited to the west of the present building, as confirmed by excavations. It had a tower with transepts. Pilgrims came to worship at the shrine of Bishop Wulfsin, who died in 1001. They included the Danish King Cnut and his Queen. She was disappointed to see the bishop's tomb 'disrupted with age and gaping with cracks' and immediately donated twenty pounds of silver for the repair of the sacred roof. Bishop Alfwold built a new church at Sherborne in the mid-11th century. In the present church there is a Saxon doorway (seen from inside and in the west wall of the nave). It led into the north transept of Alfold's church. Other Saxon remains in the present abbey church are the rough masonry of its west wall and the crossing piers. In 1840, a Purbeck marble coffin was unearthed beneath the ambulatory, believed to be the tomb of King Aethelbert, brother of Alfred the Great. The burial is recorded in the Anglo-Saxon Chronicle in the year 860. A well-known pupil at Sherborne was Stephen Harding. He was born in about 1050, eventually left for the Continent and was joint founder of a new monastery at Citeaux and thus of the Cistercian Order. He became the third abbot at Citeaux in 1108 and ruled for twenty-five years.

Reference

1.   J.H.R. Gibb, *Sherborne Abbey*, Friends of Sherborne Abbey, 2009

Wareham

As you drive into Wareham from the north, what strikes you first are its Saxon ramparts. They are immediately visible, are the finest in England and were raised on the instruction of King Alfred the Great to defend the town against the Vikings, who attacked in 876. Asser, Alfred's biographer, records Wareham as 'the safest situation in the world, except on the west side where it is joined to the mainland.'

| *Defensive Burh, Wareham*

The Church of Lady St Mary (SY925872) lies by the River Frome. It was originally Saxon but no visible trace now remains. According to William of Malmesbury, it was founded by St Aldhelm, Bishop of Sherborne, in the early 8th century. Aldhelm used Wareham as a port of embarkation for the continent. The church was obviously of major importance because the Wessex King Brihtric was buried here in 802. Asser also writes of a nunnery associated with the church and the Anglo-Saxon Chronicle records an abbess called Wulfwyn, who died in 982. There are a series of ancient stone inscriptions at the east end of the north aisle. They are Celtic, are inscribed with Welsh names, Catgug, Gongor, Gideo, Iudnerth, and Deniel, and have been dated to the 7th or 8th century. There are a number of theories as to their origin. For instance, the names have been linked with Bretons who fled to England in the 10th century to take refuge with King Aethelstan from Viking invaders in Brittany.

To the north of the town is the church of St Martin (923877). It stands on Wareham's north wall and has a Saxon nave and chancel. The church is tall – a typical Anglo-Saxon feature – and there is long-and-short work at the east end of the nave and chancel. A late Saxon round-headed window is in the north wall of the chancel and the chancel arch is late Saxon.

Reference

1. June Brown, *The Church of Lady St Mary Wareham*, Church Guide

Wimborne

Wimborne Minster (SZ00999) was founded by Cuthburga, the sister of King Ine of Wessex. She founded a nunnery here in 705. Cuthburga was followed by Gwenburga, then came Tetta. Nuns from Wimborne joined St Boniface in his task of evangelising Germany. It is said that King Alfred the Great's brother, Aethelred, was buried here after he was killed at a battle at Martin, just north of Wimborne in 871. The nunnery was finally sacked by the Vikings in 1013. Later, in 1043, Edward the Confessor founded a College of Secular Canons. There is Saxon evidence in the church – the turret tower by the north entrance is either Saxon or perhaps from the Saxon–Norman overlap period.

Reference

1. Christine Oliver, *Wimborne Minster*, Jarrold, 2002

Winterbourne Steepleton

Winterbourne Steepleton is about four miles west of Dorchester on the B3159, not far from Maiden Castle. The glory of the church of St Michael (ST629898) is a flying angel, set into the north wall of the chancel. This splendid piece of sculpture used to be outside in the open but was removed inside to protect it from weathering. Pevsner dates it to the 10th century and says it would be one of a pair. The angel's legs are bent upwards and what could be a skull is held in his hand. The face looks very male, is perfectly clear and has a halo. The nave of the church is Saxon.

Other Places of Interest

- The Church of St John the Baptist (SY847947) **Bere Regis** was founded in Saxon times. In 978, Queen Aelfthryth took refuge here after her stepson, King Edward the Martyr, was murdered at Corfe. She was the mother of King Aethelred the Unready. Bere Regis was a royal manor – hence Regis.
- It is worth visiting the church of Holy Rood (ST687053) **Buckland Newton** to see the relief of a figure above the south door (inside). It shows the figure of a man with arms stretched upwards and his right hand clutching a rope.
- On the north wall of the chancel at **Melbury Osmund** (ST574078) is a fragment from an Anglo-Saxon cross said to represent the ram in the thicket from the story of Abraham.
- In the same way as at Winterbourne Steepleton, a Saxon relief which used to be fixed to the outside west wall has been moved inside the church of St Michael (SY712910) **Stinsford**. It depicts St Michael with wings spread and striding to the left. It is badly worn.
- Part of a late Saxon cross was discovered in the churchyard of St Andrew's, **Yetminster** (ST594106) in 1938. It is now displayed inside the church and shows two figures that could be saints, both with halos.

References

1. F.P. Pitfield, *Bere Regis Church*, Church Guide
2. C.J.P. Beatty, *Guide to St Michael, Stinsford*, 2006
3. Jocelyn Berthoud and Nora Windridge, *St Andrew's Church, Yetminster*, Yetminster Local History Society, 1987.

County Durham

Durham

Durham Cathedral is forever associated with St Cuthbert of Lindisfarne. One of the most renowned saints in England, Cuthbert was born in 634, probably in the vicinity of Dunbar, now in Scotland, but then part of the kingdom of Northumbria. As a young man, he entered the monastery at Melrose. He travelled widely throughout Northumbria, preaching and spreading the Gospel. Brought up in the Celtic tradition, he nevertheless accepted the findings of the Synod of Whitby, but in 676 retreated from the world and settled on the lonely and isolated Farne Islands to live a life of austerity. His time in solitude was cut short when, on the insistence of Ecgfrith, king of Northumbria, he was recalled from his cell and consecrated at York as Bishop of Lindisfarne. Cuthbert eventually returned to his cave on the Farne Islands, where he died in 687. He was buried at Lindisfarne.

Many miracles were attributed to Cuthbert and when Lindisfarne was sacked by the Vikings in 875, the monks were determined to preserve his relics. They carried his remains with them when they fled the monastery, first settling them at Chester-le-Street. Further Viking raids compelled another move until Cuthbert was finally laid to rest at Durham. His shrine is now behind the altar at Durham Cathedral. Cuthbert's tomb has been opened on a number of occasions, the latest in 1827, and the treasury at Durham Cathedral contains items removed from it. Cuthbert's coffin is on display. It has been dated to 698 and is made from oak planks taken from a single tree. There is also his magnificent Pectoral Cross, dated to between 640–670, with inlaid garnets and a Byzantine 'Earth and Ocean' silk, dating from the 9th century.

The Venerable Bede also lies in Durham Cathedral in the Galilee Chapel. Bede died in 735 and was originally buried at his monastery at Jarrow. His remains were translated to Durham early in the 11th century.

In the Monks' Dormitory, an important collection of Anglo-Saxon stones is on display in the newly opened Open Treasure exhibition.

Escomb

The church at Escomb is one of the most important Saxon churches in the country. Escomb is a Wearside village, a couple of miles north-east of Bishop Auckland. The church stands within a housing estate. The first written mention of Escomb is in the 11th century *History of St Cuthbert* which tells us that between 990 and 995, Bishop Aldhun of Durham mortgaged Edicum (Escomb) to the Viking followers of King Sweyn. The diminutive and utterly enchanting church (NZ199302) predates this event by 300 years and was founded between 670 and 690. Its dimensions – long, tall and narrow – are typical of early Northumbrian churches such as Monkwearmouth and Jarrow. The Saxon chancel arch is tall and narrow and has bold long-and-short work in its jambs. There are five original Anglo-Saxon windows, all deeply splayed; those to the south have rounded lintels and the ones to the north have straight ones.

Interior, St John the Evangelist, Escomb

Excavations were carried out at Escomb in 1968 and the remains of a former west annexe of two storeys were discovered. At the same time a former north porticus was revealed and fragments of coloured window glass, similar to those at Jarrow.

The church also contains much Anglo-Saxon sculpture. Behind the altar is a stone cross dated to the 9th century and behind the pulpit an incised consecration cross. There are also fragments in the porch.

Outside, in the middle of the south wall, is a splendid Anglo-Saxon sundial. It has a beast-like projection above the dial with two protruding bulbous eyes. Beneath and around the dial is a serpent and twist ornamentation. The dial divides the day into the four Saxon tides, the first being breakfast and worship at 7.30am. Nicholas Beddow has written about the sundial and conjectures that it may be related to Norse mythology: Loki (god of fire) married the giantess, Angura Boda, they had three monstrous children: Hel (representing death), Fenris (representing chaos) and Jörmungand (disorder). In the sundial, the beast is Fenris and the serpent is Jörmungand. There are other interpretations such as the one from Michelle Brown, of the British Library, who maintains that the beast is a stag that has just stamped on the serpent, thus representing Christ overcoming the devil.

References

1. Nicholas Beddow, *The Saxon Church, Escomb*, Church Guide
2. Nicholas Beddow, *Interpreting the Saxon Sundial at Escomb*, Durham Archaeological Society, 1991, Vol 7, p. 109

Hart

Hart, two miles north-east of Hartlepool, takes its name from Heortnesse, in the 7th century an area north of the Tees and sometimes identified with Hartlepool. The church of St Mary Magdalene (NZ470352) is pleasantly placed with a view of the sea to the east. It was founded by the Saxons and has typical long-and-short work at the quoins at the angles of the nave. The present nave follows the line of the original Anglo-Saxon nave and above the 15th century chancel arch the outline of the arch to the Saxon chancel can be clearly seen. Above it is a triangular opening which was probably originally a door for the monks to gain access to an upper room.

Hart has an impressive display of Anglo-Saxon stone fragments including parts of a cross shaft with interlace and a cross head, decorated with a lamb. The latter was found in a nearby field by a ploughman. There are also baluster shafts very similar to the ones at Monkwearmouth and Jarrow.

Reference

1. Anon., *St Mary Magdalene Church, Hart*, Church Guide

Monkwearmouth and Jarrow

Monkwearmouth and Jarrow are without doubt 'must see' places: highlights for any Anglo-Saxon enthusiast. In 674, Benedict Biscop founded a monastery at Monkwearmouth. Later, he instructed the monk, Ceolfrith, together with fellow monks, to build another monastery on land given by King Ecgfrith of Northumbria. So was founded one monastery with two houses – St Peter's at Monkwearmouth and St Paul's at what later became known as Jarrow.

Monkwearmouth

The monastery at Wearmouth (NZ402578) is in present-day Sunderland. Benedict Biscop was born in about 628 and came from a noble Northumbrian family. At the age of twenty-five he made the first of a number of visits to Rome. On his return, he interrupted his journey at the monastery at Lérins, an island in the Mediterranean, and remained there for two years. He then went back to Rome and this time he was accompanied back to Britain by Theodore of Tarsus, newly appointed by the pope as Archbishop of Canterbury. Theodore immediately appointed Benedict as abbot at the Abbey of St Peter and St Paul at Canterbury. Benedict remained at Canterbury until the arrival of his successor, Hadrian. In 674, King Ecgfrith of Northumbria granted Benedict land on the bank of the River Wear to build a monastery. Benedict travelled to the Continent once more, this time to bring back masons, glaziers and other skilled craftsmen to build his monastery based on the Roman model. He also brought back books – hundreds of them – to stock what became one of the most famous libraries in Europe. It was here, and at Jarrow, that Bede studied and wrote his famous works.

St Peter with St Cuthbert, Monkwearmouth (Sunderland)

The original west wall of St Peter's church can best be appreciated by standing in the nave and looking to the west. High up are two small windows, each with stone balusters, and below is a doorway which leads to a room above the porch. The porch is of great interest. It is pure 7th century work and tunnel-vaulted. There are faint but exquisite carvings of birds' heads with serpent-like bodies and fish tails in the lower masonry to north and south. These designs – in the Roman style introduced by Benedict Biscop – are reproduced as a mosaic on the floor of the chancel.

Later, the original porch of Benedict Biscop's church was heightened to a tower of five stages separated by string courses. The west door has jambs of paired baluster shafts and above is a frieze which originally had animal carvings, now regrettably eroded. Above the door is a round-headed window and to the north and south at ground floor level are doorways which originally led to porticus. The outline of the gable of the original porch is visible above the window and within the outline was a figure, perhaps St Peter. There may have been smaller figures on either side. Beneath the belfry window on the west side is a small round-headed window. The belfry has openings on all three sides. They are similar and each are of two lights with a mid-wall shaft.

St Peter's has an impressive display of sculpture on display in the church, including a selection of baluster shafts and the Herebricht Stone. This was found in the porch in 1866 and dates from about 700. It consists of a cross in high relief and is inscribed: HIC IN SEPULCRO REQUISCIT CORPORE HEREBRICHT PRB, which translates as 'Here in the sepulchre rests the body Herebricht the priest'. It seems that Herebricht's name had replaced another name that was erased!

Reference

1. Stuart G. Hill, *St Peter's Church and the Wearmouth-Jarrow Monastery*, Church Guide

Jarrow

In 716 there were about 600 brethren at the joint foundation. It was here that Bede, this country's first historian, came as a seven-year-old child and remained until his death in 735.

The chancel of the present church at Jarrow (NZ339653) is original. Stone for its construction was probably taken from Hadrian's Wall or from the Roman fort at South Shields. It was probably dedicated to St Mary. Soon afterwards a second church was built to its west. Regrettably, by the end of the 18th century, it had fallen into disrepair and was demolished to be replaced by the present

Dedication Slab at St Paul's Church Jarrow

Bede's Chair (traditional) St Paul's Church, Jarrow

nave. Above the west arch of the tower is the dedication stone. It dates from 685 and is the oldest of its kind in the country. It was originally positioned to the east of the north wall in the original nave and was re-sited when that nave was demolished in 1782. There is a cast reproduction under the tower. The inscription is in Latin and translates as: 'The dedication of the church of St Paul on 23 April in the fifteenth year of King Ecgfrith and the fourth year of Ceolfrith Abbot and under God's guidance founder of this same church'.

The chancel dates from the 7th century and has three very small windows in its south wall. Two of the windows have stone shutters. The middle window is particularly interesting. It has Anglo-Saxon glass which was inserted in 1980 following its discovery during excavations in 1972. It is thus the oldest window glass in Western Europe! In the south wall of the chancel, to the west and high up, there is the outline of a blocked doorway. This would have given access to a gallery. To the east, in the sanctuary, the original aumbry can be seen on the south wall and on the opposite side is the so-called Bede's Chair. This fine piece of medieval furniture unfortunately dates from after the time of Bede. Carbon dating has put it at between 800 and 1100 years old.

To begin with the church had no tower, but when the two churches (St Mary and St Paul) were combined, the lower stages of the present tower were built. There are Saxon arches on the ground floor to north and south, the one on the south blocked. The upper stages of the tower are later and were probably added when the monastery was re-founded in the 11th century, after Viking desecration.

There are many Saxon stones and carvings exhibited in the church including the famous Jarrow Cross. It was found when Sir George Gilbert Scott restored the church in the 19th century. The shaft of the cross is incorporated into a

Roman stone inscribed in Latin, translated as: 'In this unique sign life is restored'. The inscription most probably refers to the victory of Constantine over his enemy, Maxentius, at the Battle of Milvian Bridge in 312. Constantine attributed his victory to the fact that he put the chi-rho symbol (first two letters of Christ's name in Greek) on his soldiers' shields before battle after having a vision the night before. Under the Emperor Constantine, Christianity became the dominant religion of the Roman Empire. Alternatively, the inscription might refer to the end of a plague in the 680s.

On display in the church are four baluster shafts from a total of seventeen. These stone columns may have been used to support altar rails or as part of the jambs of arches as can be seen at Monkwearmouth. There are also baluster friezes, which could have been used as lintels; also, two separate well-preserved fragments of friezes, one depicting two birds, the other a man and a beast.

The monastic buildings are to the south of the church. Nothing of the 7th century survives but there is a triangular arch, which may be Saxon.

Reference

1. Ian Hunter Smart and Mavis Dry, *The Royal Ancient & Monastic Parish Church of St Paul, Jarrow*, Church Guide

South Church

South Church is a suburb of Bishop Auckland to its south-east. The church of St Andrew Auckland (NZ217285) is usually locked and I would like to thank Mr Wharton for opening it up for me. The church is famous for its cross. It is made up of fragments. At the bottom of one broad face are three figures, all with halos and elongated fingers. At the top of the panel above are two figures, the one on the left an angel. The figure on the right is female and she holds a rod. Beneath them a central figure is bound to a cross. The cross is inscribed PAS and AND, which may refer to Paul and Andrew. Another figure to the left stands behind the cross. The head of a third figure is on the right. The reverse of this face has two bearded and shaven-headed figures; they both hold scrolls. Beneath are the worn heads of two figures. A narrow face has inhabited scrollwork; at the bottom a quadruped facing right, then above a bird, and above that another quadruped. The remaining narrow face also has inhabited scrollwork including at the bottom an archer, wearing a cap and firing upwards to a bird and quadruped.

Other Interesting Places

- Within the porch of St John's Church at **Egglescliffe** (NZ421132) is part of a Saxon cross and baluster shaft discovered in 1908 when the vestry was built.
- St Cuthbert's Church (NZ456223) **Billingham** (unfortunately locked) has a magnificent Anglo-Saxon 10th century tower. It was built later than the Saxon nave. There is no doorway on the ground floor of the tower but a small arch to the nave, which was probably the church's first entrance before the tower was built. On the first floor, there are windows and above are bell openings with recessed baluster shafts. Interestingly, in the spandrels there are openings in the shape of a star to north and south and a circle to the west. The nave is Saxon and has been dated to about 860.
- St Mary's Church at **Norton** (NZ443222) is a rare example of an 11th century Anglo-Saxon cruciform church. The crossing tower has two Saxon arches inside. There are triangular headed windows outside.
- St Mary's Church (NZ423505) lies to the north of **Seaham** and stands in a prominent position overlooking the sea. The nave has been dated to either late 7th century or early 8th century.

Cross Shaft, St Andrew Auckland Church, South Church, Bishop Auckland

East Yorkshire

Aldbrough

Aldbrough is a quiet place, close to the coast and about twelve miles due east of Beverley. It is mentioned in Domesday Book as being held by Drago de Beauvriere (a follower of William the Conqueror) but previously belonging to an Anglo-Saxon called Ulf. Within the Church of St Bartholomew (SE244387) and set on the north wall of the south aisle is a sundial, believed to be Saxon, with the Old English inscription 'ULF HET ARAERAN CYRICE FOR HANUM & GUTHART SAUL', which translates as 'Ulf raised this church for his and Guthard's souls'. The fact that the sundial divides the day into eight parts dates it to pre-Conquest.

Reference

1.   Anon., *A Short History of St Bartholomew's Church, Aldbrough*, Church Guide

Beverley

Beverley Minster was founded in about 700 by John of Beverley, a monk trained at Whitby by the Abbess Hilda. He went on to become bishop at Hexham and York and ordained the Venerable Bede at Jarrow. The original abbey was sacked by the Danes but restored in the 10th century by King Aethelstan, grandson of Alfred the Great. On his journey north to campaign against the Scots, Aethelstan stopped off at Beverley to pray. While there he placed his dagger on the High Altar and promised that if he was successful in his campaign, he would return and build the church anew. This he was and so the church was restored and converted to a minster.

The Frith Stool, Beverley Minster

Beside the High Altar is the famous Frith Stool, Saxon, and dated by Lang (CASSS) to the 7th century.

Nunburnholme

Nunburnholme lies in peaceful countryside on the edge of the Yorkshire Wolds. The Wolds Way footpath runs through the small hamlet. The Nunburnholme Cross at the Church of St James (SE848478) is justly famous and one of the finest in the country. It came to light in 1873 when alterations were carried out at the church. It formed part of the structure of the south wall and south porch of the building. The cross has now been reassembled by joining together two separate halves and is at the west end of the nave. But, according to Lang (CASSS), who has done extensive research, it has been put back together again incorrectly. He also concludes that the sculpture is the work of more than one artist.

The upper part of the east face shows a seated Viking warrior with sword at his side. Following the Viking assault on the area he is probably the new Scandinavian lord and has been nicknamed Admiral. Beneath the east face is a depiction of the crucifixion, interpreted as Christ placing His hands on the heads of Longinus and Stephaton, the Roman soldiers present at the Crucifixion.

The north face has a figure of a monk or a nun on its upper part and below is a priest administering the sacraments.

The upper west side shows the Virgin and Child; beneath is a headless figure. Both the infant Jesus and the figure below seem to be holding a similar object, perhaps a book or a harp. Beneath the headless figure there is a centaur (a mythical beast, half man, half horse) with a child on its back.

The upper part of the south face shows a saint and below are beasts and an interlace pattern.

The lower part of the north face has also been interpreted as part of the story of Sigurd, a mythical Norse story – and a gory story at that. It tells of a dragon, Fafnir, who stands guard over a hoard of gold. On the advice of Regin, Sigurd (his foster son) kills the dragon and then prepares a meal of the dragon's heart. In the process, he swallows the dragon's blood, which enables him to understand birdsong. The birds tell Sigurd that Regin is going to kill him and so Sigurd pre-empts the event by slaying Regin.

In a paper he published in 1973, Pattison has put together the cross as it should have been. Admiral would have the seated figure and centaur below him. The face with the Virgin and Child would have the Crucifixion scene below and the other faces would be similarly interchanged.

References

1. Peter Halkon, *The Nunburnholme Cross*, Church leaflet, 1996
2. I. Pattison, *The Nunburnholme Cross and Anglo-Danish Sculpture in Yorkshire*, Archaeologia, CIV, 1973

Skipwith

It is mentioned in the Domesday Survey, which tells us that at Scipewic there was a church and a priest. Skipwith is only a couple of miles from Riccall (midway between York and Selby) where Tostig and Harald Hardrada made their base in 1066. They were victorious at the Battle of Fulford but roundly beaten by King Harold at Stamford Bridge. Tostig and Harold Hardrada would have known the church of St Helen (SE657385) with its Anglo-Saxon tower. It has three stages, the upper one Perpendicular. Because of the different materials of construction of the two Anglo-Saxon stages it is likely that the lower stage, lit by double splayed

Viking Door at St Helen's Church, Stillingfleet

windows, was once a porch leading to a small nave. Then in the 11th century the second stage was added, now converting the porch into a tower. There is a typical Anglo-Saxon arch between tower and nave surrounded by a continuous pilaster strip. Above the tower arch is a blocked door which would have given access to the upper chamber of the porch.

Inside there is an interesting carving in low relief behind a panel in the north wall of the tower (now the vestry). It shows a series of gesticulating figures and a fierce animal, probably a wolf. To the left is a figure. His arms are outstretched and there is a serpent between him and the animal. It has been interpreted as having Scandinavian influence. Lang (CASSS) tells us it is probably the destruction of the gods at Ragnarök, where Thor fights with the world serpent and Odin is eaten by Fenrir the wolf.

Reference

1.   Anon., *St Helen's Church, Skipwith*, Church Guide

Stillingfleet

Stillingfleet is about seven miles due south of York on the B1222 in the valley of the river Ouse. The diminutive Stillingfleet Beck runs through the village before reaching the Ouse. The compelling reason to visit the church of St Helen (SE594411) is to view its magnificent south door. Now placed within the church for the sake of preservation, it probably predates the doorway where it once hung. Marked by the inevitable practice of nailing notices to it over the ages, it was subjected to conservation work in 1990.

Its ironwork is Viking in character with 'C' hinges, a depiction of a Viking ship, two figures with stars above, a tree and a horned figure. It has been studied by Addyman and Goodhall who have suggested a 10th century date. The figures have been interpreted as Adam and Eve and the ship as Noah's ark.

Reference

1. P.V. Addyman and Ian H. Goodall, *Archaeologia*, Vol CVI, 1979
2. Anon., Church Guide

Sutton upon Derwent

Sutton upon Derwent lies about eight miles south east of York. The church of St Michael (SE705473) is just south of the ancient bridge across the Derwent. Within there is part of a cross shaft with Viking scrollwork and the heads of beasts. On one broad side is the lower half of a Virgin and Child. Mary's head is lost but her hands clutch the Child, and she wears a broad skirt with folds. The opposite side has plant scrollwork. One narrow side has a fettered bird and the other two beasts, the upper one incomplete and the lower one in profile.

Wharram le Street

Situated in the glorious scenery of the Yorkshire Wolds, between York and Scarborough, and close to the Yorkshire Wolds Way, St Mary's Church (SE864659) has a Saxon nave and tower. The tower is unbuttressed and has four late Saxon belfry windows and slit windows below. Both the west door (now a window), the south door and tower arch are Norman in character, leading Taylor and Taylor to view them as later insertions to the Saxon original.

York

York was founded by the Romans. To them it was Eboracum, meaning a place of yew trees. And it was at York, in 306, that Constantine was hailed emperor of the West by his soldiers. He returned to Italy and went on to win the Battle of

Milvian Bridge against his rival, Maxentius. Constantine's victory is put down to the fact that, after a vision, he ordered his men to put the chi-rho symbol (the first two letters of Christ's name in Greek) on their shields. Christianity was then tolerated in the Roman Empire and as early as 314, a bishop from York was one of three who attended the Council of Arles.

The date of the founding of York Minster is usually put at 627. It was then that Edwin of Northumbria was converted to Christianity. He had married a Kentish princess who was a Christian. A condition of the marriage was that Edwin should convert and accordingly her priest, Paulinus, arrived in York with her and Edwin duly accepted the Christian faith on Easter Day. The first York Minster was then built. Five years later Edwin was killed in battle by the pagan Penda of Mercia and Paulinus fled south leaving the brave James the Deacon behind in York. The next bishop of York was the renowned Wilfrid and under him the church was rebuilt. York became an archbishopric in 732 when Ecgbert received the pallium. It was at this time that York's cathedral school thrived under the leadership of Alcuin, who later travelled to the continent to take his learning to the court of Charlemagne. York fell victim to the Vikings in 886.

There is Saxon evidence at York at the church of St Mary Bishophill Junior. It stands opposite terraced housing in a back street. Its west tower is Anglo-Saxon with reused Roman stonework.

There is a large collection of pre-Conquest sculpture at the Yorkshire Museum in York.

Other Places of Interest

- By the new wooden font at Holy Trinity Church, **Leven** (TA106453), there is a small piece of an Anglo-Saxon cross shaft with interlace.
- St James's church (TA144580) at **Lissett** has what could be a Viking age muzzled bear from a hogback, above the south door.
- The church of All Saints (SE868454) **Londesborough** has an 11th century Anglo-Danish cross head above the Norman south door.
- People come to St Martin's church (TA078607) at **Lowthorpe** to view the astonishing monument to Sir Thomas Heslerton depicting Sir Thomas and his wife. It is covered with the carving of a tree with branches on each side reaching out to their thirteen children. He

founded a chantry in 1364. Above the monument (and not part of it) is a Saxon cross head with interlace.

- All Saint's Church (TA156588) **Barmston** has a Saxon hogback tombstone with interlace and a bear biting it.
- St John the Evangelist (TA054797) **Folkton** has Saxon stonework in the tower west wall.
- St Peter's church (TA010578) **Little Driffield** has a Saxon cross head.
- The church of St Elgin (TA090535) at **North Frodingham** has an Anglo-Saxon cross head with interlace, a serpent and bird.
- St Hilda's (SE969775) **Sherburn** has fragments of Saxon stonework.

Essex

Barking

Barking Abbey was founded in 666 by Erkenwald, later Bishop of London, for his sister, Aethelberga. At the same time he founded a monastery for himself at Chertsey. Aethelberga is described by Bede as 'upright in life and constantly planning for the needs of her community'. It was originally a double monastery for both men and women. Erkenwald died at Barking and was later canonised. In 870, the abbey fell victim to the Vikings and lay desolate for a hundred years until re-founded on the instigation of St Dunstan. William the Conqueror stayed here 'while certain fortifications were built in the city against the vast and fickle population' – The Tower of London. (Next to the Tower of London is the church of All Hallows, Barking by the Tower, founded by the abbey in 675). Apart from a fragment of a cross with interlace decoration in the nearby church of St Margaret, there are no Saxon remains. The layout of the medieval abbey is marked out in the grass, north of the church, and the gate tower remains.

References

1. William Page and J. Horace Round, 'A History of the County of Essex', Vol 2 *Victoria County History*, 1907, p. 115
2. Bede, *A History of the English Church and People*, Book 4, Chapter 6

Bradwell

The chapel of St Peter-on-the-wall at Bradwell (TL032083) stands isolated and remote in a flat coastal landscape, close to where the River Blackwater enters

St Peter on the Wall, Bradwell

the North Sea. The combination of diminutive church and evocative marshland would still be familiar to its founder today. It is a wonderful place. The chapel is built of materials salvaged from the Roman fort of Orthona, which stood nearby.

By the 3rd century, the Roman province of Britannia was threatened by coastal raids of barbarian Picts and Saxons. In response, a series of forts – the forts of the Saxon Shore – were built from the Wash to the Isle of Wight. Orthona was one of these fortifications and a small community was stationed here, with a straight Roman road leading south-west to the hinterland of the country.

Although Orthona was most probably in ruins by the 7th century, it was to this spot that St Cedd was attracted, and it was here that he founded his small Celtic monastic community. Cedd was schooled by Aidan, the founder of the monastery at Lindisfarne. And it was Sigbert, king of the East Saxons, who invited Cedd, in 654, to evangelise his people. Cedd became bishop of the East Saxons and was present at the famous Synod of Whitby in 664, where he acted as interpreter. He died of plague in the same year at Lastingham, a monastery he founded in the North Yorkshire Moors. When news of his imminent death reached his flock at Bradwell, thirty of them made the sea journey north to be with him at the end but all but a child fell victim to a deadly plague and failed to make the return journey to Bradwell.

Bede called the place Ythancestir and it is recorded as Effecestra in Domesday Book, which tells us that there were fish traps and salt pans here.

We enter by the original west doorway. The church consists of just nave alone, 49½ feet by 21½ feet, and with walls 2½ feet thick. Originally there was a rounded headed, apsidal chancel and porticus to the north and south. The outline of these can be seen from outside. The chancel was separated from the nave by arches and traces can be seen, inside, on the east wall.

Reference

1.   Malcolm Carter, *The Fort of Orthona and the Chapel of St Peter-on-the-Wall Bradwell*, St Peter's Chapel Committee, 1966

Greensted

The church of St Andrew at Greensted (TL538030) is utterly unique. It is the only surviving Saxon log church in the country. The body of St Edmund, king of East Anglia, is said to have rested here in 1013, on its journey from London to Bury St Edmunds, and because of this event the church has been dated to

| *The church of St Andrew, Greensted*

that time. Archaeological excavations in 1960 have, however, revealed two wooden buildings underneath the chancel consisting of late 6th or early 7th century logs, placed vertically and resting in a trench. Thus there was an earlier church on the site, which could have been founded by St Cedd, who founded many churches in Essex, while based at Bradwell on Sea.

The nave is built of fifty-one oak logs, split into two vertical halves. Recent dendrochronological analysis (tree ring dating) have dated them to 1060. To make the logs watertight, each vertical log has two vertical grooves, one on each side, which are sealed with vertical tongues. On the base were tenons, originally fitting into a wooden sill, now replaced by brickwork dating

Portrait of St Edmund at St Andrew's church, Greensted

from the church's restoration in 1848. When originally built, the church was windowless, save for eye holes (eag thyrel in Anglo-Saxon), one of which can still be seen on the north.

The association with St Edmund is kept alive with a panel painting of the saint hanging on the north wall of the nave. St Edmund, king of East Anglia, from 855 until his defeat in battle by the invading Vikings in 869, was martyred for his Christian faith by being tied to a tree, shot with arrows till his body was 'like a thistle covered with prickles' and then beheaded.

Before St George, he was patron saint of England. His shrine, which attracted many pilgrims, is at Bury St Edmunds.

References

1. Anon., *Greensted Church Guidebook*
2. D. Attwater, *The Penguin Dictionary of Saints*, 1965

Hadstock

Hadstock lies about four miles north of Saffron Walden in pleasing, undulating countryside. Outwardly, the church of St Botolph (TL558447) is of late Anglo-Saxon date, but excavations in 1973 revealed a much older foundation. One enters through the massive oak north door which dates from the 11th century and must be one of the oldest doors in the country. It consists of a series of vertical oak boards, held by iron rivets to horizontal wooden bars on the inside. The door is framed by an arch with roll moulding. There is a legend that an invading Viking was flayed alive for committing sacrilege and the unfortunate man's skin was pasted onto the door. After a restoration, a piece of skin was actually found still intact beneath a hinge. It is now in Saffron Walden Museum and is apparently of human origin. When I visited the church, however, I was assured by the vicar that the skin came from a pig!

The nave is illuminated by Saxon double splayed windows. The tower collapsed in the 13th century but the Saxon jambs of the arch to the south transept remain. On the north, only the base is Saxon. When the floor of the church was replaced in 1973 the opportunity was taken to undertake a thorough archaeological investigation, which revealed a series of separate floors and three periods of Anglo-Saxon construction. St Botolph's is thus much older than it first appears.

There is a possible association of Hadstock with the little-known St Botolph – a man of 'remarkable life and learning' – who, according to the Anglo-Saxon Chronicle, built a monastery at Icanho, in East Anglia, which was eventually sacked by the Vikings in 869. But, where is Icanho? Iken in Suffolk is a contender but in 1144 the monks of Ely identified Hadstock as Icanho: 'that place sanctified to religion in days of old by the Holy Botolph, there at rest'. And during the excavations of 1973 a very large Saxon grave was unearthed in the south transept. It was empty and it is speculated that it once contained the body of St Botolph, which was later exhumed so that his relics could be distributed, in 970, to the abbey on Thorney Island (later Westminster Abbey), Ely, and the king's reliquary.

In 1016, King Cnut finally defeated Edmund Ironside at the Battle of Assandun. It was a decisive battle which resulted in the Peace of Alney, a treaty making Cnut king of all England, save for Wessex. Ashingdon in South East Essex has long been identified with the scene of the battle but Ashdon, two miles to the south-east of Hadstock, is also a contender – specifically, the hill which stands between the two places. The Anglo-Saxon Chronicle records:

When the king [Edmund Ironside] learned that the enemy army had gone inland, for the fifth time he collected all the English nation and pursued them and overtook them in Essex at the hill which is called Assandun and they stoutly joined battle there… There Cnut had the victory and won for himself all the English people… and all the nobility of England was there destroyed.

After the battle, Cnut built a minster of stone and lime, which, because of its extensive Saxon remains, could be Hadstock church.

References

1. Anon., St Botolph's Church Hadstock, Church guideook
2. Warwick Rodwell, *Under Hadstock Church*, 1974

Northey Island

Northey Island is an island in the River Blackwater, connected to the mainland by a causeway (TL870057). It is a mysterious place. The island is not normally open to the public but can be viewed by walking down a lane (closed to traffic) from the main B1018 from Maldon to Burnham on Crouch (at TL860055). The Battle of Maldon took place near this spot, an event that was to change the course of English history.

The story of the Battle of Maldon is told to us in a poem. It tells of the time, in early August 991, when ninety Viking ships – they could have been led by their king, Olaf Tryggvason – sailed up the River Blackwater with as many as two to four thousand men. They had already sacked Ipswich and were eager for more gold and silver from the Royal Mint at Maldon. The Vikings landed and set up camp on an island, thought to be Northey Island. On the mainland was the Saxon ealdorman, Bryhtnoth, with his army of locally recruited peasants. Bryhtnoth – tall, impetuous, religious and 'untiring in his campaigns against foes of the kingdom' – is thought to have been born in about 926, which would have put him in, 991, in his mid-sixties.

The Vikings sent a messenger to tell Bryhtnoth that if they were given booty they would sail away, but he knew from experience they would merely sail along the coast and plunder elsewhere. Either as a heroic act or, as some say, because

Northey Island

of impetuous pride, Bryhtnoth allowed the Vikings to cross to the mainland and face his army in battle. The poem takes up the story:

> then the hateful visitors started to use guile:
> they asked to be allowed to have passage,
> to cross over the ford, to advance their troops.
> Then because of his pride the earl set about
> Allowing the hateful race too much land,
> Over the chill water then began to call
> The son of Byrhthhelm [Bryhtnoth]
> 'Now a path is opened for you: come quickly against us,
> men at war. God alone knows
> who will control the battlefield?'
> Then the wolves of slaughter rushed forward
> They cared nothing for the water,
> The host of Vikings, west across the Blackwater,
> Across the shining stream, they carried their shields
> The sailors carried their lime-wood shields onto the land.

Bryhtnoth had made a fateful decision. He lost his head, removed by the Vikings, and the Saxons lost the battle. Afterwards, monks retrieved Bryhtnoth's body, which they buried at Ely with lump of wax to replace his severed head.

References

1. E.V. Gordon, *The Battle of Maldon*, Manchester University Press, 1976
2. Donald Scragg, *The Return of the Vikings*, Tempus, 2006

Strethall

Strethall is about three miles north-west of Saffron Walden, west of the motorway and in quiet countryside. The church of St Mary, Strethall (TL484397) could date from the early 11th century because the place is first mentioned in 1008 when King Aethelred sold ten hides of land at Strethle (Strethall) to the Abbot of Ely. There is Anglo-Saxon long-and-short work on the west quoins and inside there is a fine chancel arch described as 'one of the finest examples of Anglo-Saxon workmanship in smaller parish churches'. On its west side there are pilaster strips continuing over the arch and down the other side. There is a tiny Saxon window at the west of the nave.

In the churchyard (nothing to do with the Anglo-Saxons) is a charming modern gravestone which reads: 'Be kind to little animals whatever sort they be. And give a stranded jellyfish a shove into the sea'.

Reference

1. John Rutherfurd, *Parish Church of St Mary the Virgin, Strethall*, 2000

Other Places of Interest

- St Mary's church, **Chickney**, (TL575280), is in the care of The Churches Conservation Trust. It has a Saxon nave with two double splayed windows, one on each wall. Apart from an extension to the east, the chancel is also Saxon.
- The tower of the church of Holy Trinity in Trinity Street, **Colchester**, is the town's only Anglo-Saxon structure. It is built of Roman brick and has a characteristic west door with a triangular arrowhead. There are twin windows high up and below blank arcading. At the time of visiting the church was not in use.

- The north wall of the nave of the church of All Saints, **Insworth** (TL879178) is Saxon. The north and south walls of the chancel are late Saxon with two double spayed windows.
- St Katherine's church, **Little Bardfield**, (TL656307) has an Anglo-Saxon tower. There are three stages with round-headed windows in the upper two. The nave has double splayed Saxon windows.

Gloucestershire

Bibury

Bibury is a very pretty village which attracts many visitors. It entered recorded history when bishop Wilfrith of Worcester granted land to Earl Leppa and his daughter Beaga, between 721 and 743. The land was by the river Coln and was known as Beagan-byrig – hence Bibury. There was a Saxon church at Bibury. Outside, on the north wall of the chancel of St Mary's Church (SP118065), is a Saxon gravestone decorated with a series of interlocking circles with pellets within. More have been found, one of which is decorated in the Ringerike style, but these are now housed in the British Museum. The pilaster strip to the west of the south side of the chancel provides further evidence of the Saxon church. There are more pilaster strips inside, above the north arcade, showing that this wall is Saxon in origin and was merely pierced by the Normans when they built their aisle. There is also Saxon masonry in the jambs of the chancel arch and its decorated imposts; the pointed Gothic arch above them pierces the Saxon horizontal string course.

Reference

1. W.I. Croome, *A Short History of St Mary's, Bibury*, Church Guide

Daglingworth

Daglingworth is about two miles north-west of Cirencester and about half a mile west of the Roman Road (Ermin Way) which runs from Cirencester to Gloucester. Although the Church of the Holy Rood (SO994050) was restored

*Anglo-Saxon Crucifixion, Church
of the Holy Rood Daglingworth*

in the mid 19th century, there is plenty of evidence of its Saxon foundation. There are long-and-short work quoins throughout except for the north-west angle of the nave. The nave's west and south walls are Saxon as is the south doorway. Above the door is a splendid Saxon sundial. It is contained within a square stone and has a round dial of roll moulding. In the centre is the hole for the gnomon (the metal piece whose shadow displays the time). Nigel and Mary Kerr explain that the three crossed lines separate the day into three-hour tides; the vertical line represents 12 noon; the horizontal line pointing to the left is 6am, and that to the right is 6pm. There is an extra line with no cross and that indicates 7.30am. This marks the 'daeg mael' or day's marker and shows the beginning of the morning tide.

But the glory of Daglingworth is its 10th century Saxon sculptures, discovered when the chancel arch was restored. They were previously incorporated in the jambs of the original chancel arch, facing inwards. The first is a Crucifixion and shows Christ with a beard and moustache and in a long tunic. There is a halo above Christ's head with a cross within it. Soldiers are on each side – the one on the left (Longinus) holds a spear, the one on the right (Stephaton) a sponge and a jug of vinegar.

The next panel has Christ seated in a chair, once more with beard and moustache and with halo and cross. In His left hand He holds a cross and gives a blessing with his right. Next comes St Peter, holding a book in his left hand and the key of Heaven in His right hand.

There is another Crucifixion above the pulpit. It used to be outside and high up in the chancel east wall but has been removed inside to save it from the weather.

Reference

1. Anon., *The Church of the Holy Rood, Daglingworth*, Church Guide
2. Nigel and Mary Kerr, *A Guide to Anglo-Saxon Sites*, Granada, 1982

Anglo-Saxon sculpture of St Peter at Daglingworth

Deerhurst

All Anglo-Saxon enthusiasts must come to Deerhurst (SO871299) – it has two Anglo-Saxon churches, Odda's Chapel, and St Mary's Church – and the River Severn as its neighbour.

Odda's Chapel

Odda's Chapel lay hidden within the adjacent Priory House until 1885, when plaster was removed, exposing a Saxon window. Further restoration revealed a complete Saxon chapel of nave and chancel. In the Priory House, the nave was used as a kitchen and the chancel was divided into two rooms, one above the other. An inscribed slab was discovered at the same time. It reads: 'In Honour of the Holy Trinity this Altar has been dedicated'. Another inscribed slab was discovered nearby in 1675. It is now housed in the Ashmolean Museum in Oxford and its inscription tells us the exact date (1056) when the chapel was built. There is a copy of the stone fixed to the wall of the chancel and the inscription translates as 'Earl Odda had this royal hall built and dedicated in honour of the Holy Trinity for the soul of his brother Aelfric which left the body in this place, Bishop Ealdred dedicated it the Second of the Ides of April in the fourteenth year of King Edward of the English'. Odda was an important man. He was a kinsman of Edward the Confessor and was appointed earl of western Wessex in 1051. The chapel is now in the care of English Heritage.

St Mary's Church

Deerhurst was in the kingdom of the Hwicce, a sub-kingdom within the kingdom of Mercia. Aethelmund, an ealdorman of Hwicce, lost his life at the Battle of Kempsford in 802 against the neighbouring men of Wiltshire. Two years later, his son Aethleric died and bequeathed money to rebuild a monastery church at Deerhurst. Both were important men who may have attended when Charlemagne was made Holy Roman Emperor in 800 and both are probably buried at Deerhurst. Deerhurst entered national history when both Edmund Ironside and Cnut came here in 1016 after Cnut's victory at the Battle of Ashingdon. Cnut saw the need to co-operate with Edmund and an agreement was sealed at Deerhurst whereby Edmund ruled Wessex and Cnut the rest of the country beyond the Thames. The arrangement didn't last long, for Edmund was soon to die, leaving Cnut to reign over the entire country. The monastery declined in the first half of the 11th century and was given by Edward the Confessor to the monks of St Denis.

Coming first into view as the church is approached is the pre-Conquest tower. Above the entrance door is a Saxon doorway whose purpose, Arnold Porter tells us, was to give access to a balcony where the church's relics could be displayed. Then, above the inner doorway within the porch, is a splendid Virgin and Child – the Child still within the womb. On entering the church,

Anglo-Saxon Triangular Windows, west wall of nave of St Mary's Church Deerhurst

Anglo-Saxon Apse at St Mary's Church, Deerhurst

beautifully carved heads of beasts can be seen on either side of the inner door, the one on the south the finer. They were originally coloured and faint traces of colour can just be discerned.

There is a fine Saxon font, dated to the late 9th century. It was used as a drinking trough at a local farm until removed by the Bishop of Oxford. Later the stem was found at nearby Apperley Court and both then reunited at Deerhurst. The font is cylindrical and has spiral carvings in its broad centre within eight panels and plant scrollwork in bands at top and bottom. Below is the stem. This is cylindrical in its upper part and decorated with spirals, ribbon-like creatures and interlacing. The lower part is plain and octagonal.

The interesting thing about Deerhurst church is that it dates from several different Saxon periods. The first church was a simple nave and chancel of about 700. Later, a double porticus of two storeys was added to both north and south, that on the north side is readily identifiable. The upper part of the west entrance porch is later still. It has a marvellous double triangular-headed window into the nave with fluted and short pilasters beneath the abaci. The church was restored in the 10th century. The arch at the east end dates from the 10th century. It was originally a chancel arch giving access to an apse.

A window at the west end of the aisle commemorates Alphege, a famous Deerhurst monk. St Dunstan made him Abbot of Bath and he later followed St Aethelwold as Bishop of Winchester. He became Archbishop of Canterbury in

1006 but in 1012 was dragged by the Viking invaders to Greenwich. Money was demanded for his release but Alphege told his followers not to pay and his end then came. St Alphege Church at Greenwich is a reminder of his martyrdom.

There is more to see outside the church. An arrow leads to the Deerhurst Angel.

This can be seen high up on the wall to the east of the church. Also, to the east of the church is the outline of the polygonal apse.

References

1. Arnold Porter, *The Priory Church of St Mary the Virgin at Deerhurst*, Third Edition, 1992, Church Guide
2. C.R. Elrington, *Victoria County History, Gloucestershire*, Vol 8, 1969

Anglo-Saxon Cross Shaft at St Mary's Church, Newent

Newent

Inside the porch of the church of St Mary (SO723260) is part of an excellent pre-Conquest cross shaft. It was discovered in the churchyard in 1907 and shows Adam and Eve standing on either side of the Tree of Knowledge. The serpent clings to the tree and Adam holds his right arm across his chest. The church guide suggests that on the other face the sacrifice of Isaac is depicted. Finally, on one edge, David is shown cutting off the head of Goliath. The cross shaft has been dated to the 9th century and is in the Northumbrian style.

Inside the church is the Newent Stone, enclosed within a glass case. It was found in 1912 when a new vestry was planned. One side shows the Crucifixion and the Harrowing of Hell. Above Christ's head the Hand of God emerges from the clouds with a bird on either side. The piece is full of figures, including to the bottom left a body in a coffin. On the other side, there is a bishop with crozier and pectoral cross. There are figures as well, one of whom, with a cross, has been identified as the archangel Michael. The stone is carved with the name EDRED. The names of the four evangelists are on the edges of the stone: MATWEL, MARCUS, LUCAS and JOANNES. There are many interesting suggestions about the stone. It may have been a portable altar or a 'pillow stone'. The pillow-stone idea comes from the fact that when it was discovered the head of a skeleton was resting on it. This could be Edred, who may have been an abbot at Malmesbury.

Reference

1. K.M. Tomlinson, *The Church of St Mary the Virgin, Newent*, Perpetua Press, 2000

Somerford Keynes

Land at Somerford Keynes was given in 675 to the monks of Malmesbury Abbey by Bertwald, the nephew of the king of Mercia. The small village lies about four miles due south of Cirencester. Within twenty years, All Saints' Church (SU015955) was built and part of its north wall survives to this day. Within the walling is an Anglo-Saxon doorway, previously blocked but opened up in 1968 and now handsomely glazed. Seen from the outside, the jambs of the door have long-and-short work with stepped imposts above. The arch is made from one block of stone and has concentric curves of cable moulding. Inside, on the west wall, are two Anglo-Saxon sculptures carved in the reign of King Cnut. They are in the Danish Ringerike style and similar to gravestones at nearby Bibury. Two beasts face each other with their mouths in close contact and a ball in between. In 1995 they were restored by Michael Eastham.

Reference

1. Anon., *All Saints Church, Somerford Keynes*, Church Guide, 2009

Other Places of Interest

- St Mary's Church **Beverston** (ST861941) has, on the south face of its tower, a badly weathered pre-Conquest panel showing a figure of Jesus. His right hand is raised in a blessing and the resurrection banner is in His left hand.

- The church of St Mary Magdalene, **Elmstone Hardwicke** (SO920260) has a large stone, part of a cross shaft, with spiral carving very like the font at Deerhurst. It is no doubt by the same craftsmen.

- Now housed in the triforium of **Gloucester Cathedral** is a 10th century sculpture of a bust of Christ, discovered in the garden of the Bishop's Palace (now the King's School). Christ's head is surrounded by a circular border, within the left of which is a bird, maybe representing the Holy Spirit.

Hampshire

Boarhunt

The church of St Nicholas (SU604083) stands in rural isolation near to Portsdown Hill. It is pre-Conquest and has been dated to about 1060. There is a double splayed Saxon window in the chancel north wall, blocked by a stone inserted in the opening space. It can be viewed, with its cable moulding, from outside. Both the north and south doors are also blocked. A string course runs across the chancel east wall from which rises a pilaster strip to the apex of the gable. Inside, the chancel arch is typical Saxon work and is plain and unmoulded.

Reference

1. Anon., *St Nicholas Church*, Church Guide, 2000

Breamore

Breamore lies on the A338 Salisbury to Bournemouth road, in the valley of the river Avon, just over two miles north of Fordingbridge. It has an extremely important Anglo-Saxon church which is situated about one mile north-west of the main village. Breamore entered history at the time of the Domesday Survey where it is recorded that twelve families lived here. Its church of St Mary (SU153188) is much older and was founded – maybe by King Aethelred the Unready – in about 1000, probably as a minster church. There is much Anglo-Saxon evidence to appreciate.

St Mary's Church Breamore

The nave, south porticus, central tower and two north double splayed windows are Saxon. A walk around the outside reveals traces of Saxon pilaster strips and long-and-short work at the quoins of the south porticus. But there is much more. Over the south doorway, inside the porch, is an outstanding rood. It shows Christ, according to Pevsner, 'bent by suffering in a way that anticipates the Gothic', with St John on the right and the Virgin Mary to the left. Above is the Hand of God emerging from a cloud, the sun and moon, and below a serpent or snake. The rood probably fell victim to the excesses of the iconoclasts during the Reformation and is badly faded, but remarkable, nonetheless. The rood was restored in 1979 at which time it was realised that its original position was elsewhere, probably above the chancel arch. In the background, there is a landscape, although hardly discernible. On the west wall of the porch is a painting of Judas hanging from a tree.

The south porticus can be better appreciated from inside the church. It is entered by a splendid Saxon arch with an inscription that reads HER SWUTELATH SEO GECWYDRAEDNES, which translates as 'Here the Covenant is explained to thee'.

There would have been a north porticus in the original church and its outline can be seen outside on the north side of the church. There is also the faintest outline of an extension of the church to the west to a chamber. It can be seen in the west front.

Reference

1. Anthony Light and Gerald Ponting, *The Saxon Church of St Mary's Breamore*, Breamore P.C.C., 2004

Anglo-Saxon Inscription (Here the Covenant is explained to Thee) at St Mary's Church, Breamore

Corhampton

Corhampton lies on the main Alton-to-Fareham road (A32) in the valley of the river Meon. There are two strange things about Corhampton Church (SU610203). The first is that it has no dedication, it is just plain Corhampton Church; the second is that it is barely a few hundred yards from the larger Meonstoke Church. Apart from the 19th century east wall, Corhampton is a complete Saxon Church.

The church is built on a mound which could have been a fortification; the name Corhampton derives from *car*, a fortification, and *ton*, an enclosure. Dated to the early 11th century, the church has remarkably slender walls, only 2 feet 6½ inches thick, secured by long-and-short work quoins and pilaster strips. Its stone comes from the Isle of Wight and would have been delivered via the river Meon, which was navigable at the time. Regrettably, the east wall, with its large round window, collapsed in 1842 and was replaced by brickwork.

On the north side, the doorway is blocked and has been replaced by a window. The former doorway arch can be clearly discerned with a pilaster rising from the top of the arch. The arch is supported by imposts resting on pilaster strips. Inside, the chancel arch is a perfect example of Saxon work and is similar to the blocked north doorway arch.

Outside and to the right of the porch is a Saxon sundial, similar to the one at Warnford. It is not made of the same stone as the rest of the church and so could predate the church, maybe even to the time of Wilfrid, the Northumberland-born bishop, who evangelised the local heathen Meonwara. The sundial is unusual in that it has eight tides instead of twelve hours. The central hole for the gnomon is visible and at the end of each tide are tripartite leaves and bulbous shapes placed alternatively.

Reference

1.   Chris Maxse, *Corhampton Church*, Church Guide, 2000

Fareham

The Church of St Peter and St Paul at Fareham (SU582066) is predominantly 18th century but it does have a much older foundation – witness the Saxon long-and-short work in a lower part of the north wall. It is mentioned in Domesday Book: 'Ferneham… here are… a church, six serfs, two mills… woods for the pannage of ten hogs'.

Reference

1.   Alan H. Sturgess, *A Guide to the Church of St Peter and Paul, Fareham*, 1995

Headbourne Worthy

The church of St Swithun (SU486320) at Headbourne Worthy has many Anglo-Saxon features. Pilgrims would stop here on their way to the shrine of St Swithun at Winchester Cathedral. It is extremely difficult to park nearby, and due caution should be exercised. There is long-and-short work and lesenes in both nave and chancel, but the church's glory is its magnificent rood. It can be seen in the vestry to the west of the nave. Although severely damaged by the iconoclasts, its outline can be clearly seen. There are full-size figures of Christ, the Virgin Mary and St John, with above, the hand of God emerging from a cloud.

Reference

1.   Anon., *Saint Swithun's Church, Headbourne Worthy*, Church Guide

Nether Wallop

Nether Wallop lies in pleasant countryside in the Test valley, south of the main Andover-to-Salisbury road (A343) and just over one mile south west of the famous hill fort at Danebury Hill. The tiny Wallop brook – hence the village's name – runs nearby. The church of St Andrew (SU304364) at Nether Wallop was founded in the late 10th or early 11th century. It has been extensively modified since but has the oldest Anglo-Saxon wall painting in the country. The wall painting is in the Winchester School style and part of it can be seen over the chancel arch. Regrettably, when the Normans altered the shape of the arch, they destroyed a large part of the painting. The part visible today shows a series of flying angels, their fluttering hems typical of the Winchester School of Anglo-Saxon art. The tip of a mandorla can just be made out and accordingly the angels are part of a Christ in Majesty. There is a full description of the paintings in a paper by Richard Gem and Pamela Tudor-Craig in *Anglo-Saxon England*, 1981, volume 9, page 115.

Reference

1.   Richard Sawyer, *St Andrew's Church, Nether Wallop*, PCC, 1997

Romsey

The majestic abbey at Romsey (SU352212) dates from about 907 and was founded as a nunnery by Alfred the Great's son, Edward the Elder, for his daughter, Elfleda. But there is evidence of an earlier monastery, probably associated with St Boniface, who studied at the nearby village of Nursling. As part of the monastic revival, in the 960s and in the reign of King Edgar, Romsey became a monastery following the Rule of Benedict. The building is magnificent and there are two Anglo-Saxon sculptures which capture our attention. First, inside, and at the extreme east end, in St Anne's Chapel, is a Saxon cross, dated to about 960. Christ is flanked on the cross by two angels on its arms. Below are the Virgin Mary on the left and St John on the right. Further below there is Longinus on the left holding a spear, the tip of which touches Christ (Longinus is the Roman soldier who in legend pierced the side of Jesus with a spear.) Then on the right is the soldier Stephaton, holding a pole with a sponge at its end touching the body of Christ.

Outside the west wall of the south transept is the Romsey Rood: a cross 6ft 9in high and showing a bearded figure of Christ with His arms outstretched. Above, the Hand of God emerges from a cloud.

Reference

1. Judy Walker, *The Benedictine Nunnery of Romsey Abbey*
2. Judy Walker, *Romsey Abbey*, Pitkin, 2001

Steventon

Steventon lies in open countryside about six miles south-west of Basingstoke and about two miles south of the Basingstoke-to-Andover road (A3400). Jane Austen was born in the parish where her father, Rev George Austen, was the rector of the Church of St Nicholas (SU551473), which lies south-east of the village. Inside, by the pulpit, are the remains of a late 9th century Saxon cross. It was used as building material in one of the walls of Steventon Manor, which was demolished in 1970. In 1952 it was given to the church by the owner of the manor, Captain and Mrs Hutton Croft. One narrow face is decorated with interlace and winding dragons in two sections. The broader face is damaged but a dragon and interlace survive to the upper right.

Reference

1. Anon., Church Guide

Titchfield

Titchfield lies on the River Meon, two miles from the sea. It is just over one mile west of Fareham and south of the main A27. According to Bede, it was settled by the Jutes, who took their name, the Meonware, from the name of the river. Michael Hare, in the church guide, makes the point that the church was a minster, responsible for evangelising over a wide area. The church of St Peter (SU541057) is approached and dominates the view from the High Street, along Church Street. The lower part of the tower is Anglo-Saxon and was originally a porch. It is of limestone rubble with a round-headed west doorway, which was the original entrance to the Saxon Church. Above is a row of Roman tiles. The similarity of Titchfield to Monkwearmouth in Northumbria has led to speculation that its design was influenced by St Wilfrid, the Northumbrian evangelising saint who converted the South Saxons in the 680s.

Reference

1. Michael Hare, *St Peter's Titchfield: A Guide to the History of Church and Parish*, The Church Publishers, 1990

Warblington

The Church of St Thomas Becket at Warblington (SU728054) is a surprise: close to the urban sprawl of Havant and yet remote, quiet and peaceful. To the south of the churchyard is an ancient yew tree, mentioned in the Domesday Book and therefore known to Saxon worshippers. The place takes its name from Weorbald, who arrived here probably by boat (Chichester Harbour is only a few hundred yards away) and settled in Weorbling's Ton, that is 'the place of Weorbald'. The lower part of the central tower was altered in the 13th century but the second stage is Anglo-Saxon. The tower was perhaps originally a porch, the east face of which led into the nave of the Saxon church. There are round-headed doorways to north and south made of Roman tiles and within the church an opening into the body of the church, seen high up.

Reference

1. Pat Morrisey, *Warblington, The Church of St Thomas Becket*, Church Guide, 2003

Warnford

The church of Our Lady (SU622225) lies in the seclusion of Warnford Park. It can be reached on foot from a private driveway (public footpath) to the left (east) of the main A32, about half a mile south of where that road crosses the river Meon at Warnford – park with great care!

Over the south door there is an inscription in Lombardic letters which translates as 'Brethren, bless in your prayers the founders young and old of this temple; Wulfric founded it; good Adam restored it'. Adam is Adam de Port who held Warnford from 1171 until 1213; but who is Wulfric? He could be the Abbot of Newminster (Winchester) who lived in the 11th century. Alternatively, Wilfrid's name has been suggested.

Wilfrid was born in Northumberland and was educated by the monks of Lindisfarne under St Aidan. Further education in Rome was decisive in Wilfrid taking Rome's position at the Synod of Whitby in 664. As Bishop of York, he then fell into a dispute with Theodore, Archbishop of Canterbury, who wished to split the York diocese into two. This led Wilfrid to leave the north of England and travel south to evangelise the heathen men of Sussex and the Meon valley. We know from Bede that Wilfrid was in the Meon valley and there is a tradition that he made this place the base for his mission of converting the province of the Meonwaras.

There is a Saxon sundial over the south door, very like the one at nearby Corhampton.

Reference

1. C.E. Bassett, *The Church of Our Lady, Warnford*, Church Guide
2. Jim Foley, www.wilfrid-meon-pilgrimage.co.uk

Whitchurch

The church of All Hallows, Whitchurch (SU460477) has an excellent Anglo-Saxon gravestone at the entrance to the chancel. Known as the 'Saxon Stone', it was discovered during a 19th century restoration. It had been incorporated as building material in the north wall of the church built by the Normans and is similar to gravestones used by the Romans. It depicts a figure of Christ, carved in relief and framed by an arch. There is an inscription on its top which reads 'HIC CORPUS FRITHBURGAE REQUISCIT IN PACEM' that is, 'Here the body of Frithburga rests in peace'.

Reference

1. Anon., *A Brief Guide to the Parish Church of All Hallows, Whitchurch*, PCC of Whitchurch, 2002

Winchester

Winchester was the capital of Wessex; indeed, it was the capital of England before the Norman Conquest. It was the largest of King Alfred the Great's royal burghs – defensive fortifications set up by Alfred to defend against Viking incursions. As the city is entered, one is greeted by Hamo Thorneycroft's statue of Alfred. Although Hamwic (modern-day Southampton) was the main trading centre of Wessex, Winchester became the seat of a bishop when Bishop Hedda transferred the see from Dorchester-on-Thames in 676. His cathedral is now known as Oldminster. It was founded by King Cenwalh in 648 and its site is marked out on the ground to the north of the present cathedral. Winchester succumbed to a Viking attack in 860.

St Swithun was bishop of Winchester from 852 to 862. Not much is known about his life, but legends abound of miracles attributed to him. Before he died, he insisted that his burial place should be in the open air, where – according to William of Malmesbury – 'it might be subject to the feet of passers-by and to the rain drops pouring from on high'. He was thus buried according to his wish outside the west door of Old Minster. But Old Minster was rebuilt between 971 and 994 and Swithun's body was moved to a shrine within the new church. Apparently, it poured with rain on the day of the transfer, seen as a sign of the saint's displeasure. This is said to have given rise to the legend that if it rains on his feast day it will rain for forty days thereafter. Or:

> If on St Swithun's day it really pours
> You're better off to stay indoors.

Today, St Swithun lies in a shrine in the present cathedral.

After the death of King Alfred, his widow, Ealswith, founded a nunnery, Nunnaminster, later St Mary's Abbey. It lay to the north-east of the present cathedral and remains of it have been unearthed in Abbey Passage. In 903, Alfred's son, King Edward the Elder, built Newminster just a few feet to the north of Old Minster. The two churches stood side by side, so close in fact that services held in one could be heard in the other. Alfred was buried first in Oldminster and his body later moved to Newminster. Newminster later moved to the north of the town and was renamed Hyde Abbey, to which Alfred's remains were transferred once more. But the abbey was dissolved during the Reformation and today there is no trace of where his burial place might have been.

Fragment of Anglo-Saxon Wall Painting from Newminster (Winchester Museum)

Many Saxon kings and bishops were buried at Winchester and within the present cathedral there are a series of mortuary chests containing their bones, including those of King Egbert (802–839), King Ethelwulf (839–858) and King Cnut (1016–1035).

There is a fine museum at Winchester where a very large collection of sculptural remains from both Oldminster and Newminster can be viewed. These include part of a frieze from Oldminster, which shows evidence of Scandinavian influence. It may have been commissioned by King Cnut. There is also part of an Anglo-Saxon wall painting found as part of the foundation of Newminster. This was in 903 – thus dating the painting to before this date. There is also a splendid early 11th century grave marker from Oldminster. It shows a lamp between curtains which are pulled back – the lamp symbolising the resurrection and eternal life.

Other Places of Interest

- All Saints', **Hannington**, (SU539555) has long-and-short work at the north-east corner of the nave.
- The church of All Saints, **Hinton Ampner**, (SU597275), was extensively restored in the 19th century but has evidence of its Saxon foundation – see the pilaster strips on both the north and south of the nave. There is also long-and-short work at the north east of the nave. The doorway, inside, to the vestry is also pre-Conquest.

Reference

1.   Anon., *All Saints Church, Hinton Ampner*, Church Guide

- All Saints' Church at **Little Somborne** (SU383327) is diminutive but nevertheless remains the striking visual feature of the large grassed area that is Little Somborne. The church is now in the care of the Churches Conservation Trust. The nave is Saxon with lesenes on its north and south and long-and-short work to the west quoins.
- There is a Saxon Crucifixus in the Church of St John the Baptist, at **New Alresford** (SU588326).

Herefordshire

Acton Beauchamp

Acton Beauchamp is just a scattering of cottages and farms in glorious Herefordshire countryside, the name Acton meaning a settlement amongst the oaks. In the early 8th century, Aethelbald, King of Mercia, is recorded as giving three hides of land to Buca at Aactune. In 972, King Edgar granted a charter to the monks of Pershore Abbey, which confirmed that they held land at Actune.

Anglo-Saxon evidence in Herefordshire is sparse, to say the least, but the sculpture at Acton Beauchamp church (SO679503) is worth searching out. It forms a lintel for the south doorway of the tower and is 9th century. The sculpture was part of a cross shaft and so was meant to be viewed in a vertical direction. It is carved with scrollwork and has three sections; the one on the left shows an animal, probably a horse or a dog. In the centre is part of an animal and to the right, a bird.

Reference

1. Susan Shaw-Cooper, *Background of the Parish and Church of Acton Beauchamp*

Hertfordshire

St Albans

St Alban was the first British Christian martyr. He lived at the Roman town of Verulamium. There is much controversy surrounding the date of his death. Bede relates that Alban was a 'pagan who gave shelter to a Christian priest fleeing from his pursuers and when he observed the man's unbroken activity of prayer… renounced the darkness of idolatry and sincerely accepted Christ'. When soldiers arrived to arrest the priest, Alban protected him by wearing the priest's long cloak and allowed himself to be arrested instead. Alban was accordingly condemned to death and executed on a hill where St Alban's Cathedral now stands. But what was the date? Based on the evidence of Bede, a date of 304 has been suggested. The Anglo-Saxon Chronicle, however, puts it at 283. Others have placed it as early as 209. Recent scholars have suggested that a period around 250 is more likely.

There is Anglo-Saxon work at three churches in St Albans – all of them using Roman brick salvaged from Verulamium. First, the **Cathedral**. In the transepts, the triforium has two openings for each bay with baluster shafts to an Anglo-Saxon design.

According to the chronicler, Matthew Paris, the **Church of St Stephen** was founded in 948 on the instructions of Ulsinus, the sixth abbot of St Alban's. Although it has been restored, there is much Anglo-Saxon evidence in the reused Roman brick and the window, best seen from inside, just to the right of the Norman doorway and arch door leading to the parish hall.

St Michael's Church (near to the Roman remains at Verulamium) was locked when I visited. Its nave and chancel walls are Saxon.

References

1. Anon., *St Alban's Cathedral*, Jarrold, 2000
2. Bob Bonnington, *A Quick Guide to St Stephen's Church*, Church Guide

Other Places of Interest

- The Church of St Mary at Reed (TL362357) has Anglo-Saxon long-and-short work both at the south-west and north-west of the nave. There is also a Saxon north doorway. The church was mentioned in Domesday Book.

Reference

1. Anon., *St Mary's Church, Reed*, Church Guide

- The Church of St Mary, Walkern (TL293265) has a Saxon Rood.
- There is very distinctive long-and-short work at the south-east corner of the nave at St Mary's Church, Westmill (TL369272), suggesting an Anglo-Saxon foundation.

Huntingdonshire

Barnack

Barnack stands in undulating countryside on the road from Peterborough to Stamford. An Anglo-Saxon land grant of 664 states that 'the vill of Barnack had been granted by Wulfhere, King of Mercia, to Medeshamstede [Peterborough Abbey]'. It is mentioned in the Anglo-Saxon Chronicle as Beornica, meaning a warrior's oak. The famous oolitic limestone, Barnack Rag, was quarried nearby and used to build Norwich, Ely and Peterborough Cathedrals.

People come to the church of St John the Baptist (TF079051) to view its magnificent tower. It has four stages. The lower two are Saxon with three pilaster strips running up vertically on the north, west and south faces, thereby dividing each face into four sections. There is the usual long-and-short work at the corners of the tower, but this is very irregular at the bases. The south face is the most rewarding with its doorway which would have provided entry to the tower. The doorway is round-headed and framed by a hood mould. Above is a round-headed window, one of three giving illumination to the inside. Above this window is a carved

Late Anglo-Saxon Relief of Christ in Majesty at St John the Baptist Church, Barnack

sundial. The second stage has two round-headed windows between which is a panel carved with acanthus scrollwork with a bird on top. Above the clock is a triangular-headed window, within which is a slab with a carving of an endless ribbon. There is similar work on the other faces of the tower.

Inside, the tower arch to the nave is round-headed and twenty feet high. In the west wall is a recess containing a stone seat.

In the north aisle, there is a framed and seated bearded effigy of Christ giving a blessing and holding a book in His left hand. Three feet and four inches high and one foot and six inches wide, the carved effigy was discovered beneath the floor in 1931. Above Christ's head is a halo and His clothes have folds in them similar to those in Byzantine work. Controversy surrounds the date of the effigy – some say 13th century, but others Saxon.

Reference

1. Phillip G.M. Dickinson, *Barnack Church*, Chadwick Associates, 1990

Castor

The church of St Kyneburgha (a unique dedication) at Castor (about three miles west of Peterborough) is a fine building (TL125985). It stands on the site of a Roman palace and on the opposite side of the river Nene to Water Newton, where the famous Roman treasure, now in the British Museum, was discovered. Kyneburgha was the daughter of Penda, the famous king of Mercia. Her brother, King Peada (see Mercia) married the daughter of King Oswy of Northumbria with the proviso that Peada became a Christian. Kyneburgha married Oswy's son, probably with the same condition. Her faith was therefore very much in the Celtic tradition. She arrived at Castor with her sister Kyneswitha in the mid 7th century and established a Christian community of both monks and nuns with herself as abbess. She died in the late 7th century and was succeeded as abbess by her sister. Castor thus became a place for pilgrims to pray at the shrine of the two sisters. Following Viking raids, Kyneburgha's remains were moved to Peterborough in 1012 by Abbot Elsinus.

In common with many saints, there are legends about the life of St Kyneburgha. Once, she was chased by a gang of hooligans and in her haste to escape she dropped her basket. At once flowers sprang up beside her but the ruffians were trapped by thick thorn bushes and frustrated in their attempts to catch her. There is a series of carvings on the capitals of the piers which support the tower and the one on the south-west is said to represent the story.

Inside and within the north aisle is the base of a Saxon cross. It used to be outside but was brought inside to protect it from the weather. At its top, there is a socket where the cross once stood. The base is probably Roman but it is inscribed with a Saxon dragon.

There is an excellent Saxon sculpture which was found buried in 1924 during a restoration of the

Anglo-Saxon Figure of a man (St Mark?) beneath arch at St Kyneburgha Church, Castor

church and is work of the highest quality. It has been re-sited by the north aisle altar and shows a figure – thought to be St Mark – under an arch.

There is part of another figure on the right. It has been linked with the famous Hedda Stone at Peterborough Cathedral and it may have been part of the original shrine of St Kyneburgha.

Reference

1.   Helen Tovey, *St Kyneburgha's Church, Castor*, CAMUS Project, Peterborough, 2006

Fletton

Fletton is on the outskirts of Peterborough, south of the city centre. In the churchyard at St Margaret's Church (TL198972), there is a wheel-type Anglo-Saxon cross with two handles carved on its sides with animals. It is inscribed 'Radulph Filius Wilielm'. But the real glory of Fletton is inside the church. At the far east end of the chancel and beyond the altar there is a series of Anglo-Saxon sculptures of international importance. They are carved from Barnack stone. They have been linked with those at Breedon in Leicestershire and date to the early 9th century. They are discoloured slightly red, showing damage by fire; perhaps they were retrieved from Peterborough Abbey after the fire there in 1116. Once outside but now, thankfully, preserved within, they are delicate and intricate in design. In the centre are three men beneath three arches, contorted animals and abstract designs. Against the south wall of the chancel are two more Anglo-Saxon sculptures. One shows a saint and the other an angel.

Reference

1.   www.robschurches.moonfruit.com

Great Paxton

Great Paxton lies on the east bank of the River Ouse, between St Neots and Huntingdon, close to the main London-to-Cambridge railway line. Saxon coins, skeletons and pottery were found when the railway was built. The name Paxton derives from Paece or Perruc ton – the village of a person of that name – and is mentioned in the Domesday Book. The church of Holy Trinity (TL210642) is Saxon with definite Germanic influence.

Impressive sculptured yew trees welcome us as we approach Holy Trinity Church. The first clue of what awaits us are the clerestory windows – double splayed, round headed, Saxon and of iron stone. The Saxon church was cruciform and has been dated to no later than 1000. Its north transept arch is majestic, eighty feet wide at its base and twenty-eight feet high. The Anglo-Saxon nave at Holy Trinity had aisles, a rarity in common with Brixworth and Lydd. Above the arcade a string course runs horizontally, then blank walling and above this round-headed clerestory windows, two on either side. Originally there were three, as seen from outside.

Reference

1.   Phillip G.M. Dickinson, *Great Paxton, Huntingdonshire*, Church Guide, 1995

The Hedda Stone, Peterborough Cathedral

Peterborough Cathedral

Peterborough received cathedral status in 1541, courtesy of Henry VIII. Before then it was a Benedictine monastery, founded in 655 by Peada of Mercia, with Saxulf its first abbot. It fell victim to a Danish assault in 870 and was rebuilt in 965 as part of Aethelwold of Winchester's monastic revival. The Saxon church was severely damaged by Hereward the Wake in 1070 in his stubborn resistance against the Norman conquerors and further damaged by a fire of 1116. What remains of the original church lies beneath the crossing tower and south transept and is difficult to see. There is, however, the magnificent Hedda Stone, commemorating the deaths of Abbot Hedda and his monks in the Viking raid of 870. It is at the far east of the cathedral and shows standing figures (apostles) beneath arches. On its top are scrolls with interlace.

In the treasury, there is a Saxon communion cup, and in the south transept an effigy of a king and bishop.

The relic of the arm of St Oswald of Northumbria was once at Peterborough. Aidan brought Oswald's arm to Bamburgh after he was killed at the Battle of Maresfield. Then in about 1000 it was deposited at Peterborough. Its whereabouts are now unknown.

Reference

1.   The Cathedral Staff, *Peterborough Cathedral Souvenir Guide*, 2009

Wittering

The Church of All Saints, Wittering (TF057020) is at the edge of a large housing estate, west of the Great North Road (A1). The builders were in when I visited, giving the church a 21st century restoration. But, of course, the grand and imposing Saxon chancel arch remains in all its grim splendour. The capitals are not moulded and form one block with the abacus. The arch's responds have roll moulding and there is roll moulding all the way round above. The Anglo-Saxon (as opposed to Norman) date is confirmed by the pilaster strip running beside each jamb and continuing around the arch.

Other Places of Interest

- The church of St John the Baptist, **Stanground** (TL200975) has a badly weathered Anglo-Saxon cross in its churchyard, with a wheel head. There are carvings on its sides of a saltire cross.
- There are the remains of a Saxon double splayed window on the west wall of the tower (outside) at St Augustine's Church, (TL187977) **Woodston**.
- The church of All Saints at **Elton** (TL089936) has, in the churchyard to the north of the church, two fine Anglo-Danish crosses, standing next to each other, both with wheel heads.

Kent

Canterbury

St Martin's Church

Aethelbert, king of Kent, gave his Frankish wife, Bertha, a chapel to the east of Canterbury. This is the church of St Martin. She had her own priest, Liodhard, and it was to St Martin's Church that Augustine came in 597 to reconvert the English.

Augustine, his party of monks and Frankish interpreters, arrived in England at the Isle of Thanet. The traditional landing place at Ebbsfleet is marked by a cross, erected there in 1884. Aethelbert soon heard of their arrival and instructed the party to remain where it was. Bede takes up the story: 'Some days later, the King came to the island and sitting in the open-air commanded Augustine and his companions to come thither to talk with him'. Aethelbert promised to guarantee safe passage and accordingly Augustine and his party of monks made their way to Canterbury and established themselves at St Martin's Church. There 'they first began to meet to chant the psalms, to pray, to say mass, to preach and to baptise, until when the king had been converted to the faith they received greater liberty to preach everywhere and to build or restore churches'.

St Martin's Church still stands today. There is much Roman brick in its structure, which was built in two periods. The earliest is the chancel, which could well date from Bertha's time – see for instance, outside and to the south, the blocked square-headed doorway at the west end of the chancel. Excavation has shown that the door opening led from the church to a porticus. To the east there is another doorway, now blocked, which was added in the 7th

| *West Wall, St Martin's Church, Canterbury*

century. The nave was built after the chancel, perhaps after Aethelbert had been converted. The Anglo-Saxon buttresses to the nave are also typical of the period. Inside, the west wall has exposed masonry with blocked windows high up.

Reference

1.   Martin Taylor, *The Cradle of English Christianity*, St Martin's and St Paul's PCC, 2001

St Augustine's Abbey

Augustine founded an abbey soon after he arrived in Canterbury. Bede tells us 'he erected a monastery to the east of the town, in which by his exhortation he ordered a church to be erected of becoming splendour, dedicated to the blessed apostles Peter and Paul'. The abbey served as a burial place for the kings of Kent and for Archbishops of Canterbury and is situated on land given by Aethelbert, between Bertha's church of St Martin and Canterbury Cathedral. The monks obeyed the Rule of St Benedict, escaping from the evils of the world in a life of work, prayer and study and making vows of poverty, chastity and obedience. The monastery had a library, and some books were given by Pope Gregory himself.

St Augustine's Abbey, Canterbury

After the Conquest, Abbot Scolland, 'frightened by the danger that the old monastery, consumed by long decay, might collapse', demolished and rebuilt it in 1090. But what remains of the Saxon work? The Saxon monastery consisted of four separate churches arranged in an east–west direction. To the west was the church of St Peter and St Paul. Containing much Roman brick, it consisted of nave and porticus (side chapels) to the north and south. To the north is the porticus of St Gregory, preserved under a modern canopy. It contained the tombs of early Archbishops of Canterbury. (The tombs are now empty, the remains having been removed to the Norman church in 1091.) The tomb of St Augustine was in this area but is now concealed by later rebuilding. To the south was the porticus of St Martin – now below ground and not visible – which originally contained the body of Aethelbert. His queen, Bertha, lies buried nearby in the nave.

The original tomb of Mellitus, first bishop of London and founder of St Paul's Cathedral, is in St Gregory's porticus. He was among the second group of monks sent by Pope Gregory in 601 to assist Augustine and he brought with him, as a gift from the Pope, the famous St Augustine's Gospels. They are now at Corpus Christi College, Cambridge, and are still used to this day during the enthronement of new Archbishops of Canterbury.

To the east of the church of St Peter and St Paul is Abbot Wulfric's Rotunda. This unique structure was probably only partly complete when Abbot Scolland re-planned the entire abbey. It was intended to join the church of St Peter and St Paul with St Mary's Church to the east. What remains today is the crypt with the bases of eight massive piers. In 618, King Edbald, Aethelbert's son, founded St Mary's Church, most of which was destroyed during Abbot Scolland's rebuilding. To the far east and largely undisturbed by Scolland's work is the Church of St Pancras. It consists of a rectangular nave with an apsidal chancel. The Anglo-Saxon work can be identified by the reused Roman brick.

Within the City of Canterbury is St Mildred's Church, in Church Lane, near to the castle. If one stands in the field to its south the Saxon remains are immediately clear. That the nave wall is Saxon is shown by the massive long-and-short work at its quoins.

Reference

1. Judith Roebuck, *St Augustine's Abbey*, English Heritage, 1997

Dover

The church of St Mary in Castro (TR325418) at Dover Castle fell into disrepair in the 18th century, becoming roof-less and used as a coal store for the nearby barracks. In 1860, it was heavily restored by Sir George Gilbert Scott. Nevertheless, its Saxon features are clear to see. It dates from about 1000. Roman tiles are used in the three large double splayed windows on both sides of the nave. The tower arches to the east and west are Saxon but those to north and south are later. To the west of the church is the famous Roman pharos, or lighthouse.

Lydd

It has been claimed – although not conclusively – that All Saints' Church (TR043209) at Lydd, Romney Marsh, can date its foundation to the Romano-British 5th century. The section of the church in question is the north-west corner of the north aisle. Outside there is ancient walling and inside three blocked arches with a splayed arched window above; the west wall has a blocked doorway. The church has been compared with the 5th century Romano-British church excavated at Silchester and if it is indeed 5th century it is quite unique in England. If the claim is incorrect, an alternative dating of 8th century Saxon has been proposed.

Reference

1. Dudley Jackson and Sir Eric Fletcher, J. *British Archaeological Assoc.*, 1968, p. 19

Lyminge

Lyminge lies on the Downs in lovely countryside, about four miles north-west of Folkestone. The church of St Mary and St Aethelburga (TR161408) was founded as a double monastery (for both men and women) by Aethelburga, daughter of King Aethelbert of Kent. She was instrumental in introducing Christianity to the north of England when she married Edwin of Northumbria. Accompanied by her priest, Paulinus, she travelled north, and Edwin was baptised at York (a condition of the marriage). Edwin was defeated and killed by the Mercians in 633, which hastened her return to Kent with Paulinus and it was to Lyminge that she came to found a minster there.

There is evidence that when Aethelburga returned to Kent, Lyminge was already occupied by Germanic invaders: a Jutish cemetery has been excavated, yielding jewellery and weapons. The University of Reading is carrying out archaeological work at the site.

There are remains of the original church. They survive just to the east of the porch where there was an apsidal chancel. The place of Aethelburga's shrine is indicated by a sign board. Alternatively, the shrine could have been inside the present church where there is a recessed arch in the south wall. In 840 the original church was sacked by the Vikings and was rebuilt by St Dunstan, Archbishop of Canterbury, in 965. The nave and chancel of the present church is pre-Conquest – see the round-headed windows. In 1085 the relics of Aethelburga were transferred to Canterbury by Archbishop Lanfranc.

Reference

1. Anon., *Points of Interest in Church of St Mary & St Ethelburga, Lyminge*, Church Guide

Minster in Sheppey

Minster is a seaside town overlooking the Thames estuary (perhaps more accurately, the North Sea). The minster (TQ956730) was founded in 670 by St Seaxburga on land given to her by her son, King Egbert of Kent. Later she moved to Ely and became abbess there in 679. If one stands outside the north wall of the nave, in the bay to the east of the tower there is the merest trace of a blocked window. Its jambs are stone and there is the trace of two concentric circles of Roman tiles. In the next bay to the east there is a similar row of tiles, almost too hidden to make out! Inside the church and above the arches of the north aisle are the remains of windows from the original south wall of the Saxon church.

Reference

1.   Sheila Judge, *Minster Abbey*, Church Guide

Orpington

There is an ancient sundial at All Saints' Church with runic and Old English inscriptions. The top is broken off and the remainder has a central gnomon and thirteen calibration lines. There are four texts, one in runes and the others in Old English. Two Old English texts occupy the space between the cable mouldings of the sundial and the other is in the central space. Those between the cable mouldings translate as 'to count as to hold' and 'for him who knows how to seek out how'. The Roman letters OR and VM Pevsner speculates stand for orologium viattorum.

Reculver

Reculver (TR227694) lies on the estuary of the river Thames at a point where the Wantsum Channel divided the mainland from the Isle of Thanet. (The Wantsum Channel was a stretch of water – now no more – that in Roman times linked Richborough with the north coast of Kent.) Reculver was known as Regulbium to the Romans and was one of the series of forts known as the Saxon

Shore. The Saxon Shore forts were established in the 3rd century to guard against barbarian raids. Other interpretations have been proposed, such as places where Saxons settled or merely as ports for the import and export of goods to and from Europe.

There is a legend that Aethelbert of Kent, following his conversion by Augustine, moved his court to Reculver. By 669 it was in the hands of King Egbert who built a church and granted land to one Bassa to found a monastery. Egbert was implicated in the murder of his cousins and he is said to have founded the monastery to atone for his crime. As we have seen, wergild was the traditional way to recompense for a crime and the cousins' sister duly arrived from Mercia to claim it. She, Queen Ermenburga, opted for the gift of land. Accordingly, she is said to have set free her deer to wander where they would and so establish the boundary of her land. At the same time, she founded a convent at Minster in Thanet, a few miles to the south-east. Today, a deer is incorporated in the symbol of Thanet to recall these events.

Later, in 692, the abbot at Reculver, Bertwald, was appointed Archbishop of Canterbury. He was described by the Venerable Bede as 'learned in the scriptures and well versed in ecclesiastical and monastic affairs'. The minster became the parish church of St Mary the Virgin. It consisted of a nave and apsidal chancel. Much to the dismay of the parish clerk, in 1809 the Saxon church was 'scandalously' demolished. He complained that the vicar's mother 'fancied that the church was kept for a poppet show and persuaded her son to take it down'.

Much can be gleaned of its Saxon origins by inspecting the remains of the church. The towers (12th century) give access to the nave. There were doorways to the nave from north and south. At the far end of the nave, two round bases of concrete mark the position of two columns dividing nave from chancel. The columns were made of limestone from Calais. When the church was demolished in the 19th century, they were lost but later turned up in a nearby orchard and are now to be seen in the crypt (south side) at Canterbury Cathedral. Also, at Canterbury are remains of the Reculver cross, described by John Leland as 'the fairest and most auncyent', the remaining fragment showing the Ascension of Christ. Fine Saxon sculpture from Reculver is also housed in the crypt at Canterbury.

The chancel at Reculver was originally apsidal and is marked out on the ground. It was extended eastwards in the 12th century. On both sides of the concrete bases between nave and chancel are porticus (small chapels). Four more rooms were added later to the west on both sides of the nave. Much Roman brick is in evidence, presumably from the Roman fort of Regulbium which enclosed the church.

Reference

1. Susan Harris, *Richborough and Reculver*, English Heritage, 2001

Richborough

Richborough lies on the Saxon Shore Way, now a long-distance footpath running from Gravesend to Hastings, but following the coastline as it was in Roman times. Along it the Romans built a series of fortifications, including one at Richborough, to repel the invading Anglo-Saxons. Within the walls of Richborough Castle are the remains of the Chapel of St Augustine (TR322598) – now just rough masonry, barely above ground level. Excavations have also revealed a timber church of the 4th or 5th century and a font constructed of Roman tiles.

Reference

1. Susan Harris, *Richborough and Reculver*, English Heritage, 2001

Other Places of Interest

- There is a cluster of churches in the Dartford/Gravesend/Rochester/ Maidstone area with Saxon foundations – regrettably mostly locked.
- St Margaret's Church in **Darenth** (TQ561714) has a trace of a Saxon window over the north doorway, obscured by the porch.
- St Michael's Church, **Wilmington** (TQ538725) also claims a Saxon foundation.
- More convincingly, St Peter and St Paul at **Swanscombe** (TQ605740) has a splayed Saxon window with Roman tiles in the south wall of its pre-Conquest tower.
- St Botolph's Church at **Northfleet** (TQ648741) – still with the

atmosphere of a village church – has long-and-short work, thus providing evidence of its Saxon origin. The quoins can be seen to the south-west corner of the nave, by the tower.

- St Peter and St Paul's Church at **Shorne** (TQ690710) and All Saints at **Wouldham** (TQ713643) also have evidence of Saxon origin.

- The church of Holy Cross at **Bearsted** (TQ802555) may have been an aisled Saxon church.

- The tower at St Dunstan's, **West Peckham** (TQ644525) is of ragstone rubble and Saxon in origin. There are three single splayed windows in its upper stage and two on the ground floor.

- The church of All Saints (TR256628) at **West Stourmouth** dates from the Saxon era. It came under the jurisdiction of Rochester Priory and is now looked after by the Churches Conservation Trust.

- There are the outlines of Saxon windows on the north wall of St Nicholas Church at **Leeds** (TQ826533).

Lancashire

Great Urswick

Great Urswick lies south of the road from Ulverston to Barrow-in-Furness. There is part of a fascinating Anglo-Saxon cross shaft at St Mary's Church (SD268743). It was discovered in 1911 and acted as the lintel to a window in the nave. It has a runic inscription in the central panel and two figures, separated by a cross, facing each other below. W.G. Collingwood translated

Anglo-Saxon Cross Shaft, St Mary's Church, Great Urswick

the runes to read 'This cross Tunwini erected in memory of Torhtred a monument to his Lord. Pray for (his) soul' and dated the cross to the 9th century. Sir Thomas Kendrick claims it to be late Anglian in style and 11th century. Recently the study of the cross has come under more scrutiny by Steve Dickinson who asserts that the runes expand beyond the central area and run into the lower panel containing the two figures. He believes that the runes in the lower panel were intended to obscure earlier names of the two figures. He suggests that the figures are Luigne, a 7th century monk from the monastery of Elen (speculated to be in this part of Furness) and Theodore of Tarsus, the Archbishop of Canterbury. Furthermore, Tunwini, named at the head of the inscription, is an overcutting of Luibe – who presumably carved the stone.

On the other face a plant scroll rises from bottom to top. In the volutes at the bottom are round-headed creatures facing to the left. Above are two figures separated by the plant's stem. It's all very fascinating stuff and adds credence to the claim that this part of Furness is a very early Christian site. For more, see the references.

References

1. Anon., *St Mary and St Michael's Church*, Church Guide
2. Steve Dickinson, *By Water, by Stone*, Hidden Light Association, 2004
3. Colin R. Honour, *St Cuthbert and his Associations with Cumbria*, www. explorelowfurness.co.uk

Halton

Halton stands alongside the River Lune, just to the east of junction 34 of the M6 motorway. In the churchyard at St Wilfrid's Church (SD498647) is the Halton Cross. It is 11th century, of local sandstone and consists of four separate pieces fixed together in 1890. Three of the pieces are original and a fourth has been added to give an impression of the original height. At the top are the Signs of the Four Evangelists, but the more interesting features are at the bottom, showing scenes from Norse myth.

The carving tells the story of Sigurd. Sigurd was the foster son of Regin and was given the job of killing the dragon Fafnir who stood guard over a hoard of treasure. Regin instructed Sigurd to cook the dragon's heart but in so doing he burnt his fingers and, to ease the pain, put them in his mouth. Juices from the dragon enabled Regin to understand birdsong, the birds telling him that Regin meant to kill him and escape with the treasure on his horse, Grani.

The east face is divided into two, by two arches, on above the other. On the upper arch at its top are two birds on intersecting branches; below this, and still within the upper arch, is a figure (Sigurd) with his thumb in his mouth. Below is Sigurd (or possibly Wayland the Smith) with hammer in his hand; also two bellows beneath a table and, above, pincers and a headless figure. On the opposite face are two scenes enclosed within arches. Within the upper is a seated figure with squatting figures at his feet. Below is a cross with figures either side. The north face has two serpents bound together at the top and below, a quadruped, presumably Grani.

Reference

1.   Richard N. Bailey, *Viking Age Sculpture*, Collins, 1980, p. 102

Heysham

Standing in a glorious position overlooking Morecambe Bay is the diminutive Church of St Peter (SD411617). It is of ancient foundation and has an Anglo-Saxon west door. It was unfortunately locked when I visited. Anglo-Saxon sculpture is reported to be inside, including a hogback tomb. In the churchyard there are the remains of a splendid Saxon cross. It shows a gabled building with a central door and three windows above. In the windows are busts and in the doorway a figure wrapped in clothes. On each side of the central door are two doors, one above the other. Could the figure be Lazarus emerging from his tomb after being raised from the dead? On the other side is a seated figure with a halo. North of the church and sharing the splendour of Morecambe Bay on the headland is the remains of St Patrick's Chapel. It is a mere 27ft x 9ft and with a doorway dating from the 8th or 9th century, with an arch with curved grooves. Nearby are a series of rock-cut graves, again pre-Conquest; they are quite unique and have holes, probably intended to hold crosses.

One of the graves is for a child.

Pre-Conquest Rock-Cut Graves, Heysham

Hornby

Hornby is situated on the main road, midway between Kirkby Lonsdale and Lancaster at the point where the

River Wenning flows into the River Lune. St Margaret's Church (SD585685) has part of an extremely interesting Anglo-Danish cross shaft. It shows the Feeding of the Five Thousand. Below are two fishes and above them, five loaves of bread. Above again are two figures with a tree in between them. On the other face is a half figure with halo, presumably Christ, holding a book. There is the faintest trace of an inscription at the foot of this face.

Reference

1. A.J. White, *A Short History of St Margaret's Church*, 2004

Lancaster

The doorway at the west end of the nave at Lancaster Priory shows evidence of an earlier Saxon church on the site. Many pieces of Saxon sculpture have been found here and most of them are now in the museum in the Market Square. Near the entrance, however, is a 10th century slab, discovered in 1903, which at its top shows a hart, hound and snakes. The hart has large antlers, legs wide apart and biting a snake. Above is the hound, with a curly tail. The bottom section of the panel contains three concentric circles. To its left is a modern representation of what it would have looked like when first carved and full of colour.

Reference

1. Marion McClintock, *Lancaster Priory*, Jarrold, 2003

Whalley

Whalley is an ancient place. It lies on the River Calder, about three miles south of Clitheroe and first entered history in 798 when, according to the Anglo-Saxon Chronicle, a great battle was fought and Alric son of Heardbert was slain and 'many more with him'. There are three pre-Conquest crosses in the churchyard of St Mary's Church (SD734362) used in the 17th century as fence posts.

The best preserved (Whalley 2) has early 11th century decoration of scrollwork. The principal ornamentation is on the east and west faces and consists of a central rounded shaft or pole rising from the apex of a gable. At the top of the shaft are the mutilated remains of the carved central boss of the cross head.

The broad east face of Whalley 1 is divided into six panels. The second panel from the top contains a bird. Next down is a frontal figure with arms raised and flanked by serpents. Then a panel with a beast facing to the left but its head turns back to the right. The other faces are more difficult to discern because of weathering.

Whalley 3 has on all four sides heavily weathered decoration. It has a much later head.

Reference

1. English Heritage Record of Scheduled Ancient Monuments

Winwick

Lying just west of the M6 and M62 interchange is Winwick. St Oswald's Church (SJ604928) (regrettably locked) has, according to Pevsner, the horizontal bar of an Anglo-Saxon cross head in its north chapel. There is interlace and, at the rear, there are animals. There is also a man standing up with two others and a third upside down. Winwick is a contender as the site where King Oswald of Northumbria met his end at Battle of Marefield (642) at the hands of Penda of Mercia.

Other Places of Interest

- During excavations at St Michael's Church, **Aughton** (SD391054) in the early 20th century, part of a Saxon stone cross was found, dated to the latter half of the 9th century. The cross can be seen at the back of church.
- The church of Holy Trinity (formerly St Michael) (SD483678) at **Bolton le Sands** has fragments of Anglo-Saxon sculpture but was locked when visited.
- There is a collection of churches in industrial South Lancashire

which, apart from All Saints' **Childwell**, are mostly locked. **Walton,** a suburb of Liverpool, is reported by Pevsner to have a small Saxon piece. **Eccles,** just west of Manchester, has part of a Saxon cross shaft, as has **Bolton**, north of Manchester.

- The church of St John the Evangelist (SD572700) **Gressingham**, has Anglo-Saxon fragments within and a stone on the outside on the nave west wall at the south corner.

- That there was a pre-Conquest church at **Manchester** is shown by the 'Angel Stone'. This was discovered in the 19th century as part of the wall of the original south porch. It is now in the north arcade of the cathedral and shows an angel with wings holding a scroll.

- At St Wilfrid's Church **Melling** (SD597712) there is a fragment of an Anglo-Saxon cross.

Leicestershire and Rutland

Asfordby

Asfordby is a main road village, about three miles west of Melton Mowbray. There are Anglo-Saxon sculptured fragments at All Saints' Church (SK708190). The best one shows a stout figure with a large head, holding a cross, and giving a blessing. The figure is surrounded by scrollwork.

Breedon on the Hill

Breedon on the Hill (SK407233) has an outstanding collection of Anglo-Saxon sculptures of national importance. The place takes its name from the 7th century Anglo-Saxon Briudun, meaning hill, and the name is entirely appropriate for the church stands on a hill. Below are a quarry and the main A453 between Ashby-de-la-Zouch and Nottingham. Brian Williams, in his historical guide, from which the following is taken, tells us that before becoming incorporated into Mercia, in the 7th century Breedon was held by the Tomeseti. In the reign of the powerful King Aethelred of Mercia (675–716), Breedon came under the jurisdiction of the Abbey of St Peter at Medehamstede (Peterborough) and a certain Friduricus became its patron. He is recorded as building a monastery at Breedon with Hedda as its first abbot. Hedda later went on to become Bishop of Lichfield. Another important priest was Tatwine who became Archbishop of Canterbury in 731. The Anglo-Saxons loved riddles and Tatwin wrote one for his readers to solve.

> Marvellous is my fate, which I now relate to you,
> For my strength lies in two arms.

I have great confidence that I can grasp with gaping jaws
Unalarmed by anything hard, rough or hot:
With jaws gaping fearlessly I try to seize all things.
(What is it? The answer is, of course, a pair of tongs.)

In 844, in exchange for land, the Mercian King Beorhtwulf gave privileges to Abbot Eanmund. Beorhtwulf was later occupied fighting a vast fleet of Vikings who had sailed into his southern territory via the river Thames. And it is probable that Breedon would have fallen victim to the Vikings in 874 when they wintered at Repton, just a few miles away. The Vikings eventually became Christians and a charter of 966 records that – as part of Bishop Aethelwold of Winchester's great monastic revival – King Edgar granted land to the 'ecclesia at Breadone'.

According to the chronicler Hugh Candius of Peterborough, writing in the 12th century, many saints were buried at Breedon and Williams speculates that a hidden crypt, similar to the one at Repton, may lie beneath the church.

The glory of Breedon are its Anglo-Saxon carvings. Many were first located in the now-demolished west tower before being transferred to the porch. In 1937 they were moved to join the remainder inside the church. Some are set high up in the spandrels of the arches of the aisles and are difficult to appreciate

Anglo-Saxon frieze (section), St Mary's Church, Breedon on the Hill |

*Angel at St Mary's Church,
Breedon on the Hill*

without binoculars. They are all described in detail in Brian William's church guidebook and include on the south side vine scrolls containing human figures, birds, griffin-like beasts, animals and, at the south-west, a soldier kneeling with a spear. There is similar carving within the north aisle spandrels, the most interesting of which is a strip, above the pulpit, of Mediterranean pelta ornament, a series of interlocking shells; then, next to it, is a soldier on horseback with a spear.

The sculptures at eye level are easier to inspect. Starting at the east end, behind the altar is a strip of vine scrolls, within which are grapes and leaves. Then, to the south, on the east wall of the Lady Chapel is a central figure, with her head covered – probably the Virgin Mary – holding a book in one hand and giving a blessing with the other. On either side are two panels containing three saints standing within arches. Moving to the south wall and walking down from the east, first are two more saints within archways, then a pair of figures close together, one with a beard. Next is a lion with a curly tail and its face pointing towards us. Following this, a fascinating strip of frieze with, from left to right, circular interlace, weird beasts entangled with one another, a Mediterranean Greek key pattern, and a series of birds in various poses.

There are more carvings beneath the tower: to the south are two parallel strips high up, the upper with vine scroll and the lower with Greek key pattern, animals and two prancing figures. On the north side is a further length of frieze.

There is a display of parts of Anglo-Saxon crosses at the west end of the north aisle. They include a dragon with four legs, each with three toes, interpreted as in the Merovingian style and another dragon with large forked tongue, and rather than hind legs, serpentine interlace. Another cross depicts, in its lower section, Adam and Eve with the tree and serpent. The upper section has a figure giving a drinking horn to a warrior.

But the most spectacular piece is the Breedon Angel, thought to be the Archangel Gabriel.

It is thought to be the earliest sculptured angel in the country. The angel stands, dressed in robes, beneath an arch with a cross in one hand while giving a blessing in the other. There are plants, with flowers, set in the base. (The Angel on display now is a replica made by the Conservation Centre of the Museums and Galleries of Merseyside in 2001. The original is under lock and key.)

Reference

1.   Brian C.J. Williams, *St. Mary & St Hardulph, Breedon on the Hill, A History Guide*, Church Guide, 1996

Rothley

Rothley is about six miles south-east of Loughborough, just west of the main A6. There is a fine cross in the churchyard at St Mary & St John the Baptist Church (SK586126). It has been dated to the 9th century and has four sections on each side. The carving is mainly interlace and scrollwork but on one face there is an arch and a gable.

Sproxton

In peaceful and remote countryside, the Church of St Bartholomew (SK856249) has in its churchyard a complete Saxon cross with wheel head. Very weathered, it has the usual interlace carving and a relief of a beast.

Rutland

Market Overton

The tower arch at St Peter and St Paul Church (885165) at Market Overton is Saxon.

Other Places of Interest

- St James Church **Birstall** (SK597088) was locked. It has a fragment of sculpture in the east jamb of the arch leading to the vestry with a carving of a beast.
- St Bartholomew's Church (SP603950) at **Foston** was locked when I visited but it is reported to have the remains of an Anglo-Saxon window inside.
- At St Cuthbert's Church, **Great Glen** (SP652978), Pevsner reports that there are Anglo-Saxon fragments in the vestry and another small piece above the north door and just to the right.
- The Church of St Nicholas was probably **Leicester's** original cathedral. The nave is Anglo-Saxon. There are Saxon windows within on the north wall of the nave, the arches made from Roman tiles and probably, originally, a west porch, similar to that at Monkwearmouth. The church was locked when I visited.

Lincolnshire

Alkborough

Alkborough lies in the north of the county, close to where the River Trent joins the Humber. The village is better known for its maze (Julian's Bower) but the church of St John the Baptist (SE882219) is also interesting. It has a west tower of four stages, the lower three dating before the Conquest. The upper stage of the tower is Perpendicular Gothic.

Bardney

Regrettably, little remains above ground level of the once famous monastery at Bardney (TF113706), which was situated near to the River Witham in the flat but not uninteresting countryside east of Lincoln. Excavations in 2009 and 2011 have revealed its outline. It was founded as a Benedictine monastery in 697 by Aethelred of Mercia who became its first abbot in 704. But there was a monastic presence at Bardney before Aethelred's time. Bede tells us King Oswald of Northumbria was buried here in 679. Osthryda, queen of Mercia and niece of Oswald, made attempts to have the relics of her uncle, Oswald, buried at Bardney. But she was hampered at first by the reluctance of the monks. Bede takes up the story:

> In the province of Lindsey there is a noble monastery called Beardaneu [Bardney]… [Osthryda] wished that the honoured bones of her uncle should be reinterred there. But when the wagon carrying the bones arrived… the monks were reluctant to admit it; for although they

acknowledged Oswald's holiness, they were influenced by old prejudices [because] he came from a different province and had ruled over them as an alien king.

The bones duly remained outside all night until 'a pillar of light shone skywards from the wagon and was seen by nearly all the inhabitants of the province of Lindsey.' The monks saw this as a sign from heaven and Oswald's bones were admitted. Many miracles occurred: a man was relieved of an evil spirit and a child of ague.

The Anglo-Saxon monastery was destroyed by the Vikings in 870 and Oswald's remains were then taken to Gloucester Priory.

Reference

1.   Kathy Holland, *Bardney Abbey Revealed*, Lincolnshire County Council, 2011

Barnetby

The church of St Mary (TA061090) is redundant and in the care of the Churches Conservation Trust. It lies in the rolling countryside of the Lincolnshire Wolds. There is a keyhole window in the south wall which may be Saxon. Above it there is a carving of a cat, facing east but looking towards the south. Could it be Anglo-Saxon?

| *St Peter's Church, Barton-upon-Humber*

St Peter's Church, Barton-upon-Humber (Model of original church)

Barton upon Humber

The church of St Peter at Barton-upon-Humber (TA035220) is justly famous. The first Anglo-Saxons arrived here in the 7th century. They built a circular enclosure of about three hectares in an area east of the church on the remains of a Roman farmstead. Two Anglo-Saxon cemeteries have been discovered and excavated extensively. The first, some 300 yards to the south-west of the church, dates from the 7th to the 8th century. As well as over two hundred skeletons, it has yielded a rich source of grave goods. The other cemetery is later (9th to 11th century) and was excavated next to and beneath the church.

The splendid tower of St Peter's was originally the nave of the Saxon church. To its east was the chancel. This was demolished in the 11th century, but its original presence can easily be visualised by viewing the east side of the tower from inside the church – the outline of the roof-line of the 10th century chancel is clearly visible. Pevsner dates the tower to the 10th century; its upper stage and belfry, however, is Norman. Viewed from inside and looking towards the east wall of the tower, there is a round-arched doorway leading from the tower to the room above the Saxon chancel and above that a Saxon window with two triangular heads. Below is the chancel arch between the Saxon nave and its chancel. Standing within the tower, a head of Christ can be seen above the west face of the east wall. Outside, the tower has, at its lower stage, lesenes of blank arcading and at the second stage arcading with triangular heads. The tower (Saxon nave) was entered by a south doorway and there is also a triangular-headed north door, now blocked.

To the west of the tower is the Anglo-Saxon baptistry, later used as a storeroom and, in the 18th century, even as a mortuary for bodies recovered from the Humber. It has two round windows in its west wall, one above the other, the upper one lighting a room above the baptistry, and there are double splayed windows to the north and south.

Reference

1.   Warwick Rodwell, *St Peter's Church Barton-upon-Humber*, English Heritage, 2007

Broughton

The church of St Mary at Broughton (SE960086) lies east of Scunthorpe. It has a fine Saxon tower with much herringbone masonry and a sturdy south doorway, also Saxon. The stair turret to the west of the tower is not of the same stone and is therefore probably later. It is likely that the tower was the nave of the Saxon church; its arch to the nave shows Anglo-Saxon influence.

Coleby

Coleby is about five miles south of Lincoln, just to the west of the main A607 Grantham Road. There is Anglo-Saxon evidence in the tower of All Saints' Church, Coleby (SK975606); the lower part below the clock is Saxon and there is a characteristic keyhole window to the south with a hood mould above, like that at Stow. The north side of the tower also has a slit window. Inside, the original Saxon tower arch is visible in part.

Reference

1.   O.R. Clare, *The Parish Church of All Saints, Coleby*

Creeton

Creeton lies beside the River Glen and is – apart from the nearby East Coast Main Line railway – in quiet and remote countryside. The diminutive church of St Peter (TF014199) has two interesting Anglo-Saxon carved stone cross shafts in its churchyard. The one near the south doorway measures 157cm by 46cm and is decorated with interlace vine scrolls and tendrils. On the north-east face, there is a design which has been claimed to have astronomical significance – two concentric circles at top and bottom which enclose a diamond pattern. P.K. Rollings (PO Box 318, Peterborough, PE1 2YG) has produced a booklet about it at £3.14 plus postage. There is another smaller shaft to the north-west of the churchyard.

Crowland

About three miles north of Crowland, on the road to Spalding, at a crossroads (TF261149), there is part of an Anglo-Saxon cross shaft known as St Guthlac's Cross. It is about three feet in height and has an inscription which reads HANC PETRA GUTHLAC. It marks the boundary of land belonging to the Abbey of St Guthlac at Crowland and was placed here by Abbot Turketyl in the 10th century.

Crowland Abbey was founded in 716 and is forever associated with St Guthlac. He was born in 673, the son of a Mercian nobleman called Penwald and his wife Tette. His early life was spent as a soldier but at the age of twenty-four he joined the monks of Repton Abbey in Derbyshire and determined to lead a spiritual life of self-denial. Two years later, to lead an even more frugal life as a hermit, he arrived in the Fens at the marshy island of Crowland with his servant, Beccelm, and his boatman, Tatwin. There he remained until his death living in a barrow, dressed in animal skins and eating scraps of barley bread and drinking only a small cup of muddy water each day after sunset. Many came to visit this holy man and gain spiritual guidance, including Aethelbald of Mercia, at the time when he was in exile from his cousin, Coeldred. Guthlac assured Aethelbald that one day he would be king of Mercia. And so it turned out. In thanksgiving, Aethelbald founded Crowland Abbey on St Bartholomew's Day, 716. Aethelbald commissioned the monk, Felix, to write Guthlac's biography. It is also told in the 12th century Guthlac Scroll, held at the British Library.

Crowland Abbey was sacked by the Danes in 870. Many monks fled, and Abbot Theodore was murdered. His skull is preserved to this day in the Parvise

Scenes from life of St Guthlac, west portal, Crowland Abbey

Chapel. In the reign of King Eadred, the abbey was rebuilt in the mid-10th century by his chancellor, Turketyl, who remained at Crowland and became abbot. Nothing of Turketyl's building remains today. Everything was destroyed in a fire in 1091.

The story of St Guthlac is told in the quatrefoil of the west portal: the lower section shows Guthlac arriving at Crowland in his boat accompanied by Tatwin and Beccelm. In the centre, Guthlac expels two devils with his whip. On the left, Guthlac is ordained by Hedda, Bishop of Winchester. On the right Guthlac cures Egga, a Mercian nobleman, who is resting on a bed. On top, Guthlac is taken to heaven.

Reference

1. Stanley Swift and R.J. Cooke, *Visitor's Guide to Crowland Abbey*, 2007

Crowle

Crowle lies in the remote and flat lands of north-west Lincolnshire, to the west of the river Trent. At the north-west end of the church of St Oswald (SE772130) stands the Crowle stone. Probably originally part of a cross, it was used by the

Normans as an inside lintel for the west door of their church and so has been handed down to us in a good state of preservation. It was placed in its present position in 1919.

The stone, carved on all four sides, is seven feet in height and eighteen inches thick. Canon Alfred Hunt has offered a possible interpretation: the first and uppermost panel shows two wyverns or dragons facing each other. The second panel depicts two men opposite each other. They could possibly be King Oswald of Northumbria and his successor, King Oswy. (The name Crowle means 'Oswald's cross'.) An alternative interpretation is that the stone shows St Paul addressing St Anthony. Below, and difficult to make out, is a man on horseback with an oval shape behind his head, said to be a bag of earth. Beneath are Runic inscriptions. Hunt dates the stone to about 685 and says it was probably erected by Osthryda, Oswald's niece. The back of the stone is carved with a snake, consuming its own tail, a symbol of eternity.

Reference

1.   David Schofield and Donald Ramery, *St Oswald's Crowle, A Guide to the Church*

Edenham

Edenham is a main road village about two miles north-west of Bourne. There is Anglo-Saxon sculpture within St Michael's Church (TF063219). High up at both the east and west ends of the south aisle are Anglo-Saxon roundels. The one on the west is composed of foliage in the form of a cross. The one on the east is incomplete and contains foliage as well. There is also part of an Anglo-Saxon cross shaft; one side depicts the figure of a male with his head missing. He holds a book and is dressed in a belted gown and has been identified perhaps as St John. The other side shows a seated female figure below intricate pattern work.

Harmston

Harmston lies on the high ground about four miles south of Lincoln, just west of the main Grantham Road. There is part of an Anglo-Saxon cross shaft at All Saints' Church (SK972623), discovered embedded in the walls of the old

Harmston manor house. It is forty-one inches long and has two columns of interlace on both faces. One face depicts Christ on the cross with below, the Virgin Mary on the right and St John on the left. On the other side is a figure, probably Christ rising from the dead.

Reference

1. Jennifer Playford, *A Brief History and Guide to All Saints' Church, Harmston*, Church Guide

Heapham

All Saints' Church (SK877886) lies all by itself in remote countryside, east of Gainsborough. It has a late Anglo-Saxon tower of two stages separated by a string course. The lower stage has a blocked west door and slit windows above. The second stage has bell openings with mid-wall shafts. The south door is also Saxon.

Holton-Le-Clay

Holton-Le-Clay is about five miles south of Grimsby. Except for its Perpendicular upper stage, the tower at St Peter's Church (TA286027) is 11th century Anglo-Saxon. There is a keyhole window in its west wall, set within a west doorway, which has been removed and replaced with rough masonry. The tower arch to the nave is also Saxon.

Hough on the Hill

And it is on a hill, about seven miles north of Grantham in pleasant countryside. All Saints' Church at Hough on the Hill (SK923465) has an excellent west tower, the lower stages of which are Anglo-Saxon. It has a semi-circular stair turret, like the one at Brixworth. The stair projection has miniscule arched, rectangular and round windows. According to Taylor and Taylor, the nave of the church predates the tower.

One-mile south-west is Loveden Hill, the site of one of the largest Anglo-Saxon cemeteries in the country. It was also the meeting place of the Loveden Wapentake.

Lincoln (St Mary Wigford)

Lincoln, of course, is of Roman origin. The area was revived by Danish invaders as the port of Vikford – hence Wigford. Next to the railway station is the church of St Mary Wigford. Its tower has been dated to about 980 and was built by the Saxon, Eirtig. His foundation stone is set on the west front and consists of a Roman tombstone with inscription (reading from bottom to top) 'Eirtig me let pirce a n 7 fios godian Criste te Lofe 7 Sce Marie', which is to say, 'Eirtig had me built and endowed to the glory of Christ and St Mary'. The upper stage of the tower has twin bell openings, the lower stage a much-restored west door.

Marton

For those interested in looking at herringbone masonry, the church of St Margaret of Antioch (SK840817) is the place to come. The village is on the main road from Gainsborough to Newark, close to the River Trent. The tower is typically Anglo-Saxon, unbuttressed, of two stages and dating from just before the Conquest. The outline of the original nave can be seen on the east face of the tower with a doorway, now blocked, which gave access to the nave roof. The bell openings have two lights separated by a mid-wall shaft. There is what could be a carved head above the small keyhole light in the west tower. It is said to be Saxon and may represent the head of Christ. In the chancel north wall is a crucifixion showing Christ with long thin arms and feet hanging downwards. It may date from the Saxon period.

Reference

1. Anon., *St Margaret of Antioch*, Church Guide

Old Clee (Grimsby)

Holy Trinity Church (TA290085) has a splendid Anglo-Saxon tower. It has been dated to about 1050. There is a Saxon west door with two layers of wedged stones (voussoirs) forming the arch with a hood mould above. Above is a keyhole window and above that are twin bell openings with mid-wall shafts. Edward Drury, in the guidebook, points out a stone above the west door. It has the face of a man carved on it and has been named the old man of Clee.

Reference

1.   Edward Drury, *A Walk Around the Historic Parish Church of Holy Trinity and St Mary the Virgin, Old Clee, Grimsby*, Church Guide

Rothwell

Rothwell is situated in the splendid Lincolnshire Wolds, about two miles south-east of Caistor. The church of St Mary Magdalene, Rothwell (TF149994) has a fine Anglo-Saxon tower of two stages separated by a string course. Each face of the upper stage has twin bell openings with mid-wall shafts. The lower stage has three narrow, internally splayed windows. Its west doorway is similarly Saxon with a hood mould over the tympanum.

Stow

Stow is in pleasing countryside, midway between Gainsborough and Lincoln. Its early history is a bit complicated. Even though it is many miles away, land at Stow (SK883820) and the area surrounding once

St Mary's Church, Stow (Interior)

St Mary's Church, Stow (Exterior)

belonged to the vast see of the Bishop of Dorchester-on-Thames, the original see of the bishop of the West Saxons. (It was moved to Winchester in 660.) All this arose because of Viking raids on Leicester causing its bishop to transfer his see to Dorchester (now in Mercia). In consequence the see at Dorchester was re-founded in the late ninth century.

In 975, Bishop Aelfnoth built a church here to serve Stow and its surrounding countryside. Aelfnoth's church fell victim to a fire and was later rebuilt by Bishop Eadnoth in the mid-11th century. A charter of 1054 tells us that Leofric, Earl of Mercia, and his wife, the renowned Lady Godiva, endowed the church and installed priests to sing 'in the choir in the same way as at St Paul's Cathedral in London'. After the Conquest, the Normans began a policy of moving sees in rural and outlying districts to larger centres of population. Hence in 1073 the Norman Bishop Remigius moved the see from Dorchester to Lincoln, built his majestic cathedral there and Stow reverted to an ordinary parish church.

Looking at the church of St Mary's from the south, the Anglo-Saxon south transept has a narrow slit window with hood mould above. It was built by Bishop Eadnoth. Other windows in the transept are later. One's breath is taken away on entering the church – the interior is huge, and the eye is immediately drawn to the crossing and transepts. Here is the oldest part of the building. There was once a Saxon tower, now demolished. It was supported by the round and outer arches of the crossing. The pointed arches were added later to hold up the present tower.

There is an excellent Saxon doorway in the north transept, part of Aelfnoth's work. It has typical long-and-short work on its left side. Most interesting of all, for me, is the carving of a Viking ship on the south pier of the chancel arch. It is the earliest known depiction of a Viking ship in England and dates from the 10th or 11th century.

Reference

1. Anon., *St Mary's Stow in Lindsey*, Church Guide

Other Places of Interest

- There are fragments of Anglo-Saxon sculpture in the west wall of the nave of the church of St Andrew at **Burton Penwardine** (TF119422). They include parts of a cross shaft and grave covers carved in a variety of interlace styles.
- The church of St Michael (TF403954) at **Conisholme** was locked when I visited. It is recorded by Pevsner as having a 'very interesting head of an Anglo-Saxon wheel cross, with a tiny, very primitive Crucifixus, interlace above His head, three discs by his feet.' A UFO has been sighted here, allegedly!
- All Saints' Church, **Greetwell** (TF013716) was locked but a Saxon keyhole window is visible on its south side.
- The church of St Peter at **Lusby** (TF341679) has evidence of an Anglo-Saxon foundation. At the time of the Conquest, Totti of Lusby was Lord of the Manor. The stumps of semi-circular shafts on each side of the chancel arch are Anglo-Saxon. There is also a keyhole window in the chancel north wall.
- The Anglo-Saxon tower at St Giles, **Scartho** (TA267063) is similar in many ways to that at Old Clee. The west door (now with a window within) is Saxon and there are the usual twin bell openings with baluster shafts.
- The church of St Martin, **Waythe** (TA284007) is redundant. It has an Anglo-Saxon central tower with twin belfry openings with mid-wall shafts. It is in the care of the Churches Conservation Trust.
- The tower at the Church of All Saints (SE928187) at **Winterton** has three stages, the lower two dating from before the Conquest.

Norfolk

Bessingham

The tiny village of Bessingham is in peaceful countryside five miles south west of Cromer. St Mary's Church (TG167370) has a Saxon round tower dated to about 1050. It is built of carstone in its lower and upper part and flint in between. There are four typical twin bell openings with triangular heads in the upper carstone stage and one single splayed window in the flint stage. Inside, the tower arch is Saxon with a triangular-headed window above.

Reference

1. Anon., *The Parish Church of St Mary the Virgin, Bessingham*, Church Guide

Gissing

Gissing lies about four miles north of Diss, just to the west of the main railway line to Norwich. St Mary's Church (TM146853) at Gissing has a round tower, fifty-four feet in height. Is it Norman or is it Saxon? The three double splayed round-headed windows halfway up certainly point to a Saxon builder. But the belfry windows look more Norman. Apparently, Saxon foundations have been discovered beneath the north porch.

Reference

1. Richard Butler-Stoney, *St Mary's Church, Gissing*, Church Guide, 2003

Great Dunham

The small village of Great Dunham is situated in lovely Norfolk countryside, about three miles east of Castle Acre. The church of St Andrew (TF874147) is a splendid Saxon building containing much Roman brick. There is typical long-and-short work in the quoins of the tower. The belfry windows are of two lights with a central baluster, with above to the west and east two circular openings, usually known as sound holes. Beneath the bell openings are double splayed windows, two on the south and one on the north. The north wall of the nave has a similar double splayed window. The west doorway (now blocked) has a triangular head. It would have been the original entrance to the church. The surprise at Great Dunham comes inside; there is blank arcading to both the north and south walls of the nave. The tower arch to the chancel also has Saxon features.

Reference

1.   Richard Butler-Stoney, *St Andrew's Church at Dunham*, Church Guide

North Elmham

North Elmham is a place of some importance to the Anglo-Saxon enthusiast. It lies south-east of Fakenham. Felix of Burgundy arrived in East Anglia from his homeland in about 615 and is recognised as bringing Christianity to the East Angles. Sigbert was ruling East Anglia at the time and had been converted to Christianity while in exile in Gaul. According to Bede, 'Sigbert laboured to bring about the conversion of his whole realm'. In this he was assisted by Felix who 'reaped a rich harvest of believers'. Felix was ordained bishop of a place called Dommoc in 630. Dommoc has been identified by many as the coastal village of Dunwich. Others, however, claim it to be at Walton. Felix died in 647 and soon afterwards, in 672, Theodore of Canterbury divided the see and a second diocese was founded at North Elmham. The see at Dommoc finally lapsed when the Vikings invaded.

There was thus a Saxon cathedral at North Elmham, and its ruins (TF987216) are there for us to see today. They are mixed up with the later remains of a manor house but are well worth inspecting. The late 10th century north and south transepts and the apse are clearly visible. Excavations to the north of the village have revealed a series of Saxon buildings confirming North Elmham as a place of importance. In 1075 the diocese moved to Thetford and finally, in 1094, to Norwich.

Tasburgh

Tasburgh is about six miles south of Norwich just to the west of the main road to Ipswich. St Mary's Church (TM201958) has a round tower with Anglo-Saxon workmanship, as shown by the blank arcading and the three narrow rounded-headed windows in the centre of the tower, to the south, north and west.

St Mary's Church, Tasburgh

There are two tiers of blank arcading, with the upper tier beginning at the apices of the lower tier. Excavations have revealed the existence of a sizeable Anglo-Saxon settlement at Tasburgh.

Thorpe next Hadiscoe

Thorpe next Hadiscoe is the tiniest of hamlets on the edge of marshland and the River Waveney to the east. The upper part of the round tower at St Matthias' church (TM436980) is Norman but the lower stages are Saxon. There is Saxon blank arcading with small slit windows beneath the Norman stage.

Weybourne

Weybourne is a couple of miles west of Sheringham and close to the sea. The remains of the original axial Anglo-Saxon church tower to the east of the present priory church – albeit a picturesque ruin – is still there today for us to see (TG112431). There are the usual round sound holes and below, a blind arcade.

Reference

1. C.L.S. Linell, *Weybourne Priory and Parish Church*, Church Guide

Whissonsett

The village is about four miles south of Fakenham in peaceful Norfolk countryside. The church of St Mary (TF919233) has part of a ringed Anglo-Saxon cross to the south of the chancel arch. It was found buried in the churchyard in 1902 and is decorated in the upper part of its shaft with interlace.

Reference

1. Richard Butler-Stoney, *The Church of St Mary the Virgin, Whissonsett*, Church Guide

Other Places of Interest

- St Peter's Church at **Guestwick** (TG061270) was founded in pre-Conquest times. Parts of its tower are Saxon; this was once the central (i.e. axial) space of an earlier church.
- The church (TL995960) at **Rockland All Saints** was locked when I visited. It has Anglo-Saxon long-and-short quoins to the nave. Inside, Pevsner reports an Anglo-Saxon coffin lid with crosses at top and bottom connected by a shaft. Between are interlace patterns.
- All Saints' Church (TM366918) at **Kirby Kane** has a round tower with the remains of pilaster strips at its base, a typical indication of Anglo-Saxon work.
- Set adjacent to the bishop's modern cathedra at **Norwich Cathedral** are fragments from the cathedra at Thetford and/or perhaps North Elmham.

North Yorkshire

Bedale

St Gregory's Church at Bedale (SE266884) (about six miles south-west of Northallerton) has on display part of a hogback tombstone of 10th century date. It was discovered in 2003 in the crypt and its interest lies in the fact that it is one of only three Wayland stones in the country. (The other two are at Leeds and Sherburn, near Filey. It is also referred to on the Franks Casket.) It depicts the Viking myth of Wayland the Smith. He was captured by a king who cut his hamstrings to prevent him running away. Wayland then made a flying machine which he used to make good his escape. The fan-like tail of the flying machine can be seen at the bottom of the carving as well as one of its wings; Wayland is represented with his feet, legs and body secured by Celtic knots. There is what could be a nativity scene on the end of the tombstone.

In the south aisle is a fragment of an Anglo-Saxon column with typical knotwork.

Reference

1. Anon., *St Gregory's Church, Bedale*, Church Guide

Brompton-in-Allertonshire

Patricia Turner, in the guidebook to St Thomas' Church (SE374965), has written an excellent and detailed description of the Saxon crosses and hogback

Viking Hogback Tombs, St Thomas' Church, Brompton-in-Allertonshire

tombstones found in the church during a restoration in 1867. Many may be seen here, and others are on display in Durham Cathedral Library. Brompton is just over a mile north of Northallerton.

The earliest Anglo-Saxon cross is the Cock Shaft. Two cocks are clearly seen in two panels, a reference to St Peter's denial of Christ. Beneath are men or beasts who appear to be fighting. On the opposite face a figure, perhaps St John the Evangelist, holds a book. One of the narrow faces is divided into three panels; the upper one shows part of a bird, below is a full-length figure, probably a cleric, holding a book in both hands. The bottom panel is less distinct and shows a head. The other narrow face has intricate plant scroll mouldings. There are also good examples of wheel head crosses.

But the glories of the church are its hogback tombstones. They were intended to resemble dwelling places, with the roof of the house raised in the centre, and to act as grave covers; many are decorated with stylised roof tiles. Ten were found; five are preserved here and the remainder are at Durham Cathedral Library. In contrast to the more usual type – where hogs lie on their backs at the end of the stones and bite plaits which run the length of the stone – at Brompton there are bears. It is speculated that the bears may have been intended to guard the dead or refer to the occupant's fighting prowess.

Reference

1.   Patricia Turner, *A Brief Guide to the Church of St Thomas, Brompton-in-Allertonshire*, Church Guide, 2004

Hackness

Hackness lies in wooded and hilly countryside about four miles north-west of Scarborough. Bede tells us that a nunnery was founded at Hackness (SE969905) by St Hilda of Whitby in 680. Hilda died in the same year and, in one of those mysterious medieval stories, Bede relates that a devout nun at Hackness, called Begu, was awakened by a bell and a vision of the soul of Hilda being borne up to heaven on the very day that she died. Begu immediately informed Prioress Frigyth and so when monks came from Whitby with the news of Hilda's death, it wasn't really news at all.

In 1830, the remains of a Saxon cross were discovered, acting as a gatepost. It is now in the south aisle and has inscriptions in Latin, runic and Ogham script. (Ogham is a medieval script, sometimes called Celtic Tree Alphabet. It is mainly found in Ireland and the west of Britain.) The cross is of two pieces; the upper depicts the head of Christ, interlace and scrolls; the lower depicts parts of griffins.

There is a display board in the church which interprets the inscriptions:

The uppermost stone reads OEDILBURGABEATA AD SEMPERTERECOLANT AMANTES PIE DEPOSCANT REQUIEM VERNANTEM SEMPITERNAM SANCORUM PIA MATER APOSTOLICA, translated as 'Blessed Oedilburga, may they always remember thee, dutifully loving thee; may they ask for thee, the verdant everlasting rest of the saints, O loving Mother Apostolic'.

Next... FIB... GA SEMPER TEAMENT MEMORES DOMUSTUAETE MATERAMANTISSIMA, translated as 'Hudetburga, may thy houses always love thee, remembering thee, Most loving Mother'.

The lowest stone has TRECEA, ORA, (PRO EO) ABBATISSA OEDILBURGA ORATE PRO, translated as 'Trecea, pray for him; Abbess Oedilburga pray for her'.

Oedilburga is probably Aethelburga, the great niece of Hilda and abbess at Hackness, who founded the monastery in 680.

The church of St Peter has a Saxon chancel arch with interlace in its northern impost.

Reference

1. Bede, *A History of the English Church and People*, Book 4, Chapter 23
2. James Winterbotham, *Hackness and its Church*, 2000

Hovingham

Hovingham lies in quiet countryside midway between Malton and Helmsley. All Saints' Church (SE667757) at Hovingham was restored in 1860 but mercifully the Saxon west tower was left intact. The Domesday Book tells us that the original church was built on land owned by Orm (the same Orm whose inscription is on the sundial at nearby Kirkdale). The tower has three stages and is unbuttressed. There are two light bell openings with mid-wall shafts. The guidebook points out that there are reused stones in the south-west quoins with the obvious implication that they come from an earlier church on this site. Above the bell opening on the south is a carved cross, again probably from an earlier church. The west doorway is also Saxon and has one order of shafts and roll moulding. It is late Saxon work and above it is an Anglian Cross.

In the south aisle is a sculptured Saxon stone slab carved in high relief, quite like the Hedda Stone at Peterborough Cathedral. Until 1924 it formed part of the masonry of the tower. There are eight arches within the slab, all containing figures. Within the first two arches on the left an Annunciation scene is depicted, the Angel Gabriel on the left and the Virgin Mary on the right. Next is the Visitation, Mary on the left and Elizabeth on the right. The remaining figures are difficult to discern but have been interpreted as two women at the sepulchre, and an angel and the Virgin Mary. Beneath is a panel of vine leaves inhabited by birds, all a little difficult to decipher. Elsewhere in the church there is a fragment of a cross.

Reference

1. Patrick H. Vaughan, *All Saints' Church, Hovingham*, Church Guide, 2006

Kirkdale

St Gregory's Minster at Kirkdale (SE677867) is all by itself by the tiny Hodge Beck stream just over one mile south-west of Kirbymoorside and north of the road between Pickering and Helmsley. It is the proud possessor of an Anglo-Saxon sundial, sited above the church's south door. It was discovered in 1771, happily covered with plaster, which had protected it from erosion. It is in the centre of a stone slab, eight feet long by twenty inches in height. An inscription reads: 'This is the day's sun-marker at every hour' and 'Hawarth made me and Brand the priest'. There are further inscriptions on both sides. They read 'Orm the son of Gamel acquired St Gregory's Church when it was completely ruined and collapsed, and he had it built anew from the ground to Christ and St Gregory in the days of King Edward and in the days of Earl Tostig'.

The phrase 'in the days of Earl Tostig' enable us to date the building, for Tostig (son of Earl Godwin of Wessex and brother of King Harold) was the Earl of Northumbria between 1055 and 1065. Thus, the church was 'built anew' during this period.

Inside, a Saxon arch divides nave from tower, this arch being the likely entrance to the church that Orm 'built anew'. Investigations during drainage work have also revealed the remains of part of an Anglo-Saxon apse. Surviving from the church that was 'completely ruined' are two stone tomb slabs dating from the 8th century.

But what of Orm and Gamel? They are both Scandinavian names. We know that Orm was an important nobleman in the 11th century. He married Aethelthryth, daughter of Ealdred, Earl of Northumbria, between 1025 and 1038. Orm held considerable amounts of land in the area and was brother-in-law to Siward, Earl of Northumbria (1041–1055).

Reference

1.   Richard Fletcher, *St Gregory's Minster, Kirkdale*, Church Guide, 2003

Lastingham

Lastingham lies in glorious countryside, about four miles north-east of Kirbymoorside and one mile east of Hutton le Hole, with Spaunton Moor as neighbour to its north. Lastingham is an important place (SE728905). A monastery was founded here by St Cedd in 654. Cedd and his three brothers, Cynebil, Caelin and Chad, were all pupils of Aidan at Lindisfarne. Bede writes that on the instructions of Aethelwald, son of King Oswald of Northumbria, Cedd (more famous as the bishop of the East Saxons) founded his monastery 'among some high remote hills, which seemed more suitable for the dens of robbers and haunts of wild beasts than for human habitation'. This, said Cedd, was to fulfil the prophesy of Isaiah: 'in the habitation of dragons where each lay, shall be grass, with reeds and rushes'. Ten years later he returned at the time of a plague, died and was buried there. When news of his imminent death reached his flock at Bradwell (Essex), thirty of them made the sea journey north to be with him at the end but all save a child fell victim to the deadly plague and failed to make the return journey to Bradwell. Cedd handed over the abbacy to his brother Chad who later became well known as the Bishop of Lichfield. The Anglo-Saxon church of St Mary was rebuilt in 1078 by Stephen, abbot of Whitby. It has a remarkable and memorable crypt within which there are several pre-Conquest cross shafts.

Reference

1. Anon., *St Mary's Lastingham*, Church Guide, 1997

Levisham

Levisham is about five miles north-east of Pickering and west of the main road to Whitby. St Mary's Church at Levisham (SE833901) lies deserted. It had an Anglo-Danish gravestone, now removed to the new church of St John the Baptist in the village. For those intent on visiting, St Mary's lies in the valley and can be accessed from a bridleway just before the hairpin bend that leads to the village.

Masham

Masham lies midway between Ripon and Leyburn. Outside the south porch of St Mary's Church (SE226807) is a sandstone 9th century cross shaft. It is badly weathered and carved in four levels with figures within arches. Below are animals; in the two sections above are Old Testament scenes, difficult to discern, but said to represent Samson and the Gaza gates, and King David and his lyre – a unique pre-Conquest example of this musical instrument. At the top are figures, very likely to be Christ and the Apostles.

Reference

1. David Cleaves, *St Mary's Church, Masham*, Church Guide

Middleton

The small village of Middleton is about one mile north-west of Pickering. St Andrew's Church at Middleton (SE782854) is famous for its splendid collection of Viking crosses. But first, its tower. It is Anglo-Saxon up to the string course and has a Saxon door in its west wall. Above is an Anglian cross of the 8th century, from the centre of which radiate petals of flowers. There is another cross built into the south wall of the tower, beneath the lowest window and to the right. The tower also has typical long-and-short work to its quoins.

The Viking crosses inside the church are justifiably famous. They have been displayed in Denmark, the British Museum, the Metropolitan Museum of Art in New York and the Institute of Arts in Minneapolis. They are numbered A to E.

A. is ring-headed with a hunter holding a spear in his right hand. Beneath him is a stag with giant antlers and to the left two hounds, one above the other. The other side shows a snake, bound with rope. It is in the Jellinge style.

B. B depicts a warrior with axe, sword and spear. He wears conical-shaped headgear. On the rear is a snake-like creature, once more bound. Both A and B were originally incorporated into the tower.

C. C has animal heads and scrollwork.

D. D is similar to B but here the warrior has a beard.

E. E is two joined-up fragments, the top, a ring head cross and the bottom, the upper part of a man with pointed helmet.

Reference

1. Jenny Richmond-Brown, *St Andrew's Church, Middleton near Pickering*, Church Guide

Osmotherley

Osmotherley is about nine miles north-east of Northallerton and under one mile east of the main trunk road from Thirsk to Stockton and Middlesbrough. St Peter's Church (SE456972) was founded in the Anglo-Saxon era. Excavation has revealed an Anglo-Saxon apse. The church also contains a fragment of a Saxon cross shaft. A legend tells of a Saxon prince called Osmund who was warned of his impending death by drowning. To avoid this fate, his mother took him to the top of nearby Roseberry Topping in the Cleveland Hills, in the belief he would be safe there. But by a miracle water flooded from the hill and drowned poor Osmund. He was buried at St Peter's Church, from the legend the place gets its name – 'Osmund lies here', corrupted to Osmotherley.

Oswaldkirk

Oswaldkirk is about five miles south of Helmsley in splendid countryside. Pevsner points out the unusually long stone quoin in the south-west corner of St Oswald's Church (SE621789), which he identified as a Saxon cross shaft. In the porch there are stones from the Saxon and Viking era, including one with an excellent Mother and Child from a hogback tomb.

Reference

1. Anon., *St Oswald's Church Through the Ages*, Church Guide

Stonegrave

As with Hovingham and Oswaldkirk (above), Stonegrave lies on the road between Malton and Helmsley. Holy Trinity at Stonegrave (SE656779) was founded as a minster church in the 8th century. Its abbot (or abbess) ruled over the local countryside including nearby Coxwold. Stonegrave Minster witnessed an early clash – so familiar in later years – between church and state. It is recorded that in 757 an abbess recommended a certain Forthred to be her successor, but the king of Northumbria overruled her and a lay abbot, Aethelwold Moll, was appointed instead. The matter was brought to the attention of Pope Paul I who wrote sternly to the king:

> The abbot Forthred reported to us that three monasteries had been granted to him by a certain abbess, namely the monasteries called Stonegrave, Coxwold and Donaemuth and that your excellency took these monasteries from him by force and gave them to a certain patrician, Moll by name… Therefore, we exhort you and warn you by the admonition of the Apostolic See that with true obedience you restore to the aforesaid abbot Forthred those three monasteries that he may be allowed to enjoy them without any troublesome molestation.

The church has a well-preserved 10th century wheel-headed cross. It was found during a restoration of the church in 1863, incorporated within the north wall of the chancel. There are three carvings on its face. At the bottom there is a priest. He has a bag hanging from his neck which probably contained chalice, paten and Bible. Above is a cross and at the top a figure sits in prayer with a book held high.

The cross stands on a 13th century coffin lid which itself stands on an Anglo-Danish slab, difficult to discern but interpreted as an archer shooting an arrow at a stag.

Reference

1. Vaughan Hazlehurst, *A Short History of Stonegrave Minster*, 1988
2. Lorna Pobjoy, *People of the Minster*, 1989

Other Places of Interest

• All Saints' Church (SE735735) at **Appleton-Le-Street** has a 10th century west tower with two tiers of bell openings with mid-wall shafts.

- St Peter's Church (NZ289099) at **Croft** has what is described by Pevsner as the finest cross shaft in the county. Unfortunately, the church was locked when I visited.

- The Church of St Mary and All Saints, **Cundall** (SE423731) (locked) has, according to Pevsner, an Anglo-Saxon cross shaft beneath the tower.

- The tower at St Mary's Church, **Hornby** (SE223937) dates from the Saxo-Norman overlap period.

- Pevsner reports Anglo-Saxon sculptures at **Kirkbymoorside** (697866).

- Pevsner records that, within the porch at St Martin's Church, **Kirk Leavington** (NZ432098), there are many Anglo-Saxon fragments. The church was locked when I visited.

- St Oswald's Church, **Lythe** (NZ85132) has a large collection of Anglo-Danish sculptured remains.

- St James Church, **Melsonby** (NZ201085) dates from before the Conquest as shown by an Anglo-Saxon opening between tower and nave. There are also Anglo-Saxon sculptures, reported to be in excellent condition. Regrettably, the church was locked when I visited.

- There is an Anglo-Danish fragment beneath the tower of All Saints' Church, **Pickhill** (SE347837) in the style of Jellinge with dragon and interlace.

- The church of St John the Baptist (NZ185120), at **Stanwick**, has fragments of Anglo-Danish sculpture.

Northamptonshire

Brigstock

St Andrew's Church at Brigstock (SP946852) is worth a journey. Brigstock is included in the Domesday Book as Bricstoc – meaning stockade of the birch trees or shrine by the bridge. It is a main road village in pleasant East Northamptonshire between Corby and Thrapston. The splendid tower is Saxon with long-and-short work quoins and a circular stair turret to the west. The upper part of the tower is Decorated Gothic. There is also typical long-and-short work at the nave's south-west and north-west corners, indicating that the nave of the original church was pre-Conquest. Further confirmation can be seen inside where there is a blocked Saxon window above the later north arcade. Inside there is a grand Saxon tower arch which Pevsner dates as late Saxon. But other scholars (Taylor and Taylor) have dated the lower parts of the tower and the nave to early Saxon, in which case the tower arch is a later insertion. It has a pilaster strip running vertically upwards, continuing around the arch and down the other side. Inside the tower there is a triangular-headed doorway and single splayed windows above.

Reference

1. L.G. Davies, with revisions by G.R. Loxston and R.D. Howe, *Historical Guide to the Church and Village of Brigstock*, Guidebook

Brixworth

'Perhaps the most imposing architectural monument of the 7th century yet surviving north of the Alps' was how Sir Alfred Clapham described the Saxon

church at Brixworth. The village is about six miles north of Northampton, on the road to Market Harborough. The immediate impact of the building is its size. It is vast. Evidence for a 7th century foundation comes from the pen of Hugh Candidus, a 12th century monk at Peterborough, who wrote 'when Saxulf was made bishop of the Mercians from the great monastery at Peterborough, called Medeshamstede, many daughter houses were founded… as at Brixworth'. Saxulf was made bishop in 675.

The church of All Saints (SP747712) we enter today is later, built between 750 and 850, maybe in the reign of King Offa of Mercia. The nave, fully thirty feet wide and over a hundred feet in length, has four arches, blocked now, and supported by enormous pillars. Originally, the arches would have led to porticus, small areas, perhaps containing an altar. Above are clerestory windows situated on top of the spandrels. The arches are of Roman brick, two semi-circles, one on top of the other, and set in a jumble, rather than in the neater and more usual wedge shapes. Above the doorway at the west end of the nave is a blocked door. It is speculated that there was once a wooden gallery attached to the tower and protruding into the nave, with the door allowing villagers to enter it from the tower. Further above is a triple arch with baluster shafts.

Near the pulpit is a fragment of a late Saxon red sandstone cross. Found in the vicarage garden in 1897, it is difficult to make out, but the design, with Scandinavian influence, shows a dog facing to the left; its head, however, is

All Saints' Church, Brixworth (Nave)

missing. Also, in a compartment to the left of the entrance porch, is a sculptured block of oolitic limestone known as the Eagle of St John, also Saxon.

In the 15th century the apse of the Saxon church was rebuilt and given a square end but during the restoration of 1865 the apse was reinstated. What is interesting is the ring crypt, best seen from outside. It would have been entered by worshippers via a doorway in the chancel, now blocked. The tower has a south doorway with double curved rows of Roman brick. It was heightened in the later Saxon period and has an attached staircase tower to the west. There is much herringbone masonry.

It seems likely that the monastery at Brixworth, mentioned by Hugh Candidus, fell victim to the Viking raids of 870. The Anglo-Saxon Chronicle states that: 'In this year the host went across Mercia into East Anglia and took winter quarters at Thetford; and in the same winter St Edmund the king fought against them, and the Danes won the victory, and they slew the king and overran the entire kingdom and destroyed all the monasteries to which they came.'

Apart from its imposing architecture, there are mysteries to engage us at Brixworth. In 1809, while the pews were being rearranged, workmen found a reliquary containing a wooden box. Inside were a human throat bone and a slip of paper. Unfortunately, the slip of paper – which may have revealed the name of the owner of the bone – disintegrated on exposure to the air. But that has not prevented scholars from speculating who the owner of the throat bone might

All Saints' Church, Brixworth, (Nave West Wall)

be and St Boniface is their choice. While not standing up to rigid scientific scrutiny there are, in fact, compelling reasons to favour St Boniface. He was born near Exeter in 675 and baptised with the name of Winfrith. He entered a monastery at a young age and later went as a missionary to continental Europe as Boniface. Never returning to England, he became Archbishop of Mainz and was a leading figure in the Frankish church. Subsequently, in 747, an important church council was held in England at a place – the location of which is a mystery – known as Clofesho. Boniface was not present at the council but had written to Archbishop Cuthbert of Canterbury beforehand and had a definite input to its deliberations – the decisions arrived at bearing a great similarity to those of earlier Frankish councils. Some have identified Brixworth as the site of the Council of Clofesho. The topography of the area, south of the church, includes a deep cleft and from this Clofesho (meaning cleft height) has been assigned to Brixworth.

But back to the throat bone; the hypothesis is that, although Boniface was buried at Fulda in Germany, monks at Brixworth would have desired the relic because of his influence at Clofesho. The case is strengthened because there was medieval guild of St Boniface at Brixworth, unique in the country, and as well as that, an annual fair, dating from 1253, and held on the feast day of St Boniface. There are many leaps of faith in the hypothesis – you can decide.

References

1. Rena Gardina, *Look at Brixworth Church*, Church Guide, 1995
2. Stephanie James, www.earlybritishkingdoms.com/adversaries/archaeology/brixworth02
3. David Parsons, *The Mystery of the Brixworth Relic*, Brixworth PCC, 1983

4. David Parsons, *St Boniface – Clofesho – Brixworth*, Reprinted from Baukunst des Mittelalters in Europa, ed. F.J. Much, Stuttgarter Gesellschaft fur Kunst und Denkmalpflege, 1988

Earls Barton

Earls Barton is a large village between Northampton and Wellingborough. It is recorded in Domesday as Bartone or Buartone, that is, a place where barley was grown. The prefix, Earls, was added later and refers to the Earl of Huntingdon.

The place is justly famous for the Saxon tower of All Saints' Church (SP852637) standing unbuttressed to a height of nineteen metres and on a base 7.3 metres square. Local legend asserts that it was built by the same workmen who built St Peter's, Medeshamstede (now Peterborough Cathedral).

The ragstone of the pilaster strips and long-and-short work at each corner come from Barnack, near Peterborough. It is now accepted that, when first constructed, the church did not extend much to the east, in other words it was without a nave and had only a short and narrow chancel attached to the east. The tower is late Saxon and a date of 970, or thereabouts, is frequently quoted, that

All Saints' Church, Earls Barton

231

is, in the reign of King Edgar the Peaceful. The earliest documentary mention is in 1637, when it was said that 'the steeple is crasye, cracked very much in divers places and in great danger whiche will require a long tyme for the mending of the same'.

The tower has been mended and we can be grateful for that. There are four stages, each one set back from the preceding lower one and separated by string courses. Decorated by vertical pilaster strips throughout each stage, there are semi-circular strips at the base of the second stage and triangular ones in the third and fourth. The strips are in fact the edges of blocks of Barnack stone inserted into the thickness of the wall and as well as being decorative serve a structural purpose.

The church was entered from the west door. Here, it can be clearly seen that the slabs forming the jambs of the doorway extend inwards to fill the entire wall, their capitals decorated with finely carved blank arcading. On the bottom stage of the south face of the tower there are two windows with carved balusters and lights in the shape of a cross. To the left of the windows is a disc, carved with a cross. Above, there is a door and it has been surmised that this could be an observation lookout. Alternative explanations are that relics could have been displayed here for the faithful to observe standing below, or even that it could have been an entrance, accessed by a ladder, provided for the villagers in case of attack. The upper stage has bell openings on all sides of the tower, five narrow arches with carved balusters.

There has been much speculation about Berry Mount, the mound and ditch north of the church. Pevsner insists it a Norman defensive motte. In which case its bailey would have contained the Saxon tower within its precincts and Pevsner argues that the builder of the fortification would have intended to dismantle the tower later, but never – to our undoubted relief – got round to it. Andrew Hart, the author of the church guidebook, disagrees and discounts the theory that it is a motte. There are various legends surrounding the mound and ditch – some say an army is buried beneath, others that it is part of a Saxon defensive site. Unfortunately, excavations have been minor, and nothing has been found.

Andrew Hart wonders if the tower could have served a secular purpose as well as a religious one. In which case, Barton could have been held by a thegn – a man of some importance in Saxon Britain. As a thegn, he would have been required to possess five hides of land, a fortified residence (the Saxon tower) and a chapel. If the theory is correct, the lower part of the tower would be reserved for worship while the upper part, with its separate entrance, would act as residence, a place of storage and for observation. We can only speculate!

Reference

1.   Andrew Hart, *All Saints' Church, Earls Barton, A Brief History and Guide*, 2006

Green's Norton

Green's Norton is to the west of the main Roman road, the Watling Street, north-west of Towcester. The Church of St Bartholomew (SP669499) dates from the Saxon era, as shown by the typical long-and-short work quoins of the nave, seen outside to the north-west and south-west. Inside, traces of the jambs of an original window can be seen above the chancel arch.

Nassington

Nassington is in open countryside, about six miles west of Peterborough, close to the river Nene. The church of St Mary & All Saints at Nassington (TL063962) is Saxon. Inside, in the west wall of the nave, there are two openings: below, a large window in outline and above a triangular window or door. There is also long-and-short work, but the glory of the church is the splendid remains of a Saxon cross. The excellent guidebook tells us it was discovered in 1809 and then again (presumably it was lost in the interim) when the church was restored in 1883. It has been dated to the 10th century and consists of two panels. The Crucifixion is depicted in the lower part with the sun and moon on either side of the cross. Below there is a man holding a sponge on a reed and a soldier with spear. The soldier is Longinus who pierced the side of Jesus with a spear. By tradition the man holding the sponge soaked in vinegar is Stephaton. Above, in the upper panel is a figure (missing above the waist) – probably representing the Ascension.

Reference

1.   Anon., *A Guide to St Mary & All Saints' Church, Nassington*, Church Guide

Northampton

Northampton was a place of some significance in pre-Conquest days. It was in Mercia and as a place name is mentioned in the Anglo-Saxon Chronicle in 913. Hamtuncir means a bend in a river, in this case the river Nene. Northampton can thus be compared with South Hamtuncir, i.e. Southampton. Anglo-Saxon remains have been found during excavations just east of the church of St Peter, Marefair, and reveal a building of considerable size of three bays, probably a nobleman's palace. Other pre-Conquest traces have been found at the site of the castle.

In the mid-11th century the priest at St Peter's was a man called Bruning. He was assisted by a Norwegian who longed to make a pilgrimage to Rome. At every attempt, he was dissuaded by the vision of an old man who always led him back to St Peter's. There, he was directed to the burial site of an obscure saint, Ragener, the nephew of Edmund of East Anglia. Miracles occurred, and a shrine was duly erected, decorated with the finest precious stones.

At the end of the south aisle of the church is a splendid grave slab, retrieved from its previous use as a door lintel and then a mantelpiece. Could it be the grave cover of St Ragener's tomb? It has intricate carving of birds, a bearded man's face and animals.

Reference

1. Paul Woodfield, *Church of St Peter, Marefair*, Churches Conservation Trust, 2007

Other Places of Interest

- According to Pevsner there is part of a Saxon cross at St Giles Church, **Desborough**, (SP803830). The church was locked when I visited.
- People go to **Geddington** to view its excellent Eleanor Cross. The Church of St Mary Magdalene (SP895830) dates from Saxon times but was locked when I visited.
- In the tower (inside) of St Peter's Church, **Lutton** (TL112878) there is a small piece of Anglo-Saxon sculpture.
- Pevsner reports a Saxon wheel cross head at All Saints' Church, **Mears Ashby** (SP838667).

- The church of St Mary (SP574490) at **Moreton Pinkney** has part of a Saxon cross shaft in the south-east corner of the churchyard.
- The church of St Peter and St Paul, **Moulton** (SP784664) has in the south aisle remains of an Anglo-Saxon cross shaft with a beast biting its own tail.
- There is Anglo-Saxon long-and-short work quoins to the nave – seen outside from both south-east and north-west –of the church of Holy Cross (SP672543) at Pattishall.
- The church of St Michael, **Stowe-Nine-Churches** (SP638577) stands in a commanding position with extensive views to the north. It was locked when I visited, but its Saxon tower is striking with its vertical lesenes, high up at the bell-stage.

Northumberland

Bamburgh and the Farne Islands

Bamburgh was the ancient capital of the kingdom of Bernicia. It is on the coast, about thirty-five miles south of Berwick-upon-Tweed. It was invaded by the Angles in the mid-6th century and their leader, Ida, is generally recognised as the first king of Bernicia. Just off the coast are the Farne Islands. St Cuthbert came here for solitude in 676. He initiated laws to protect the birds of the islands, in particular the eider duck. Cuthbert eventually became Bishop of Lindisfarne but returned to the Farne Islands to die.

Birtley

The tiny hamlet of Birtley is about sixteen miles north-west of Hexham, east of the North River Tyne. The Church of St Giles (NY878780) has a stone in the chancel north wall inscribed with a cross and the letters ORPE. It was discovered in 1884, has been dated to 700AD and interpreted as OR (ATE) P (RO) E (DMUNDO), 'pray for Edmund'.

Bolam

There is a fine 11th century Anglo-Saxon tower at the church of St Andrew at Bolam (NZ092825), about seven miles west of Morpeth. It is unbuttressed and has two light bell openings with a shaft between. Above are small windows. High up there is herringbone masonry. Inside the tower, an original west window can be seen above the existing later window.

Reference

1.   G.W.D. Briggs, *The Church of St Andrew, Bolam*, Church Guide, 2003

Bywell

Bywell, about four miles south-east of Corbridge, is a tranquil and picturesque spot on the north bank of the Tyne, and takes its name from byge-wella, meaning a spring in the bend (of the river). It has two churches, St Peter's and St Andrew's, just a stone's throw from each other. Both are of Saxon origin. But it is St Andrew's (NZ048613), now in the care of the Churches Conservation Trust, which takes our attention.

It may have been founded by Wilfrid in the 7th century and it is said that Egbert was consecrated bishop here in 803 following his flight from the Viking assaults on Lindisfarne. The tower is one of the finest in Northumberland and is probably constructed of reused Roman masonry. It was built over two periods divided by a string course, the lower part before 850 and the upper part in the late 10th or early 11th century. The belfry has mid-wall shafts with circular openings left and right. On the south face is a round-headed door and below this, small Saxon windows on the south and west face. There is a fragment of a Saxon cross shaft in the chancel.

Reference

1.   *St Andrew's Church, Bywell*, Church Guide, The Churches Conservation Trust, 2005

Corbridge

When the Angles came to Corbridge they built a small settlement to the east of the old Roman military town of Corstopitum and used stone from there to build a monastery dedicated to St Andrew (NY988644). The lower part of the tower was originally a porch which led into the Saxon nave. It has a blocked doorway, above which is a Saxon window. The tower arch to the nave is particularly interesting and was almost certainly taken en bloc from Corstopitum. The outline of the early church is defined by the arches of the aisles and probably measured about 47ft in length, 17ft wide and 34ft high. Much damage would have been inflicted on St Andrew's Church by the Danish warrior Halfden in his raids of 875.

On the north face of the tower, taking measurements from the buttress at the end of the nave, four stones up and four stones to the left (west), there is a Roman stone with an eagle's beak and head.

Reference

1. Brian Gordon, *A Visitor's Guide to St Andrew's Parish Church, Corbridge*

Hexham

The church of St Andrew at Hexham was founded in 674 as a Benedictine Monastery by the fiery Wilfrid, who at the time was Bishop of York. It was built on a grand scale on land granted to him by Aetheldreda, queen of Northumbria. The magnificent crypt of Wilfrid's church remains to this day and was discovered in 1725 when the medieval tower was being restored. Hexham's first church would almost certainly have been modelled on Roman designs, for it was Wilfrid who was largely responsible for the Roman church prevailing over the Celtic Church at the Synod of Whitby. The church is vividly described by his biographer, Eddius Stephanus, as having 'crypts of beautifully dressed stone, the vast structure supported by columns of various styles and numerous side aisles, the walls of remarkable height and length… we have never heard of the like this side of the Alps'.

Wilfrid was not the easiest man to get along with and throughout his life he was involved in disputes, quarrels and appeals to Rome. He fell out with Ecgfrith, king of Northumbria, probably because of his encouragement of Ecgfrith's wife, Aetheldreda, to flee to Ely, where she founded a religious community, later to become Ely Cathedral. Theodore of Tarsus, the newly appointed Archbishop of Canterbury, took advantage of the falling out to implement his plans to break up the huge see of York into smaller areas. A new bishopric was therefore established at Hexham in 681, much to the displeasure of Wilfrid. Despite appealing to the Pope – and indeed having his claims recognised – Wilfrid was still rejected by Northumbria. Sussex was to gain from Wilfrid's expulsion, for it was at Selsey that he began the conversion of the pagan South Saxons. In 686 Wilfrid was back in Northumbria, but only to more disputes. He then spent time in Mercia until he was finally restored to Northumbria to end his days at Hexham and Ripon. He was succeeded at Hexham by Acca. Danish raids in 821 brought the see of Hexham to an end.

Saxon work is evident at St Andrew's in the west wall and the bases of the north wall of the nave. Excavations have also revealed a Saxon apse to the east of the crossing. The church is entered via the south transept and on the right are two carved crosses. The larger is known as Acca's Cross and is thought to be the headstone of Acca's grave. It is 8th century and carved with vine patterns. Acca, Bishop Wilfrid's successor, is recorded by Bede as creating 'a very complete and excellent library'. In the choir is the Frith Stool, or Wilfrid's throne, a bulky stone chair of 7th century date. It is one of only two in the country (the other is at Beverley Minster) and was probably used by Wilfrid. On display in the south aisle of the choir is a Saxon chalice of copper gilt. Also from Wilfrid's time is the rosette on the north side of the nave.

The glory of Hexham, however, is the Saxon crypt. It is entered from the centre of the nave via steep steps giving access to a tunnel-vaulted chamber. There are chambers leading off to north and south.

The crypt is constructed from Roman masonry, much of which bears inscriptions. One tells of a granary built by Septimius Severus and his two sons on their way to Scotland.

Anglo-Saxon Crypt, Priory Church, Hexham

Reference

1. Jessica Hodge et al., *Hexham Abbey*, Scala Publishers, 2008

Lindisfarne

In 635 St Aidan came to Lindisfarne from Iona at the invitation of King Oswald of Northumbria. Lindisfarne, also known as Holy Island, then became a base for the Celtic Church. Later, St Cuthbert spent much of his life at Lindisfarne, became bishop and was buried there in 687. His body was subsequently moved to Durham Cathedral. The famous Lindisfarne Gospels were illuminated here, perhaps by Bishop Eadfrith. They are now housed in the British Library.

The monastery at Lindisfarne fell victim to the Vikings in 793, as recorded in the Anglo-Saxon Chronicle:

> In this year, fierce, foreboding omens came over the land of Northumbria, and wretchedly terrified the people. There were excessive whirlwinds, lightning storms and fiery dragons were seen flying in the sky. The signs were followed by great famine and shortly after in the same year, on January 8th, the ravaging of heathen men destroyed God's church at Lindisfarne through brutal robbery and slaughter.

There are no remains of the Saxon monastery visible in situ today, but the Priory Museum has a splendid collection of Anglo-Saxon remains, including parts of cross shafts and grave markers.

Rothbury

Rothbury is about twelve miles south-west of Alnwick. The glory of All Saints' Church (NU057016) is the pedestal supporting the font. It is part of an Anglo-Saxon cross dating from about 800 AD. The east side shows a scene from before the Fall of Man with an animal between branches of fruit. The north side shows the Ascension of Christ with angels either side. The apostles are looking upwards and hold the gospels. It is claimed to be one of the earliest carvings of this subject in the country. On the west are beasts facing up to one another, i.e., after the Fall, and on the south, is elaborate Anglo-Saxon knotwork. There are other parts of the cross in the Museum of Antiquities at Newcastle upon Tyne.

Reference

1.   G. Burn and J Eddershaw, *The Church of All Saints, Rothbury*, Church Guide

Warden

The tiny church at Warden sits quietly where the North River Tyne departs from the main South River Tyne. Tradition tells us that St John of Beverley founded an oratory here in 704, where he would retreat for prayer and solitude. Warden takes its name from Waredun, a nearby hill with cairn and Iron Age settlement. It means a lookout hill. The church of St Michael and All Angels (NY915655) has, apart from its belfry stage, an 11th century Saxon west tower with small slit windows. The tower arch to the nave uses Roman masonry.

In the porch is the well-known 'Warden Man', dating from the early 11th century. It shows the outline of a man, carved in relief on Roman altar stones. Outside there is a pre-Conquest stone upright with cross on top.

Reference

1.   Jean Briddon, *The Church of All Hallows and St Michael, Warden*, PCC of Warden and Newbrough

Warkworth

Warkworth lies on the south bank of the River Coquet just before it reaches the sea at Amble. The name Warkworth derives from Wercewode and means the palisaded enclosure of Werce. Werce was an abbess who gave a shroud of linen to the Venerable Bede. The church of St Lawrence (NU248063) enters history in 737 when Ceowulf, king of Northumbria, gave it to the monastery at Lindisfarne. As with so many churches facing the North Sea it fell victim to Viking raids. In 875, the Viking leader Halfden 'cruelly wasted the land from sea to sea and sailed to Wrycesfade which he destroyed'. There is a fragment of Saxon cross on the windowsill in the chancel.

Just off the coast from Warkworth is Coquet Island. It was here, in 684, that St Cuthbert met Aelfled, sister of king Ecgfrith of Northumbria and abbess of Whitby. Cuthbert told her that Ecgfrith had only twelve months to live and would be succeeded by a king she would treat as a brother. This was Aldfrith, a son of her father, Oswy, by an Irish princess.

Aelfled knew that king Ecgfrith wanted Cuthbert to be a bishop, a position Cuthbert confessed he would accept but added, 'in the short space of two years I shall find rest from my labours'. This was indeed the case: Cuthbert retired to his cell on the Farne Islands and died there in 687.

Reference

1.   Anon, *A Guide to the Church of St Lawrence Warkworth*, Warkworth PCC, 1997
2.   John Crawford Hodgson, *History of Northumberland*, Vol 5, 1899

Whittingham

Whittingham (NU067120) lies on the tiny River Aln in glorious countryside about eight miles west of Alnwick. It takes its name from Hwit-ing-ham, the home of Hwita's people and claims to be the place where, in 684, the saintly Cuthbert was appointed Bishop of Lindisfarne. Later, in 757, Ceowulf, king of Northumbria, gave up his land at Hwitingham to the monastery at Lindisfarne and at the same time renounced his crown to become a monk.

There is a tradition that when the Viking leader Halfden died in 880, the Abbot of Lindisfarne had a vision in which Cuthbert appeared to him and instructed him to tell the Vikings to appoint as their king a Christian slave boy owned by a widow of Whittingham. This they duly did and named him Cnut (not the same Cnut of later fame). He thus brought peace to Northumbria by uniting the two warring factions of Angles and Vikings.

The church of St Bartholomew dates from the 10th century. There is a Saxon arch from tower to nave and, in the north-west corner of the nave, the clear outline of a Saxon arch. It may be the entrance to a porticus. The original church can be visualised by standing outside to the west of the tower. At about three feet distance from each side of the tower are distinctive vertical long-and-short work quoins marking out the outline of the original Saxon building.

Reference

1. G. Peberdy and B. Winstanley, *Church of St Bartholomew, Whittingham*, Church Guide, 2004

Yeavering

Yeavering (NT9330 approx.) was situated in the ancient kingdom of Bernicia. It can be found about four miles north-west of Wooler. In 1949, aerial photographs revealed the markings of an ancient site which was then meticulously excavated by Dr Brian Hope-Taylor. What he found was evidence of a series of wooden buildings and a structure very like a grandstand. The buildings dated from the end of 6th century to the mid-7th century and included what is thought to be the grand hall of Edwin, king of Northumbria. The hall was indeed great, measuring eighty feet in length and forty feet in width. Yeavering has thus been identified as the royal residence at Ad-Gefrin, and it was here that Paulinus, priest of Edwin's wife, Aethelberga, came in 627. Bede takes up the story:

Yeavering, Northumberland

So great was the fervour of faith and desire for baptism among the Northumbrian people that Paulinus is said to have accompanied the king and queen to the royal residence of Ad-Gefrin (Yeavering) and remained there thirty-six days constantly occupied in instructing and baptizing. During this period, he did nothing between dawn and dusk but proclaim Christ's saving message to the people, who gathered from the surrounding villages and countryside; and when he had instructed them, he washed them in the cleansing waters of Baptism in the nearby river Glen.

The grandstand captures our imagination. Could this be the place where local people heard addresses from their king and listened to the message of Paulinus? The answer is almost certainly yes. Yeavering faded as a place of importance by the end of the 7th century. Regrettably, there is nothing for the visitor to see apart from a display board, but it is still a very atmospheric place.

Other Places of Interest

- The church of St Andrew (NZ134669) at **Heddon-on-the-Wall** is claimed to date from 680AD and it is certainly of Saxon origin – probably built of stone salvaged from nearby Hadrian's Wall – as shown by the massive quoins at the south-east corner of the nave. It was locked when I visited.
- The church of The Holy Paraclete (NY700494) at **Kirkhaugh** is set in idyllic countryside. In the churchyard is a Saxon cross.
- The church of St Mary, **Ovingham** (NZ085637) has an 11th century unbuttressed Saxon tower. The bell openings have two lights with a circle above and there are Saxon windows below. It is similar to nearby Bywell. Pre-Conquest sculpture is also reported.
- The Church of St Mungo (NY871735) at **Simonburn** has part of an ancient Anglian cross shaft in its porch. It is carved with scrollwork and grapes.
- The Church of St Mary, **Woodhorn** (NZ302888) is reported to have fragments of Anglo-Saxon crosses.

Nottinghamshire

Carlton-in-Lindrick

Carlton-in-Lindrick is in the north of the county, about two miles north of Worksop. The name Carlton-in-Lindrick probably derives from a tun (enclosure) of the carls (freed men) in the lind (lime) ric (wood). Apart from its buttresses (15th century) and belfry, the tower at St John the Evangelist (SK588839) is Saxon, or if not, dates from the Saxo-Norman overlap period. The tower has four stages. There are two-light bell openings on its east and west sides.

Over the Priest's door at the south end of the altar rail is a stone, known as the sun stone. It shows the sun, the moon and two stars.

Reference

1. Melville Williams and Antony Lambert, *The Parish Church of St John the Evangelist*, Church Guide

Shelford

Shelford lies close to the winding river Trent, due east of Nottingham. The church of St Peter (SK662424) has an excellent piece of Anglo-Saxon sculpture, a relief of the Virgin and Child in profile. On the other side is an angel with a book. The sculpture was probably part of a cross.

Stapleford

Stapleford is about seven miles west of Nottingham, north of the main A52 Derby road. St Helen's Church (SK488373) has a Saxon cross in its churchyard dated to about 1000AD. It was discovered lying abandoned in the churchyard in 1760 and then placed in the centre of the town on the corner of Church Street and Church Lane by the Old Cross Inn. Because it disturbed the free flow of traffic, it was moved to its present site in 1928. On one face there is a figure, identified by some as St Luke and by others as an angel. There is also interlace decoration. The cap at its top is modern.

Reference

1. C.J. Bull, *A Guide to St Helen's Church Stapleford*, Church Guide

Other Places of Interest.

- At St Margaret's Church, **Bilsthorpe** (SK655604) (locked), Pevsner records the presence of a cross slab in the porch.
- There is a small part of a Saxon cross at St Peter's Church, **East Bridgford** (SK691431). It was found in 1778, incorporated into the church wall.
- There is a Saxon cross shaft at St Mary and All Saints' Church, **Hawksworth** (locked) (SK754434).
- The church of St Luke at **Hickling** (SK692293) has, according to Pevsner, a Saxon coffin lid with interlacing and the heads of beasts.
- St Bartholomew's Church (locked) (SK704643) at **Kneesall**, has small pieces of an Anglo-Saxon cross shaft with interlace.
- The church of Holy Trinity (SK743525) at **Rolleston** was locked, but Pevsner reports fragments of a Saxon cross inscribed Radulfus me fe (cit), i.e. 'Radulfus made me'.
- There are two pieces of a Saxon cross at St Mary's Church (SK781446) in the tiny hamlet of **Shelton**.

Oxfordshire

Bampton

Bampton is situated on the main road between Witney and Swindon. The church of St Mary (SP313034) was founded in the Saxon era and has Saxon work in its tower. In 614, the Anglo-Saxon Chronicle records that Cynegils, the king of Wessex, fought the Welsh at Beamdune (Bampton) and killed 2065 of them. Then in 1046, Edward the Confessor granted land at Bampton to Leofric, who became Bishop of Devon, thus explaining why, until the 19th century, Bampton belonged to the see of Exeter.

Reference

1. www.bamptonoxon.co.uk

Caversfield

Caversfield lies in open countryside north of Bicester. The church of St Lawrence (SP581252) at Caversfield lies within the grounds of Caversfield House. There is access from the main B4100 (Bicester-to-Banbury road) but only via a small gate off the main road and there is no safe parking. The lower part of the west tower is Saxon and probably of the 10th century. There are double splayed windows in both the north and south faces of the tower.

Dorchester

In the Anglo-Saxon era, Dorchester was a very important place. It is between Oxford and Henley-on-Thames, just east of the meandering river Thames. In 635, Pope Honorius sent Birinus to Britain to convert the West Saxons, whose king at the time was Cynegils. Birinus arrived in Dorchester and met both Cynegils and King Oswald of Northumbria. Oswald, already a Christian, wished to marry the daughter of Cynegils, presumably to cement an alliance with the West Saxons against the warlike Mercians. The meeting ended with both kings granting land to Birinus to build a cathedral and found an episcopal see. He thus become the first bishop of the West Saxons. Birinus died in 650. By 676 another see had been created at Winchester and Birinius's body was translated there in 690 by Bishop Hedda.

When Dorchester was absorbed into Mercia further bishops were installed, before sees were established at Lindsey and Leicester. Then, following the Danish incursions, Dorchester once again became a see, its jurisdiction extending over the vast area stretching from the Thames to the Humber. After the Norman Conquest, the see at Dorchester was replaced by that at Lincoln.

Reference

1. Jean Cook, in Jean Cook and Trevor Rowley eds., *Dorchester through the Ages*, Oxford University for External Studies, 1985

Langford

Langford is located in quiet countryside, about three miles north-east of Lechlade-on-Thames. St Matthews Church (SP249026) was probably built by Aelfsige of Faringdon who, at the time of the Domesday survey, also held land in Langford. Therefore, the tower probably belongs to the Anglo-Saxon/Norman overlap period. It is of three stages divided by string courses and has twin bell openings on all four sides. Below are double splayed windows to north and south. There are characteristic pilaster strips to north and south, which on the south incorporate a stone slab carved in low relief. It is difficult to make out, but the guidebook says it shows two men, with bare heads and sharp-pointed beards, wearing cloaks and supporting a sundial. Inside, the tower is tunnel-vaulted and if Saxon is one of only three in the country. Pevsner considers it, however, to be more likely to date from the 14th century.

Anglo-Saxon Crucifixion, St Matthews Church, Langford

The glory of the church, however, is its Saxon sculptures. The south porch carries a figure of a bearded Christ with the Virgin Mary and St John. They have been reset (incorrectly) and may predate the church. Christ's arms have been inverted so instead of stretching upwards they hang down. Also, both Mary and St John face away from the cross rather than towards it. They too, in the reset, have been placed on the wrong sides of Christ.

On the east face of the porch is the Langford Rood. Christ is shown triumphant with arms outstretched and clad in a tunic.

Reference

1. RMSB, *St. Matthew's Church, Langford*, Church Guide, 1996

North Leigh

St Mary's Church, North Leigh, lies north of the modern village (SP387136), which, itself, is about three miles north-east of Witney. Its Saxon tower, dating from 1000 to 1050, can best be appreciated from the west of the church. It is at once apparent that, although now a west tower, it was originally in the centre of the church. The line of the gable end of the former nave (which was originally to the west of the tower) is clearly visible. The outline of the former arch from tower to nave is also evident above the 14th century window. The tower has typical round-headed double bell openings on all four faces and round-headed windows below to north and south. It may also have served as a lookout.

Reference

1. Charles Batey, *A Short Guide to St. Mary's Church North Leigh*, Church Guide

Anglo-Saxon West Tower, St Michael's Church, Oxford

Oxford

In the heart of Oxford, on the corner of Ship Street and Cornmarket Street, is the Church of St Michael with its Anglo-Saxon west tower. The church is referred to in the Domesday Book which says, 'the priests of St Michael's owned two houses paying 52 pence'. The tower was originally detached from the church. It stood in the north of the ancient city, adjacent to the defensive earthen bank, the forerunner of the city wall, and may have served as a lookout tower. Dating from between 1000 and 1050, it is built of rubble with typical long-and-short work quoins. There are bell openings on two levels with bulky balusters and a blocked west door. The tower was carefully restored in 1986. It is twenty feet square and sixty-three feet in height with walls four feet thick.

St Frideswide's Church at Oxford (now Oxford Cathedral and the chapel of Christchurch College) was the scene of the St Brice's Day massacre. In 1002, King Ethelred the Unready ordered that all Danes in England should be massacred on St Brice's Day, 'because he had been told that they intended to kill him and all his counsellors; and afterwards to possess his kingdom'. The Danes took refuge in the church. To no avail; they were massacred by the local

Saxons. Gunnhild, the sister of Swein Forkbeard of Denmark, was amongst those killed and her death must have strengthened Swein's desire to conquer England.

In Christchurch Chapel there is a magnificent stained-glass window by Edward Burne-Jones. It depicts the life of Frideswide, who founded a monastery at Oxford, later to be the college chapel and Oxford Cathedral. The romantic story, with its many variations, tells of her being pursued by Algar, a king of Mercia.

Reference

1. Vivian H.H. Green, *The Tower and Church of St. Michael at the North Gate*, Church Guide.

Swalcliffe

Swalcliffe is about eight miles west of Banbury in glorious Cotswold countryside. At the church of St Peter & St Paul, Swalcliffe (SP378379), there are two typical Saxon round-headed windows above the arches of the nave to both north and south. It can therefore be concluded that there was once a Saxon nave at Swalcliffe, the walls of which were cut through when the present aisles were built.

Reference

1. L. Rudge, F. Hitchings and S. Digby Firth, *The Church of St Peter & St Paul, Swalcliffe*, Church Guide, 1989

Waterperry

The church of St Mary at Waterperry (SP629063) can be combined with a visit to the pleasant Waterperry Gardens, within which the church is located. It is about eight miles east of Oxford, just east of the M40 motorway. The name means a collection of pear trees and the Domesday Book says the manor was worth 100 shillings in King Edward the Confessor's time.

It was the Rev John Todd, appointed vicar of Waterperry in 1925, who suspected that his church was pre-Conquest. He therefore removed the plaster above the 14th century chancel arch to reveal the Saxon arch beneath. He also excavated under the chancel and discovered that the original Saxon building had an apsidal east end. What we see today is the Saxon chancel arch, blocked, and rising above the 14th century addition. It is still clearly discernible.

Reference

1. J.S., *Waterperry Church*, compiled from the papers of Rev. John Todd, 1955

Shropshire

Diddlebury

In glorious Shropshire countryside, Diddlebury lies between Corve Dale and Wenlock Edge, about eight miles north of Ludlow. It takes its name from an Anglo-Saxon called Dudela. The most striking thing about the inside of St Peter's Church (SO508854) is the north wall of the nave, which consists of a complete expanse of herringbone masonry. It is probably pre-Conquest, but many have questioned this and maintain it is Norman work. Martin Speight, in the church guide, favours a pre-Conquest date and points as evidence to the double splayed Saxon window, which is integral to both the inside wall of herringbone and the outer wall of ashlar masonry. Further east, in the jamb of the window, is a fragment of Saxon carving and a further fragment is beyond. One of the carvings shows a tree with two figures trying to climb it for fruit. The blocked north doorway, seen from outside, is Saxon.

Reference

1.   Martin Speight, *St Peter's Church Diddlebury*, Church Guide

Much Wenlock

In about 680, Merewalh, brother of King Wulfhere of Mercia, endowed a nunnery at Wenlock with his daughter, Milburgha, as abbess. It was destroyed by the Danes in about 874 and re-founded by the famous Leofric, Earl of Mercia, in 1050. Excavations have shown a small late 7th century building with an apse, but there is nothing above ground to see today.

Stanton Lacy

Stanton Lacy stands beside the tiny river Corve, about three miles north-west of Ludlow. There is a legend that the Saxon church of St Peter (SO496788) was founded by St Milburgha, granddaughter of Penda of Mercia and Abbess of Wenlock Priory, see Much Wenlock above. It is one of those wonderful tales so beloved of our ancestors. Milburgha was blessed with good looks and she aroused the attention of a virile and lustful Welsh prince. Milburgha found his interest unwelcome and was forced to flee, with the prince in hot pursuit. Milburgha fell to her knees as she crossed the river Corve and to her relief it swelled with water to halt the prince in his tracks. In gratitude, she founded a church on the spot – St Peter's. It is cruciform and the west and north walls of the nave have characteristic Saxon pilaster strips, as do the walls of the north transept. The north doorway is also Saxon.

Reference

1.   Peter Klein, *A Guide to St Peter's Church, Stanton Lacy*, 1989

Stottesdon

The tiny village of Stottesdon is in splendid, hilly Shropshire countryside about twelve miles south of Bridgnorth. Inside the tower at St Mary's Church (SO673829) is a lintel which could be Anglo-Saxon, although Taylor and Taylor dispute this. Above it is a tympanum more likely to be early Norman. The lintel shows two beasts, lying on their backs and, on the right, what appears to be a lion. Did the lion kill the two beasts? Pevsner speculates that the lintel is upside down – but the tail of the beast in the centre has its tail pointing downwards (by the force of gravity) and so my conclusion is that the lintel is correctly placed. The carving can be seen by going through the door into the tower.

Reference

1.   D.O. *St Mary's Church Stottesdon the Tower and Bells*, Church Guide, 2006

Other Places of Interest

- The chancel at St Giles's **Barrow** (SJ658000) is Anglo-Saxon and has been variously dated to the 8th, 10th and 11th centuries. Within the north wall is a double splayed north window. The chancel arch is also Saxon.
- Holy Trinity Church at **Uppington** (SJ597094) has been extensively restored but there is a splendid 11th century tympanum. It shows dragons.
- People visit **Wroxeter** to see its impressive Roman remains, capital of Britannia Secunda. The Church of St Andrew (SJ563082) dates from Saxon times. High up on its north wall is a fragment of Anglo-Saxon cross shaft.

Somerset

Athelney and Aller

Following his setback, in 878, at the Battle of Chippenham, King Alfred sought refuge in the lonely Somerset marshes at Athelney. According to tradition, he stayed at the home of a swineherd and it was here where his absentmindedness was supposed to have allowed the cakes to burn. Perhaps Alfred's mind was on the more important task of regaining his kingdom. Burnt cakes or not, he soon rallied his men and was victorious at the Battle of Eddington. Afterwards, the Danish leader Guthrum made peace with Alfred and was baptised, with Alfred as his sponsor, at the nearby church at Aller (ST396288).

Monument to King Alfred the Great, Athelney

In so doing he changed his name to Aethelstan. In thanksgiving, Alfred founded a monastery at Athelney in 888. There are no remains standing today but the spot is marked by the King Alfred Monument at (ST357294).

Reference

1.   Jack Ward, *The Parish Church of St Andrew, Aller*, Church Guide

Bath

Bath Abbey was founded in 675 by Osric, king of Hwicce (a sub-kingdom of Mercia) and given to Abbess Berta to establish a convent. It is famous for being the place of the coronation of King Edgar in 973. There are elements of Edgar's coronation in the present-day ceremony.

Cadbury

Cadbury Castle (ST6225 approx.) is situated about ½ mile south of the main A303, about four miles west of Wincanton. It began as a small Bronze

View from Cadbury Hill Fort

Age settlement. It was enlarged in the Iron Age and became a hill fort of considerable size. There was a major re-fortification in about 500AD and excavations in the 1960s by Leslie Alcock revealed a hall, associated by some with King Arthur. Cadbury has been cited as a possible centre from where the legendary king is supposed to have led his forces to battle at Mount Badon in 537.

It was John Leland, the 16th century antiquary, who in 1542 wrote that 'at the very south ende of the chirch in South Cadbyn standith Camalatte, sumtyme famose town or castelle. The people can telle nothing ther but that they have hard say that Arture much resorted to Camalat'.

Who knows whether King Arthur was here?

Glastonbury

Glastonbury is a place of myth. There are the stories of Joseph of Arimathea bringing the Holy Grail, King Arthur being buried here and more. But it is a place with much Anglo-Saxon history: King Edmund was buried here in 967, King Edgar in 975, and Edmund Ironside in 1016.

A church was built here by King Ine of Wessex in 712. It was sacked by the Danes in the 9th century and rebuilt in the mid-10th century by Dunstan, who introduced the Rule of St Benedict to Glastonbury Abbey. There are no Anglo-Saxon remains above ground but the Abbey Church of St Peter and St Paul has been excavated and much pre-Conquest material found. Not only was evidence of Ine's and Dunstan's church found but also remains from an altogether earlier era. The chronicler William of Malmesbury has recorded three earlier foundations. First a church built by missionaries in the 2nd century, with later additions by Paulinus, then a church built by St David of Wales and finally one built by holy men from the north.

Reference

1. C.A. Ralegh Radford and John McIlwain, *Glastonbury Abbey*, Pitkin, 1999

Milborne Port

Milborne Port was obviously a place of some importance in pre-Conquest times. It is at OS ST676185, about three miles east of Sherborne on the main A30. Its name derives from the port (or town) on the borne (or stream); it was perhaps an Anglo-Saxon burgh and is recorded as having a church by 950. There was also a mint between the years 997 and 1035, further confirmation of its importance. The Church of St John the Evangelist has Saxon evidence, although Pevsner places it within the Anglo-Saxon/Norman overlap period. Outside, the chancel south wall has pilaster strips, or lesenes, high up, above a doorway, bearing comparison with those at Bradford upon Avon.

References

1. A.P. Baggs and M.C. Siraut, in *A History of the County of Somerset* (eds. C.R.J. Currie and R.W. Dunning), Victoria County History, 1999

Other Places of Interest

- There is a portion of a Saxon cross-shaft at St Nicholas Church (ST698669) at **Kelston** dating from the late 8th century. One side, divided in two by roll moulding, has interlace below and scrollwork above with leaves.
- There is a fragment of an Anglo-Saxon cross shaft at All Saints' Church, **Nunney** (ST737456), two faces decorated with birds.
- The parish church of St Dubricius at **Porlock** (SS886468) has small fragments of a Saxon cross shaft.
- St Michael's Church (ST450586) at **Rowberrow** has a fragment of an Anglo-Saxon cross decorated with a ribbon-type animal whose tail gives way to an interlace pattern. It is dated to the 9th century.
- The Church of St George (ST225238) at **Wilton**, in a suburb of Taunton, dates from pre-Conquest times. It has long-and-short work in the quoins of the west wall of both the south and north aisle.

Staffordshire

Ilam

The church of Holy Cross (SK133507) is idyllically placed in the heart of Staffordshire's Manifold valley. The church, although restored, dates from Saxon times as shown by the blocked Saxon doorway in the south wall. There are also Saxon fragments in the south chapel and the west wall of the north aisle. Outside there are two Anglo-Saxon crosses, one with patterning, made of three parts fixed together. It has three figures in its lower broad panel and a single figure in the lower narrow panel; above is interlace. The other is badly worn but has the remains of a cross at the top and a circular band halfway down; the upper part is decorated within a rectangular panel.

The church is associated with St Bertelin. He was a Mercian prince who, while travelling in Ireland, met a beautiful princess. He brought her back to Staffordshire, married her and she had a child. But while Bertelin was away hunting, wolves attacked and killed his princess and child. Bertelin then abandoned all worldly affairs and lived as a hermit in and around Ilam. He was buried in the church and there is a memorial in the south chapel. His remains were later transferred to Stafford.

Reference

1. *Church of the Holy Cross, Ilam*, Church Guide

Leek

The church of St Edward the Confessor, in the centre of Leek, has two fine Anglo-Saxon preaching crosses in its churchyard. The church guide dates them to the 7th and 8th century, but Pevsner puts them at the 11th century and compares them to those at Penrith. The larger one, near the vicarage, is round at its lower end and tapered towards the upper part. There is a circular band of interlace two-thirds of the way up. Above is a rectangular section with scroll patterns and interlace. A local legend maintains that the cross sinks into the ground a little bit every year. A local rhyme relates:

> When the churchyard cross shall disappear,
> Leek town will not last another year.

There is also a display of parts of Anglo-Saxon crosses in the north-west corner of the church. One shows two figures, one of whom carries a cross.

Reference

1. Nigel and Mary Kerr, *A Guide to Anglo-Saxon Sites*, Granada, 1982
2. Malcolm Sperring-Toy, *The Parish Church of St Edward the Confessor, Leek*, Church Guide, 2009

Lichfield – the Staffordshire Hoard and Lichfield Cathedral

On 5 July 2009, Terry Herbert, a keen metal detector enthusiast with many years' experience, was hard at work in a field near to the small village of Hammerwich, close to Lichfield. He soon struck gold – literally. Over a period of five days he was to unearth what turned out to be the largest hoard of Anglo-Saxon treasure ever found. Very soon archaeologists from Staffordshire County Council got involved and the cost of further excavations was funded by English Heritage. Over an area of nine metres by thirteen metres, a staggering total of 1,662 objects were found. A geophysical survey was conducted over surrounding land to ascertain the extent of the find and to make sure that the entire hoard had been recovered.

The find is unique. It consists of 712 gold objects, 707 silver and 73 copper alloy with 93 other specimens. It is almost entirely military ware and, significantly, with no female ornaments. It probably dates between the years 650 and 700 and therefore could have belonged to the warlike Mercian kings, Penda,

Wulfhere or Aethelred. Alternatively, the hoard could be trophy collected from Northumbria or East Anglia, Anglo-Saxon kingdoms which were frequently at war with Mercia.

Many helmet parts were found as well as sword fittings, many inlaid with garnet. Remains of four Christian crosses were recovered. Penda was a pagan but both Wulfhere and Aethelred were Christians and so the hoard could have belonged to one of them, unless it was trophy taken from Penda's battles with Christian Northumbria. There is an intriguing strip of gold with the biblical quote 'Surge domine et disepentur inimici tui et fugent qui oderunt te a facie tua', which translates as 'Rise up, O Lord, and may thy enemies be dispersed and those that hate thee be driven from thy face'. The Hoard may be viewed at Birmingham Museum and Art Gallery.

The 8th century St Chad's Gospels are on display at Lichfield Cathedral. This beautiful book consists of 236 folios, eight of which are illuminated, and contains the Gospels of St Matthew and St Mark with part of the Gospel of St Luke. There was a second volume, probably destroyed in the Civil War. Uniquely, there are examples of early Welsh prose in the margins. The origin of the Gospels, also known as the St Teilo's Gospels, is unknown. Their source may have been Wales, Ireland, Northumbria or indeed Lichfield itself.

Also, at the cathedral is the recently discovered, early 8th century Lichfield Angel, revealed in excavations in 2003. The limestone sculpture is in three parts and was probably the corner of the shrine chest of St Chad, built by Hedda in about 800. The angel – almost certainly the Archangel Gabriel – gives a blessing with his right hand and holds a sceptre with his left. The fact that the angel had been buried for so long has prevented weathering and left red and white pigment intact.

Reference

1. Kevin Leary and Roger Bland, *The Staffordshire Hoard*, British Museum Press, 2009
    www.lichfield-cathedral.org

Rolleston

When I visited the Church of St Mary (SK236277), repairs were being conducted and its Anglo-Saxon cross head was obscured by scaffolding. The village is about two miles north of Burton Upon Trent. Pevsner reports that the cross head comes from Tatenhill and is of the wheel type. It was placed here by Sir Oswald Moseley (father of the fascist). Rolleston was first mentioned in an Anglo-Saxon charter of 942.

Stafford

The name Stafford is derived from staith (a landing place) and ford (a crossing). In 913, Aethelfleda, Lady of the Mercians and daughter of King Alfred the Great, created a burgh here as a defence against Danish raids. Pilgrims came to worship at the shrine of St Bertelin, who was said to have founded Stafford in about 700AD.

The church of St Mary stands on an ancient site. To its west are the remains of the foundations of the Anglo-Saxon church of St Bertelin. It stood here until 1801 and was a simple two-cell church. In 1954, excavations revealed remains of an earlier wooden church.

Reference

1.   Michael Fisher, *St Mary's Stafford, History and Guide*, 2009

Wolverhampton

King Aethelred II granted land in these parts to Lady Wulfrun and she, in turn, by a charter of 994, endowed a minster church. Lady Wulfrun also gave her name to the town: Wolverhampton. Evidence of the Collegiate Church of St Peter's Saxon heritage is the impressive cross in the churchyard. It is 9th century and 14ft high. There are pendant triangles, rather weathered, on its lower part, and acanthus decoration. Above are a series of frames. The first has lozenges containing quadrupeds with bird-like creatures above and below in triangles. Next (above) is a narrow section of acanthus followed by a broader section of acanthus. Then come a section where quadrupeds and birds are alternately displayed in a round plant scroll. The top section has uninhabited plant scroll. A plaster cast has been made of the cross, which is now in the Victoria and Albert Museum.

Reference

1. J.C.B. Hall-Matthews and Ian Shields, *The Collegiate Church of St Peter, Wolverhampton*, R.J.L. Smith and Associates, 1993

Other Places of Interest

- The church of St Mary, **Bushbury** (SJ925025) has a fragment of a Saxon cross in its churchyard.
- The church of All Saints, **Chebsey** (SJ860285) has a weathered Anglo-Saxon cross in its churchyard which has traces of interlace.
- There are three fragments of Anglo-Saxon cross shafts in the churchyard of St Mary's Church (SK028379) at **Checkley**. The one furthest from the church has two figures in its lower part with a central and larger figure between them. The shaft in the centre has interlace decoration.
- Holy Trinity Church (SJ827293) at **Eccleshall** is reported to have two Saxon fragments depicting Adam and Eve and a horseman with a spear.

Suffolk

Debenham

Debenham is a beautiful and picturesque small town about twelve miles north-east of Stowmarket. The tower of St Mary's Church (TM175633), at its lower stage, has long and short cornerstones, typical of the Anglo-Saxon period. William White's *Directory of Suffolk*, of 1844, tells us: 'In Saxon times the Kings of East Anglia occasionally held their courts here'. There is a tradition that King Edmund of East Anglia was shot with arrows and killed nearby in 869 by the marauding Viking army.

Gosbeck

The church of St Mary's (TM151556) stands all by itself, west of the hamlet of Gosbeck and about six miles south of Debenham. It is mentioned in the Domesday Book and has Anglo-Saxon long-and-short cornerstones to the east of the nave. There is a Saxon single splayed narrow window high up on the north wall of the nave. The church guide tells of a fragment of Saxon carving, recovered during the restoration of 1883, and reinstated into the building to the right of the west window.

Reference

1. Anon, *A Brief Guide to St Mary's Gosbeck*

Halesworth

Halesworth takes its name from the Saxon, Halesuworda, meaning a place between two rivers near woodland. In the church of St Mary (TM387774), set into the east wall of the chancel, is the Dane Stone, dating from the 9th century and showing hands grasping a leafy bough.

Reference

1. John Willem Olink, *St Mary's Church, Halesworth*, Church Guide

Sutton Hoo

Mrs Edith Pretty, a lady with a very inquisitive and enquiring mind, lived at Tranmere House near the river Deben, close to Woodbridge. On her land were ancient burial mounds and in the late 1930s she asked Ipswich Museum to investigate. Basil Brown, a well-known local archaeologist, was duly released from the museum and went to work for Mrs Pretty. He began digging in 1938 but his discoveries were minor – many of the mounds had been looted before. He returned in 1939 but this time with the help of the estate gardener and game keeper unearthed the most astonishing Saxon burial hoard ever discovered in this country, the famous Sutton Hoo ship burial (TM288487).

Burial Mound, Sutton Hoo, Suffolk

The British Museum was at once contacted and excavations were continued under the direction of Charles Phillips. The wonderful discovery was the outline of a ship, twenty-seven metres in length, complete with metal rivets and containing a vast collection of treasure. High levels of phosphate were found in the soil, indicating the presence of a body. But who was he? The most likely contender is Raedwald, king of East Anglia, who died in 625.

An investigation was made to determine whether the hoard was treasure trove. At the time of the discovery (the law governing treasure has now been changed), treasure trove was the property of the monarch. It was defined as gold and silver that has been hidden in soil and where the original owner cannot be found, but it must have been his original intention to return. Other precious objects, for example grave goods or accidental losses, are not treasure trove and belong to the finder. Given that the finds at Sutton Hoo were a burial, and therefore there was no intention of anyone to return to dig them up again, they were not treasure trove and belonged to Mrs Pretty. She could have become a very rich lady but instead made the generous gift of all the finds to the nation. They now reside in a special gallery at the British Museum.

The finds include a helmet, with 'eyebrows' inlaid with silver wire, also with square-cut garnets and a gilt bronze 'nose' and 'moustache'. Many items were imported, for example, spoons inscribed 'Saulus' and 'Paulus', an obvious Christian reference, which clearly showed the importance of the person buried. They could have been baptismal gifts (Raedwald had converted to Christianity, even though he was into lapse to paganism). There are items of Celtic origin – a Hanging Bowl and Royal Sceptre. But most amazingly beautiful of all are the gold buckle and the remains of a purse with the most intricate of hinges. Inside the purse were coins, thirty-seven in all, from all over Europe.

There are a total of seventeen burial mounds at Sutton Hoo. Mounds 1 and 2 were investigated by Basil Brown and further excavations were conducted by Rupert Bruce-Mitford between 1965 and 1967. Between 1983 and 1991, the University of York, under the direction of Martin Carver, continued research at Sutton Hoo. Mound 2 was investigated in greater detail. Regrettably, looters had disturbed much of the mound but the scattered remains of the rivets of a ship were unearthed, beneath which was the grave of a man. The team from York investigated other mounds and discovered many other burials dating from between the 8th and 11th century including, from mound 17, a high-status man, aged about twenty-five, with sword, shield and the remains of his horse together with fragments of lorinery.

In 2000, Suffolk County Council Archaeological Society carried out excavations and unearthed another burial site. A National Trust visitor centre was opened at the same time

Reference

1. Martin Carver, *Sutton Hoo: The Burial Place of Kings?* British Museum Press, 1998
2. Stephen Plunket, *Sutton Hoo*, National Trust, 2002
3. www.suttonhoo.org

Thorington

Thorington is the tiniest of hamlets, in peaceful countryside, about three miles south-east of Halesworth. In the early 19th century, St Peter's Church at Thorington (TM423742) was visited by the antiquarians David Elisha Davy and Henry Jermyn before 'improvements' had been made in the 1830s. They described St Peter's distinctive flint round tower as having four windows, each consisting of two small arches supported by three round Saxon pillars. Although the church may date from the Saxon-Norman overlap period, the blank arcade of eleven arches circling the tower halfway up points to an earlier Anglo-Saxon date.

Reference

1. Anon, Church Guide

West Stow

West Stow (TL815705) is about four miles north-west of Bury St Edmunds, east of the river Lark. In 1847, farm workers digging the land uncovered the remains of many skeletons and discovered urns and other domestic remains. A series of excavations then began, including one in 1940 by Basil Brown, who in the late 1930s had made the stupendous discoveries at Sutton Hoo. There were other major excavations at the site between 1965 and 1972. Many objects were preserved because of the non-acidic soil and it was soon realised that the site of

Anglo-Saxon Village, West Stow (Recreation)

an Anglo-Saxon village had been uncovered. In 1972, the West Stow Anglo-Saxon Village Trust was established to manage the site.

When the Anglo-Saxons settled in the area they grouped themselves together in a series of villages spread out along the river Lark. Here they would have a ready supply of water and a source of fish to eat. They would graze their cattle, sheep and pigs and live off a diet of bread, meat, milk, cheese and eggs.

What we see today is a recreation of the Saxon village that was occupied between about 450 and 650AD. Afterwards, the site was abandoned. All the houses were made of wood; the Anglo-Saxon builders of the time were unaware of the use of stone, tiles, bricks and mortar. There were two types of house, typically a large one – perhaps a hall for communal gatherings – surrounded by smaller ones. Post holes, discovered by the archaeologists, determined the size of each recreated house. Within each house was a pit, but the Saxons did not live in pit dwellings; instead, planks of wood would be placed across the pit with a space beneath. The entire site at West Stow is an experiment in archaeology to test theories about building development. There is also a museum.

Reference

1.   Stanley E. West, *Understanding West Stow*, Jarrold, 2000

Other Places of Interest.

- The church of St Peter at **Blaxhall** (TM357569) has a fragment of Saxon interlace carving set in its west wall. A welcome feature of the church was the coffee, tea and squash laid on for the weary visitor!
- The church of St Peter, **Claydon** (TM137498) is in the care of the Churches Conservation Trust. There is Anglo-Saxon long-and-short work in the west cornerstones of the nave, the core of which is also Saxon.
- There is Saxon long-and-short work to the east of the nave at St Peter's Church, **Fakenham Magna** (TL910766), confirming the church to have an Anglo-Saxon foundation.
- In St Mary's Church (TM201598) at **Framsden** is the horizontal figure of a man, set in the wall by the chancel north west window. One arm rests on his waist and the other is raised. It could be Anglo-Saxon.
- The church of St Gregory, **Hemingstone** (TM145536) has long-and-short Anglo-Saxon quoins at the west end of the nave, indicating an Anglo-Saxon foundation.
- The derelict church of St Peter and St Paul (TL884722) on private land at **Little Livermere** has, according to Pevsner, Anglo-Saxon long-and-short work.
- The ruins of a church, at **South Elmham St Cross** (TM307826) – often referred to as a minster – lie ½ mile SSW of South Elmham Hall. Pevsner makes the point that it may not be a minster at all. The ruins probably date from the 11th century. They should not be confused with those at North Elmham in Norfolk, which was an early minster church.

Surrey

Compton

Compton is about three miles west of Guildford, south of the main A3. The glory of the Church of St Nicholas (SU955470) is its two-storied chancel. But this is Norman; the sturdy tower, however, is Saxon, unbuttressed and constructed of Bargate stone. Compton means 'valley farm' and Domesday records: at 'Contone there is a church; in the time of King Edward it was valued at £8, afterwards £6, and at present £9'. The nave of the Saxon church ran along the line of the piers of the present church as seen from the stonework outside in the west wall. The squint in the north wall of the chancel is also probably pre-Conquest. It was perhaps built for an anchorite.

Reference

1. Alan Bott, *The Parish Church of St Nicholas, Compton*, Church Guide, 2000

Thursley

Thursley lies ½ mile west of the main A3, between Milford and Hindhead. The name may derive from Thunor's Leah, a grove where the pagan god Thunor (Thunder) was worshipped. Before the conquest it was held by Earl Godwin, father of King Harold. The church of St Michael and All Angels (SU901394) has a vast Saxon tub font made of Bargate stone. It has ring moulding around its centre and chevron carvings on top. In 1927, the outline of two windows, seen from outside the north wall of the chancel, was investigated by the vicar. Inside they were hidden by a monument. They proved to be two double-splayed Anglo-Saxon windows, still with their oak frames intact, a rare survival.

Reference

1. Alan Bott, *The Parish Church of St Michael and All Angels, Thursley*, Church Guide, 2003

Witley

Witley is about three miles south-west of Godalming on the main A283. The nave at All Saints' Church (SU946397) contains Saxon work. The name means 'Witta's grove' or clearing. Like Thursley it was held by Earl Godwin. There are double-splayed windows in the south and west walls of the nave. They came to light in the early part of the 20th century and still have their oak frames, as at Thursley.

Reference

1. Alan Bott, *The Parish Church of All Saints, Witley*, Church Guide, 2003

Other Places of Interest

- There is the merest trace of a pre-Conquest capital set in the south window of the tower of St Michael's Church, **Betchworth** (TQ211497) – eight circular roll mouldings, one above the other.
- St Mary's Church (Quarry Street) in **Guildford** has a pre-Conquest tower of flint. The church was locked but Anglo-Saxon evidence is visible in the pilaster strips seen from the outside.
- St Mary's Church (TQ129585) at **Stoke D'Abernon** has Anglo-Saxon foundations.

Sussex

According to the Anglo-Saxon Chronicle, the first Saxons arrived in Sussex in 477. This period is confirmed by characteristic late 5th century burials in the area. But Christianity was late in coming to Sussex; it was the last Anglo-Saxon kingdom to be converted. When it did come, it came via Wilfrid, the fiery monk from Northumbria. In 680, Caedwalla, king of the West Saxons, granted land to Wilfrid: 'I Caedwalla, King by Grace of God have been asked by the Venerable Bishop Wilfrid to be so good as to grant him a little land for the support of himself and his followers'.

A charter granted three years later tells us that Wilfrid was given land to build a monastery at Selsey.

Arlington

The church of St Pancras (TQ543074) has the Cuckmere River as a neighbour with a view of the Downs to the south. It is about eight miles north-west of Eastbourne and dates from before the Conquest. The nave has long-and-short work quoins at its north-west, south-west and south-east ends and there is a small Anglo-Saxon splayed window containing Roman bricks to the right of the porch.

Reference

1. F.H. Foster, *A Visit to Arlington Church*, Church Guide

Bexhill

The Church of St Peter is set back from the coast in the Old Town. It dates from the time of Offa, king of Mercia. A deed dated 772, a copy of which is on display in the church, tells us that Offa granted land at Bexhill to build a monastery:

> Wherefore I Offa, King of England for the good of my soul and for the love of God… grant in eternal possession of Almighty God and to the venerable Bishop Oswald a certain piece of land in Sussex that he may construct a monastery there and endow a church… that is eight hides in a place which is called Bixlea [Bexhill].

To remind us that Sussex was evangelised by Wilfrid in the late 7th century, there is a mural depicting the saint by Alan Sorrel. Also on display is what Pevsner describes as 'a fine Anglo-Saxon coffin lid'. An alternative explanation is that it is the cover of a reliquary. It was found concealed in the wall of the Saxon church in 1878 and, interestingly, is made from sandstone of a type not found in the south of England. This has given rise to the theory that it might have been brought south by Bishop Wilfrid on his mission to convert the South Saxons, only ninety years before the monastery at St Peter's was founded.

Reference

1.   Edward Bryant, *Bexhill Parish Church of St Peter*, Church Guide, 2006

Bishopstone

Bishopstone is a small South Downs village about one mile north-west of Seaford. The church of St Andrew at Bishopstone (TQ472010) is entered through the south porch, leading to a nave of Anglo-Saxon foundation. The porch is Anglo-Saxon and was originally an 8th century porticus with no entrance from outside. Above is a Saxon sundial with the name Eadric inscribed on it. It has been suggested that the cross on the dial indicates that Eadric may have been a bishop. In 2006 the church underwent a major restoration for which we should be grateful because an Anglo-Saxon window, previously hidden beneath plaster, came to light above the war memorial. In pre-Conquest days, the church would have been entered from the west. In the 12th century, the Normans built the tower at the west end and entrance to the church was then gained from the south porch, i.e. via the previous porticus.

Reference

1.   Anon, *Welcome to St Andrew's Church, Bishopstone*, Church Guide

Bosham

Bosham, with its easy access to Chichester Harbour, is a place of much significance in Anglo-Saxon history. There is documentary evidence of an early 7th century Christian community at Bosham. It is from the hand of Bede, who, while recording Bishop Wilfrid's conversion of the South Saxons, tells of:

> An Irish monk named Dicul who had a very small monastery in the place which is called Bosanham, a spot surrounded by woods and sea. In it were five or six brethren who served the Lord in a life of humility and poverty. None, however, of the natives of the country cared either to imitate their life or listen to their preaching.

In the 11th century, the manor of Bosham was held by the powerful Earl Godwin and after his death by his son, Harold (later King Harold). Bosham Church is shown on the Bayeux Tapestry. Harold is seen riding with his followers towards the Church. The text records 'Ubi Harold dux Anglorum et sui milites equitant ad Bosham' – 'Where Harold, Earl of the English, and his retinue ride to Bosham'. He enters the church and after prayers and feasting in a hall departs for Normandy, allegedly to confirm Duke William of Normandy as Edward the Confessor's successor.

The tower of Holy Trinity Church (SU804039) is of four stages. The lower two are late Anglo-Saxon with typical long-and-short work in the quoins. The third stage is also Saxon but a little later. Inside, the tower arch is Saxon, as is the triangular-headed doorway and the round-headed doorway above it. According to Pevsner, the chancel arch is also pre-Conquest, but the most recent surveys have concluded that it is more likely to have been constructed after the Conquest.

It is rumoured that a daughter of King Cnut lies buried within the church, but there is no definite evidence. Another rumour is that King Harold himself lies buried here!

Reference

1. Joan Langhorne, *Holy Trinity Church, Bosham*, Church Guide

Botolphs

Set in peaceful countryside – except, that is, for the cement works on the other side of the river Adur – is Botolphs (TQ194093). The chancel wall is Saxon, as is the chancel arch, with its moulded responds similar to, but not so accomplished, as those at Sompting. In some ways, its simplicity, particularly the chancel, enables one all the better to imagine our Saxon ancestors who worshipped in this place.

Reference

1. Anon, *The Parish Church of St Botolph*, Church Guide

Chithurst

Chithurst sits in idyllic West Sussex countryside, about two miles west of Midhurst, with the river Rother as its neighbour. It is often difficult to say with precision whether a church is Norman or Saxon. The church at Chithurst (SU842231) is one such example. Taylor and Taylor argue for Anglo-Saxon based on the tall, thin walls, the narrow chancel arch and the small splayed window. The church's position – remote and on the bank of the river Rother – makes a visit rewarding.

Clayton

Clayton sits at the foot of the South Downs, just over two miles south of Burgess Hill. The church of St John the Baptist at Clayton (TQ299140) is visited more for its magnificent wall paintings than its Saxon features. The diminutive church has long-and-short work and a fine chancel arch, of which comparisons have been made with Worth.

Reference

1.   W.J.M., *Clayton: A Guide to the Parish Church*, Church Guide

Elsted

The tiny village of Elsted, about three miles west of Midhurst, is in glorious countryside looking south to the escarpment of the South Downs and Beacon Hill. The church of St Paul (SU817197) is another example of the Saxon-Norman overlap. It has magnificent herringbone masonry on its west and east side and on the entire north wall. The church was restored in 1951 after a tree that fell on the nave in 1893 had made it unusable.

Reference

1.   Anon, *St Paul's Church, Elsted*, Church Guide

Hardham

Hardham (TQ038175), less than one mile south-west of Pulborough and in a side road off the main A29, is visited more for its magnificent wall paintings. It is almost certainly of Saxon origin and all of a piece. There are three original windows, two on either side of the nave and one in the north wall of the chancel.

Reference

1.   Anon, *Hardham, Its History and its Church*, Church Guide

Jevington

Jevington is wonderfully situated on the South Downs, about two miles south of Polegate. There is a fine flint Anglo-Saxon west tower at St Andrew's, Jevington (TQ562045). It was built between 900 and 950. At the time, the south coast was experiencing attacks by Viking marauders. The Anglo-Saxon tower had, therefore, a dual purpose – both as a place of worship and as a lookout and refuge against attack from Vikings who came ashore at nearby Cuckmere Haven. There are typical Saxon bell openings with baluster shafts in the tower and in both the north and south walls there is evidence of the original windows, each headed with Roman brick.

In 1785 a magnificent Saxon sculpture was discovered under the floor of the tower. It has been surmised that it was hidden there during the Commonwealth period to save it from destruction. It shows Christ in a loincloth holding a long staff resting on an animal. An alternative explanation is given in the guidebook, which says Christ holds a sword and thrusts it into the beast as a symbol of good triumphing over evil.

Reference

1. R.E. Hodge, *St Andrew Church, Jevington*, Church Guide, 2003

Lyminster

Lyminster lies in the flat land of the valley of the river Arun, north of Littlehampton, (TQ023048). At first sight the church of St Mary Magdalene looks anything but Saxon, but first impressions are deceptive. The church's Saxon heritage soon becomes apparent when we enter. St Mary's has a tall, narrow and commanding nave and chancel, dated by John Slegg to about 1040. Also Saxon is the blocked south door.

Alfred the Great left Lullyngminster to Osfred, his nephew, and this is history's first mention of the place. The church formed part of an Anglo-Saxon Benedictine Nunnery, which stood just to its south, on the site of the adjacent farm. Apart from the church, all traces have now gone. It is recorded that, between 925 and 939, Aethelstan, king of Wessex, came to Lyminster with the Witan to deliberate on local issues. This would have been in a building which may have been just north of the church.

There is a legend associated with Lyminster and dating from Saxon times about a dragon. A tombstone (not Saxon) by the font is thought to be that of one Jim Pulk, who may have slain the sea-water monster which was terrorising the local neighbourhood. The beast lived in a pond, thought to be bottomless, which lies a short distance to the north-west of the church, along the path to Arundel. The pond is known as the 'Nucker Hole', taking its name from 'Nicor

Hole', that is, Anglo-Saxon for 'the hole of the sea-monster'. It was the brave Jim Pulk, a local farm hand, who gets the credit for slaying the ferocious dragon and ridding the good people of Lyminster of its evil powers.

Reference

1.   John E. Slegg, *The Parish Church of St Mary Magdalene Lyminster, A Short Guide*, 2001

Selham

What strikes us first about the diminutive church of St James at Selham (SU933206) is its herringbone masonry. It lies in pleasant countryside, in the valley of the river Rother, one mile south of the Petworth to Midhurst road. But as in so many places, there is debate about whether the church is Saxon or Norman; but one way or the other there is certainly much Saxon influence here. At the time of Domesday, it contained 'woodland for 10 hogs and a mill of 10 shillings and 100 eels'. The name, which is of Saxon origin, means the home (ham) of a hall (sel). Before the Conquest, the manor was held by Codulf from Earl Godwin, father of King Harold.

St James Church, Selham

*Capital of Chancel Arch at
St James Church, Selham*

We enter by the north door, which is undoubtedly Saxon, and are at once confronted by the remarkable chancel arch. The carvings on the imposts, abaci and capitals of the chancel arch deserve special examination. Both the church guidebook and Taylor and Taylor surmise that 'the work was executed without a comprehensive design and using such materials as were to hand from some earlier building'.

There is thus a mixture of styles. Working from the top, the impost on the south side has rope ornamentation and a serpent looking to the west; below, the abacus has leaf ornamentation and below this, the capital shows a snake and serpent intertwined, with the serpent devouring its own tail. On the north side, the impost has, according to Taylor and Taylor, what could be a section of reused Roman string course or architrave. The abacus has interlace decoration and the capital volutes.

Reference

1.   Anon, *St James Church Selham*, A Church Guide, 1998

Sompting

The church of St Mary, Sompting Abbots, is justly famous for its Saxon tower. The church lies north of Worthing at TQ162057, a few yards along a lane leading north from the main A27 and approached along the A27 from the west.

The tower is the only Saxon one in this country with a pyramidal cap in the German style – or with a Rhenish helm, as it is sometimes known. Nairn – surely the topographer with the keenest and most descriptive eye – describes it in the *Buildings of England* series as elegant, dainty, fresh and alert. It was built in stages, but as a whole it is unbuttressed with attached pilaster strips from its base to the gables of the cap. The first stage, built around 1000AD, terminates in a string course and is thought to be the west end of the original nave. The second stage dates from fifty years later and has bell openings on all four sides, those to the east and west with triangular heads and those to the north and south with two-light round-headed windows. The Romans were obviously hereabouts, for Roman tiles can be seen near the west and north window and inside the tower.

St Mary's Church, Sompting

Inside, it is the tower arch which grabs our attention. It is offset, probably because the original entrance to the church would have been from the tower and there was an altar in its wall, north of the arch. The capitals are worth inspecting – the inner orders have leaf designs while the outer orders have a scroll with a pomegranate in their centre.

Fixed to the north wall of the nave is a stone. In fact, it is two stones, one on top of the other. On the west side, there is interlace pattern and on the other, Christ in Majesty, the latter dated, however, to the 13th century. There are other Saxon fragments in the chancel, particularly the triangular headed piscina; then in the south transept a stone carving of an abbot or a bishop with a crozier, dated at various times between the 6th and 12th century. Colin Excell postulates that it may be St Wilfrid. Finally, high in the south wall of the nave is a window, discovered in a 1967 restoration.

Reference

1. Colin Excell, *A Brief History of St Mary the Virgin, Sompting*, privately printed, 2006

Stopham

Stopham – 'the home of Stoppa' (TQ026189) is set in lovely countryside, west of Pulborough. The church of St Mary has vast north and south doorways probably dating from the Saxon-Norman overlap period.

Reference

1. Anon, *Stopham, Its History and its Church*, Church Guide

Stoughton

Stoughton lies in wonderful South Downs countryside in a secluded valley to the west of Bow Hill at SU801115. The church of St Mary is reached up a narrow track and lies in a commanding position overlooking the village below. It is thought that the church, with its characteristic high and narrow nave, was built between the end of the Viking assaults (1016) and the Norman Conquest. Apart from later windows, its doors and the belfry, it is a complete Saxon church. There is long-and-short work and herringbone masonry on the east and west walls of the nave. Inside, the chancel arch bears many similarities with that at Bosham. Its capitals are decorated with what look like crosiers or ferns. There are double splayed windows in the west walls of the transepts.

Reference

1. E.A. Killick, *The Parish Church of St Mary, Stoughton*, Church Guide, 1997

West Dean

Just off the main Midhurst-to-Chichester road is West Dean. The church (SU861126) fell victim to fire in 1934 but its walls date from Saxon times. There is a blocked tall and narrow door on the north side of the nave, which is certainly Saxon. In 1001, Sussex came under ferocious Viking attack and the church at West Dean may have fallen victim to its destructive force. The Anglo-Saxon Chronicle tells us that 'in this year there were constant hostilities in England because of the pirate host and they harried and burnt almost everywhere, so that in one continuous drive they penetrated inland as far as Aethelinga dene'. West Dean could very well be Aethelinga.

Worth

Worth is a suburb of Crawley. An avenue of lime trees – known as the Ten Apostles – leads to the church of St Nicholas (TQ302363), one of the finest late Anglo-Saxon buildings in the country. With an apse at its east end, the church is cruciform and is entered from the west door. Immediately one is confronted with an unmistakable Saxon interior. An immense Saxon arch – 22ft high and 14ft wide – divides nave from chancel. It has semi-circular responds and cushion capitals. The arches to north and south transepts are also Saxon.

The north and south doors of the nave face each other and the church guidebook speculates that this arrangement would allow a mounted horseman to enter, bow to the altar and then leave by the other door without dismounting! (The north door is now blocked.)

High up on the walls are two-light windows separated by baluster shafts. There are two on the north and one on the south and they are unique because

St Nicholas Church, Worth. (Interior)

they are the only ones of this type in the country in such a position. It is very likely, given the position of the later Perpendicular window, that there were originally two Saxon windows on the south side of the nave. There are the typical pilaster strips, rising to a string course which runs around the entire building. The church may have been a daughter church of the great Abbey at Chertsey in Surrey.

Reference

1. Anon, *St Nicholas Church, Worth*, Church Guide, 2007

Anglo-Saxon Window and Pilaster Strips, St Nicholas Church, Worth

Other Places of Interest

- **Buncton** (TQ145138) lies about half a mile north of the Steyning-to-Storrington road and is approached through woodland by walking into a ravine. Its church of All Saints is simple and rewarding and is either late Saxon or early Norman.
- The church of St John-under-the-Castle at **Lewes** is Victorian. There was a medieval church and from it was taken an Anglo-Saxon doorway, now to the east of the church.
- The church of St Peter (SU881062) at **Westhampnet** has herringbone masonry on the south wall of the chancel, which is probably of the Saxon-Norman overlap period.
- That the church of All Hallows, **Woolbeding** (SU873227) is Saxon becomes immediately apparent as it is approached between a row of box-shaped yew trees. There are characteristic pilaster strips to both north and south. Within, however, it has been largely restored.

Warwickshire

Berkswell

Berkswell is about six miles west of Coventry. The church of St John the Baptist (SP244791) is predominantly Norman, as is its fine crypt. It is 12th century and of two halves with an octagon at the western part. The church is said, however, to have had Saxon origins. Leland, writing in the 16th century, records it as the burial place of St Milred, the Bishop of Worcester, who died in 772. Another theory is that it could be a shrine to St Mildred, Abbess of Minster on the Isle of Thanet in Kent. She died in 725 and was buried at Minster and then her remains were transferred to Canterbury. Aethelbald, king of Mercia, was a kinsman of Mildred and it is conjectured that he may have removed some of her relics from Canterbury to Berkswell.

Reference

1. Anon, Berkswell Church Guide

Tredington

Tredington lies in pleasant countryside on the road from Oxford to Stratford on the west bank of the river Stour. Outwardly, the church of St Gregory (SP259435) looks to be post-Conquest. But inside there is a surprise. Above the arcades are remains of eight Anglo-Danish windows and doorways. There was once a west gallery and this was accessed by outer stairs to the two ancient Anglo-Danish doors, thirteen feet above the ground. The church guide tells us that the first church of stone to be built at Tredington was in 961.

Reference

1.   Anon, *A Short Guide to St Gregory's Church, Tredington*, Church Guide

Wooton Wawen

Wooton Wawen is about seven miles north-west of Stratford-Upon-Avon, close to the River Alne and the Stratford-Upon-Avon Canal. Warwickshire is not particularly well endowed with Saxon architecture but St Peter's (SP154633) is an exception. The region was originally called Stoppingas, perhaps after a man named Stoppa. It was in Hwicce, a sub-kingdom of Mercia, and a minster church was founded here in the early 8th century. A charter of King Aethelbert of Mercia describes how 'at Wudu Tun, an estate in the woods, near the River Alne, in the midst of royal territory called Stoppingas, the king of Mercia gave his blessing to Aethelric, a sub-king of the people of Hwicce, who had founded a minster there'.

The church we see today is outwardly post-Conquest but inspection inside reveals substantial Anglo-Danish work. There are characteristic long-and-short quoins to the tower, the lower part of which is pre-Conquest, and doorways to north and south leading into previous porticus. The tower (as seen from inside) is clearly early 11th century and its four contemporary arches show that the original church was cruciform. A notice outside informs us that St Peter's church is the oldest in Warwickshire and invites us to view the Saxon Sanctuary, which is a most excellent exhibition outlining the history of the village.

Reference

1.   Donald Graham, *The Saxon Sanctuary*, Wooton Wawen PCC, 1999

West Yorkshire

Bardsey

Bardsey lies on the road between Leeds and Wetherby. The tower at All Hallows Church (SE366431), apart from the battlements, is Anglo-Saxon, as shown by the two double belfry windows on its south face. The entrance to the church was originally from a porch, dating to the 9th or 10th century, its cornerstones clearly seen on the west face of the tower, as is the outline of its gable above the rectangular west window. Later, in the 11th century, the porch was enlarged to form the present tower.

References

1. Anon, *Welcome to the Parish Church of All Hallows, Bardsey*, Church Guide
2. Anon, *Historic Churches of West Yorkshire, Bardsey Church*, West Yorkshire Archaeology Service, 1987

Hartshead

On a public footpath on Hartshead Moor (SE176237), about seven miles north-east of Huddersfield, is the Walton Cross. It is a massive piece and quite badly weathered. It has been dated to the 11th century.

The east face has a series of interlace frames within which, in the centre, is a panel with scrollwork, leaves and birds. The opposite west face has a circular design at its top, below which two beasts face up to each other. The north and south faces have interlace ornamentation.

| *Walton Cross, Hartshead*

Ilkley

All Saints' Church at Ilkley has a splendid collection of ancient Anglo-Saxon crosses. They were originally in different parts of the churchyard and in the 1870s were placed together, in line on the south side of the church. Inevitable weathering and pollution prompted their removal to inside the church and they now stand beneath the tower. There is a group of three. The tallest dates from the 9th century and is made up of four panels. Christ gives a blessing at the top and beneath in the next panel two beasts confront each other. Next down, a beast faces to the left and at the bottom a quadruped advances to the right but looking back to the left. On its other side are depictions of the four evangelists, symbolised as beasts as in chapter 4 of the Book of Revelation, i.e. from the top, eagle (John), ox (Luke), lion (Mark) and man (Matthew). They are difficult to decipher but the guidebook tells us that, unusually, and in a similar way to Wirksworth in Derbyshire, the evangelists have the heads of beasts but the bodies of humans and hold a book not a scroll. The head of the shaft is not part of the original.

One face of the second-tallest cross shaft also has a series of panels. From the bottom, birds inhabit vine scrolls, above, two quadrupeds confront each other, face to face. The two upper panels are less distinct. The upper one has been interpreted as showing Adam and Eve.

The smallest cross shaft has, at its base, a figure (perhaps an angel) and at the top an animal.

Reference

1. Dick Watson, *A Guided Tour of All Saints' Parish Church, Ilkley*, Church Guide

Kirk Hammerton

Kirk Hammerton is situated in pleasing flat and open land between York and Knaresborough, south of the main A59 and north of the river Nidd. The Church of St John (SE465556) at Kirk Hammerton is a complete Saxon church apart from

Detail of Anglo-Saxon Cross Shaft, All Saints' Church, Ilkley

the 19th century extension to its north. The tower is unbuttressed with, high up, double belfry windows on each of its faces. Below is a string course, separating the bell stage from the much larger lower stage, within which is a narrow west doorway and small slit windows on the tower's north, south and west faces. The south doorway has a pilaster strip running around it and careful inspection to its east reveals another doorway, albeit blocked, which may have led to a porticus. Inside, the tower arch and chancel arch are both of Saxon origin.

Laughton-en-le-Morthen

The South Yorkshire village is situated in the country, about seven miles south-west of Rotherham. There is an Anglo-Saxon north door at the church of All Saints (SK516883) with pilaster strips located on each side of the jambs. Later, a medieval door was inserted within the original Saxon opening. One interpretation of the name en-le-Morthen is 'place of death', and this has given credence to the place being a contender (among many others) for the site of the Battle of Brunaburgh, a great and bloody slaughter in 937. The combined forces of the Vikings, and the Kings of the Scots and Strathclyde were decisively defeated by the English King Aethelstan and his brother Edmund. The cause of the battle was the fear of King Constantine of the Scots that, following Aethelstan's victory in 928 against the Vikings, Aethelstan might capitalise on his success and invade Scotland. Constantine therefore made treaties with the king of Strathclyde and the Vikings to thwart any possible attempt. King Aethelstan's victory was a watershed moment in history as the first time that all Saxon kingdoms of England were united.

Ledsham

The small village of Ledsham is about one mile west of Junction 42 of the A1(M), north of Castleford. The church guide speculates that All Saints' Church (SE457298) could have been a church mentioned by Bede. He wrote of the existence of a stone altar from an earlier wooden church (possibly at Doncaster) 'preserved in the monastery that lies in Elmet Wood and is ruled by the most reverend priest and abbot Thrydwulf'.

The church has been dated to the 8th century. The lower part of the tower is Saxon and originally served as the entrance porch. The porch would have been entered originally by the south doorway of the present tower. To its right are two small windows, one above the other, the upper one lighting an upper room in the original porch. The nave walls are Saxon and there are blocked Saxon windows to the east and west of the present entrance porch, two on the left and one on the right. This present-day entrance porch was originally a porticus and there was probably another leading from the opposite north wall. The tower door was pleasantly restored in 1871. The chancel arch is Saxon, but the tower arch is a Norman replacement. Above it is an Anglo-Saxon window for the upper room of the tower.

References

1. Anon, Church Guide
2. Anon, *Historic Churches of West Yorkshire, Ledsham Church*, West Yorkshire Archaeology Service, 1987
3. Bede, Book Two, Chapter 14

Leeds

St Peter's in Kirkgate has a magnificent Anglo-Saxon cross. It is made up of separate pieces fixed together, found when the original medieval church was demolished in 1838. It is much travelled. Bailey tells us that the architect who carried out the restoration (R.D. Chantrell) took the fragments home and placed them in his garden. After a while, he moved to Newington Butts in South London, then eventually to Rottingdean on the south coast where he took the fragments with him. After he died the cross remained in Rottingdean, and so desperate were the good people of Leeds to see their cross, they were reduced to climbing on ladders to peer into the suburban garden. Eventually, £25 changed hands and the cross came home.

One broad face has a figure in the bottom fragment looking to his left towards a bird. Another figure is at the mid-point of this face. At the bottom of the other broad face, the Germanic heritage of the people who inhabited this area is demonstrated by figures from German mythology. It shows the escape of Wayland the Smith. A poster at the church tells the story. Wayland was captured by Nithad, hamstrung and made to work as his smith. Wayland took revenge by murdering the two sons of Nithad and giving their skulls to him as drinking cups. He also made Beaduhild, Nithad's daughter, pregnant. Wayland managed to escape in a flying machine, which is shown strapped to his body. He is shown surrounded by the tools of his trade and reaching to seize Beaduhild.

An alternative explanation is that the figure is Elijah who ascended to heaven in a fiery chariot.

Reference

1. Richard N. Bailey, *Viking Age Sculpture in Northern England*, Collins, 1980 p. 23

Middlesmoor

The Church of St Chad (SE092741) stands high up, overlooking stupendous Nidderdale scenery. There is an Anglo-Saxon cross head which has double cross bars, a shape known as hammerhead, and has been attributed to the 11th century. Pevsner states that the cross marks a holy site and is not in commemoration of a deceased person. W.G. Collingwood has interpreted the inscription on the cross as 'Cross of St Chad' – Chad being the famous Celtic monk who took Christianity to Mercia and became Bishop of Lichfield.

Reference

1.   Muriel Swires, *The Church of St Chad, Middlesmoor*, Church Guide

Otley

The Parish Church of All Saints has a fine collection of Anglo-Saxon crosses, displayed on a pedestal. To the left of the pedestal is part of a shaft with two figures, both of which are holding a book. Above is part of another figure. When complete, the cross could therefore have shown the four Evangelists. On the back are scrolls of leaves, fruit and a man holding a staff. W.G. Collingwood has ascribed this cross, the Angel Cross, to about 750.

To the right of the pedestal is part of a cross with two wyverns (a mythical viper with wings, two forelegs and a serpent's tail). It is sometimes known as the Dragon Cross. Beneath each viper is a haloed figure of a man. The narrower sides have beasts tied together with their tails. The cross was salvaged in 1851 from part of the chancel arch. It dates from about 800. There are other fine examples of Anglian sculpture and other fragments outside.

Reference

1.   F. Morrell and D. Peel, *All Saints' Parish Church, Otley*, Church Guide

Ripon

The story of Ripon Cathedral (SE315390) begins with Eata, a monk from Melrose Abbey. Aelhfrith, son of King Oswy of Northumbria, gave him land nearby to build a monastery. Within a year, in 658, Wilfrid (see Northumbria) became abbot and moved the monastery to its present site. Wilfrid spared no expense in decorating his church. It was said by his biographer, Eddius, to be 'built of smoothed stone with many columns and porticus and adorned with gold and silver and varied purples. While the High Altar was vested in purple woven with gold thread'. As we have seen (see Northumbria) Wilfrid spent much of his time in exile. He eventually returned as Bishop of Hexham and lies buried at Ripon. Another tradition asserts that Archbishop Oda (see Deerhurst, Gloucestershire) removed Wilfrid's relics to Canterbury – unless, as is sometimes claimed, he mistakenly took the remains of someone else. There is a modern (1977) stained-glass window by Harry Harvey in the north transept, showing St Wilfrid and scenes from his life.

When Wilfrid died, Ripon became a place of pilgrimage. Pilgrims would have filed round the ancient crypt, built between 660 and 670. It lies beneath the High Altar of Wilfrid's church and the tower of the present church. The York Archaeological Trust have excavated and found that the roof of the crypt was made from stone ribs and mortar, the first use of this architectural technique in this country. The roof of the passage uses Roman masonry from Aldborough or York and the eastern niche was probably reserved for relics.

The Treasury at Ripon contains the Ripon Jewel. It was found close to the cathedral in 1976 and is a small gold roundel. The back is plain gold with settings for gems on the front. Square cells are filled with amber and the triangular ones with garnets.

As an act of revenge for accepting Viking rule, King Eadred sacked the church and monastery in 950.

Reference

1. Allan Barton and Mark Punshon, *Ripon Cathedral 1300 Years of Worship and History*, Dean and Chapter of Ripon Cathedral

Other Places of Interest

- At St Peter's Church (SE218263) **Birstall** (locked) there is a fragment of the base of an Anglo-Saxon cross.
- St Oswald's Church, **Collingham** (SE390461) (locked) has, according to Pevsner, important Anglo-Saxon crosses.
- All Saints' Church (**Dewsbury Minster**) has an excellent collection of Anglo-Saxon sculptures. Unfortunately, as with so many town centre churches, it was locked when I visited. But, there is very good description of them on the church website. www.dewsburyminster. org.uk.

- At St Andrew's Church (SD933539) at **Gargrave** there are the remains of Anglo-Saxon crosses.
- The name **Monk Fryston** derives from monks' freestone, and refers to the free stone, quarried here and used to build Selby Abbey. St Wilfrid's church (SE505298) (locked) has an Anglo-Saxon west tower with twin bell openings. Unusually, the tower has two horizontal corbel tables.
- In the churchyard at St Matthew's Church, **Rastrick** (SE138216) is the base of an Anglo-Saxon cross of the 11th century.
- St Michael's Church (SE255188) at **Thornhill** was in the process of a major restoration when I visited and so the church's Saxon sculptures could not be seen.
- There is a portion of an Anglo-Danish cross at St Peter's Church, **West Marton** (SD908507). Pevsner reports that it comes from Scriven Park, it has human figures and monsters enclosed within interlace patterns.

Westmorland

Great Ormside

Ormside refers to 'the seat of Orm'. It is in magnificent countryside south of Appleby-in-Westmorland with the river Eden as its neighbour. Orm was a Viking and maybe a kinsman of Halfden, the notorious Viking who pillaged this area around the year 915.

The Church of St James (NY702176) has a blocked south doorway, now with a later window within. It has a vast lintel and tympanum above, which is probably pre-Conquest. The tower arch is also probably Saxon.

A Viking sword was found in the churchyard and is now in the Tullie House Museum in Carlisle. The famous Ormside Bowl was also found in the churchyard in 1823. It is now in the Yorkshire Museum at York, but there is a descriptive display in the church telling its story. It is 8th century and consists of two pieces – an inner bowl of silver bronze and an outer bowl of silver gilt – riveted together with blue glass and silver. The outer bowl is decorated with interlace and fruit, animals and bird patterns. It was originally a liturgical object but later used in a secular context.

Reference

1.   Anon, *A Guide to St James' Church Ormside*

Heversham

Heversham lies close to the estuary of the river Kent, between Kendal and Carnforth. The first Christian presence at Heversham was probably an early Anglian monastery. The 11th century *History of St Cuthbert* relates that between

901 and 925, Tilred, abbot at Heversham, bought land, half of which he dedicated to St Cuthbert, in the hope that he could become a monk at Lindisfarne. The other half he gave to Norham to enable him to become abbot there in his place. Heversham was probably attracting the attention of the ravaging Vikings and Tilred's wish to leave Heversham is therefore perfectly understandable.

There is part of a cross shaft in the church of St Peter (SD496834). It has a likeness to those at Bewcastle and Ruthwell. It has four volutes and bunches of berries. Within is a quadruped biting a bunch of berries.

Reference

1. W.T. McIntyre and John Hancock, *The History of St Peter's Church, Heversham,* Church Guide

Kirkby Stephen

Kirkby Stephen sits on the banks of the river Eden and has the glorious expanse of the fells as neighbour. Just inside the church of St Stephen (NY775088) is its famous 'Loki' stone or 'Bound Devil Stone' – part of an Anglo-Danish cross shaft of the 10th century with a chained, horned and bearded devil. Loki was an ancient Norse god, and not a particularly nice god at that, more a devil. He was a mischief-maker, player of unpleasant jokes and responsible for the death of Odin's son. This last piece of mischief led him to be imprisoned below ground in chains. The Loki Stone is the only one in this country and one of only two in Europe. It reminds us of the Viking presence in this area in the 10th century.

Reference

1. Anon, *Kirkby Stephen Parish Church*, Church Guide

Long Marton

The church of St Margaret and St James (NY666240) is south of the village of Long Marton, which is about two miles north of Appleby-in-Westmorland. It was probably founded in pre-Conquest times – see the typical Anglo-Saxon long-and-short work of the north-east angle of the nave. The chief point of interest is the tympanum over the south doorway. It is of unknown date but may well be 7th or 8th century. It shows a dragon with twisted tail, a winged ox in what could be a boat and a winged shield with cross. Inside (and much more difficult to make out) is another tympanum over the door to the tower. In Winterburn's excellent guide he informs us it depicts a dragon, a merman, a club and a cross.

Reference

1. G.H. Winterburn, *Long Marton*, Guidebook

Lowther

Lowther is about five miles south of Penrith. The church is north of Lowther Castle near the tiny river Lowther. There is a hogback tombstone at St Michael's Church (NY519244). The long section shows a serpent at the bottom. Above on the left is a boat with eight sailors. In the centre is a half figure and to the right a group of warriors.

Morland

Morland sits in pleasant countryside about eight miles south-east of Penrith. There is only one Anglo-Saxon west tower in Westmorland (and Cumberland); it is here at the church of St Laurence (NY598225), Morland, and has been attributed to the great Siward, Earl of Northumberland. At the bell stage it has double headed windows and mid-wall shafts typical of the period, the smallest of windows below and a Saxon arch to the nave. The upper part of the tower is later.

Reference

1. Anon, *The Parish Church of St Laurence, Morland*, Church Guide

Other Places of Interest

- St Michael's Church, **Bonegate** (NY689199) at Appleby is now in private hands. Pevsner reports that the north doorway has a hogback as the lintel.
- The church of St James, **Burton in Kendal** (SD530770) was locked but according to Pevsner has parts of a cross shaft depicting Christ and other figures, described by Kendrick (many years ago) as 'in its final stage of disintegration'.

Wiltshire

Alton Barnes

The tiny church of St Mary, Alton Barnes (SU108620) is in quiet countryside about nine miles south-west of Marlborough and next to a farmyard. Apart from the 18th century chancel it is Anglo-Saxon as revealed by the characteristic long-and-short work at its west end. There are also pilaster strips, both here and on the north and south walls. Alton Barnes came into history in 825, when King Egbert, who had just been victorious in battle against the Mercians, gave land in the village to the see of Winchester.

Reference

1. *All Saints, Alton Priors and St Mary's Alton Barnes, A Short History*, 2009

Avebury

Avebury, about seven miles west of Marlborough, is of course more famous for its prehistoric standing stones. But the Saxons were also here. There are two Anglo-Saxon windows at the west end of the nave at St James' Church, (SU109700). Then, in the clerestory to the north, are three circular windows, also Saxon.

Reference

1. Carol Davies, Church Guide

| St Lawrence Chapel, Bradford-Upon-Avon

Bradford-on-Avon

Bradford-on-Avon is about two miles north-west of Trowbridge. The tiny chapel of St Laurence (ST825609) came to light in 1856 when Canon Jones, the vicar of nearby Holy Trinity Church, realised that the building – then used as a school room and a cottage – was in fact Anglo-Saxon. Based on the 12th century chronicles of William of Malmesbury, the church is assumed to have been founded in the 6th or 7th century. The chronicles record that 'today at that place there exists a little church which Aldhelm is said to have built to the name of the most blessed Laurence'. It is also mentioned in a deed of 705, the time when St Aldhelm was Abbot of Malmesbury.

The church was restored in the 1870s by J.T. Irvine, who maintained that the building was late Anglo-Saxon. Since then, there have been other theories, such as there being two periods of construction. The weight of evidence seems to point, however, to an early 11th century foundation. In 1001, a charter of King Aethelred granted Bradford to the nuns of Shaftesbury and the church could well date from this time, but the debate continues. There are suggestions that St Laurence's houses the relics of Aethelred's brother, Edward the Martyr, or, indeed, the body of St Aldhelm, in a now hidden crypt.

The church, extremely high in proportion to its width, consists of nave, 25ft in length, chancel of 21ft and a north porticus. There was originally a porticus to the south but now only the entrance door remains. The west wall dates from the restoration of 1875. Outside, the walls are decorated with the usual pilaster strips and are divided into tiers, the upper tier with blind arcading. There are double splayed windows in the south wall of the nave and chancel and the west wall of the north porticus. Sculptures of two angels are high up on the east wall of the nave and there are fragments of Saxon work in the altar.

Reference

1.   Jonathan Pitt, *The Church of St Laurence, Bradford on Avon*, Church Guide, 1998

Britford

The church of St Peter is about two miles south-east of Salisbury and close to the river Avon. It is approached by turning left down a lane off the A338 Bournemouth Road (SU163285). Referred to as Bretforde in the Anglo-Saxon Chronicle, the manor was held by King Edward the Confessor. He was here in 1065 with Tostig, the brother of Harold Godwinson, and it was at Britford that they both heard news of a rebellion in Northumbria – news that would have disturbed Tostig for he was Earl of Northumbria. By the time of the Domesday survey the church was held by Osbern. It had one hide of land worth forty shillings.

The nave – or at least its lower part – is Saxon, dated to about 800, and there is a Saxon south door. But the real interest at St Peter's lies in the entrance arches to the two side chapels or porticus, revealed by G.E. Street's restoration of 1873. The south arch is the cruder of the two. It has Roman bricks as voussoirs. The north arch is much more accomplished with vertical posts within which are square slabs. The posts are richly decorated with vine scrolls and the grapes are clearly visible. The slabs house knotwork and rosettes.

Reference

1.   C.L. Rowe, *The Parish Church of St Peter, Britford* (1968 edition of previous guides by E. Mary Woodall and W.G.C. Addison)

Codford St Peter

Mercifully, the main A36 Bath-to-Salisbury Road bypasses Codford St Peter and peace has been restored. Codford means the 'fording place of Codda', an Anglo-Saxon who perhaps held land here. The place is mentioned in a charter of 906 as Codda's Ford – the ford being a passage over the nearby river Wyle. The church (ST965399) was restored in 1863 and the original Norman chancel arch removed. What was revealed is the glory of Codford, the magnificent 'dancing man'. Dated to the early 9th century and made of Bath stone, it stands alongside the north wall of the chancel.

Anglo-Saxon Cross Shaft, St Peter's Church, Codford St Peter

The tapered shaft, four feet in height, depicts a man with moustache, his head bent backwards so that he gazes upwards. In his left hand, he holds a mallet (or maybe a rattle), and his right hand grasps a branch, laden with fruit. Careful inspection reveals the handle of his knife above his belt and his smock is secured with a long pin. There is a panel at the bottom of the sculpture but without inscription. On the eastern side of the shaft are two eels, an otter and two fish. On the west side are leaves, perhaps comfrey. But what does it all mean? Some have suggested he is a jester and that the shaft is his memorial, others an archer, and yet others that he is a symbolic harvester.

References

1. Anthony F. Bainbridge, *The Parish Church of St Peter, Codford, Wiltshire*, Church Guide, 2012

2. K.G. Forbes, *Wiltshire Archaeological and Natural History Magazine*, 1967, 62, 34–7

Colerne

Colerne is about eight miles south-west of Chippenham, north of the main A4 Bath road. The church of St Mary (ST821712) has two excellent fragments of Anglo-Saxon crosses. They are mounted on the north wall of the nave and date from the 9th century. In the Jellinge style, they clearly show beautifully carved intertwining dragons. In one, the dragons cross each other, their legs clutching the other's neck. Their toes are visible to left and right. The other panel is less distinct and has two or maybe three creatures. A poster in the church says that the sculptures were part of a Saxon cross erected to commemorate St Aldhelm, bishop of Sherborne, who died in 709 and whose body rested at Colerne on its way to burial at Malmesbury Abbey, of which he was a former abbot.

Inglesham

The church of St John the Baptist at Inglesham (SU205984), one mile south of Lechlade-on-Thames, is in the hands of the Churches Preservation Trust. It was a firm favourite of William Morris as is recorded in an inscription in the church: 'This church was repaired in 1889/9 through the energy and with the help of William Morris who loved it' – praise indeed. On the south wall of the nave is an Anglo-Saxon sculpture showing the Virgin and Child and above, the hand of God, with finger pointing to the infant child. Christ gives a blessing with His right hand and holds a book in His left. Above is an inscription with the word MARIA above Mary's head.

Knook

A small lane leads south-west off the main A36 Bath-to-Salisbury Road, five miles east of Warminster. After a few hundred yards the tiny hamlet of Knook, close to the river Wyle, is reached (ST936418). The church of St Margaret is entered by the north porch, but it is the south doorway which commands our attention. Its tympanum, carved in low relief, is Saxon in style – but whether Saxon or Saxon-Norman overlap is a matter of debate. Two beasts face each other, to the right is a lion and to the left a griffin. They both appear to be biting the scrollwork.

Inside the diminutive church there is a band of Saxon interlace behind the altar and fine intricately carved capitals to the chancel arch. Although thought by some to be the work of a Saxon mason, Pevsner maintains they are Norman.

Netheravon

Netheravon is situated in the valley of the river Avon, about five miles north of Amesbury. The tower at All Saints' (SU148484) looks decidedly Saxon, although Pevsner concludes that it may date from the Saxon-Norman overlap period. He also speculates that the tower may originally have been a central tower with nave to its west and chancel to the east; in which case, it is probably Anglo-Saxon. To the north and south of the tower are doorways (blocked to the north) which could have led, in a Saxon church, to porticus.

Ramsbury

Ramsbury is about five miles north-west of Hungerford, north of the river Kennet. Anglo-Saxon settlers came to the area around Ramsbury (SU274715) after the battle of Barbury Castle, near Ogbourne St John, in 556. Barbury Castle is an Iron Age hill fort and was captured by the early settlers of Wessex at a battle with the native Romano-British. Evidence of a Saxon settlement was found in 1974 when a 7th or 8th century iron smelting forge was discovered. Ramsbury was originally known as Hraefn's Burgh, that is raven's fortified town, and is thought to have been given to the church by a grant from King Offa of Mercia.

In 900, Ramsbury came to prominence when a bishopric was founded here. The first bishop was Aethelstan who had jurisdiction over Berkshire and Wiltshire. He was succeeded by a Dane, Oda, who later became Archbishop of Canterbury, as did, in 990, Sigeric the Serious, who is credited with advising Aethelred the Unready to pay off the Danes with Danegeld and buy peace. In 1058 the sees of Ramsbury and Sherbourne were combined and later in 1075 the bishopric transferred to Old Sarum.

The present church of Holy Cross stands on the site of the Saxon Minster. During restoration in 1891, Saxon stones were revealed which have been reconstructed as a cross. It is Viking in style and made up of three parts. The top slab has two full roundels and a half roundel containing dog-like creatures, each with pointed toes. In the middle slab are two reptiles and in the lowest slab is a single serpent-like creature consuming its own body and decorated with chevrons.

Reference

1. Barbara Croucher, *The Village in the Valley*, privately printed, 1986

Other Places of Interest

- Pevsner reports that there is a 9th century cross head on display in the church of St Mary and St Melor (SU152415) at **Amesbury**. It was locked when I visited. In 980, Amesbury Abbey was founded by Aelfthryth, wife of King Edgar, allegedly to atone for her part in the murder of Edward the Martyr.
- The church of St Martin, **Bremhill** (ST980730) has long-and-short Anglo-Saxon quoins at the north-west end of the nave, indicating a pre-Conquest foundation.
- The chancel at St John the Baptist, **Burcombe** (SU073312) is Anglo-Saxon as seen by the long-and-short work quoins to the east. Please note – the church is on the main A30 road and partly hidden. Cars can be parked in the small lane opposite, leading to Burcombe village. Cross the main road with care.
- The Abbot of Glastonbury is recorded as building the first church at **Mildenhall** (SU210695) in 804. The lower part of the tower at the church of St John the Baptist is Saxon.
- There are long-and-short work quoins at the north-west angle of the nave of St Mary's Church, **Upton Scudamore** (ST865477) pointing to an Anglo-Saxon foundation

Worcestershire

Cropthorne

Cropthorne (SO001452) is mentioned in Domesday Book and refers to Croppa's land. It is about four miles west of Evesham, just south of the river Avon. It was given by King Offa of Mercia to the Priory of Worcester in 786 and Offa also had a hunting lodge here. It remained a royal residence and in 841 King Beorhtwulf signed a charter here in the presence of Queen Saethryth giving land at Wychwood to Bishop Heahbeornt of Worcester.

The Church of St Michael has a magnificent Anglo-Saxon cross head displayed in the north aisle. It was found in the south wall of the Sanctuary in the 18th century and dates from about 800 AD. Pevsner describes it as 'the best piece of Anglo-Saxon art in the county', and it was on show at the British Museum in their 1991 exhibition of Anglo-Saxon art. One face has in its lower arm a quadruped. There are birds and foliage in the side arms and a winged creature in the upper arm with fruit in the centre, which has a recess, probably to house a jewel. The other face also has a quadruped in its lower arm, fruit in the centre and dog-like/quadruped creatures in each side arm. The upper arm has a curving stem, possibly ending in a frog. The style of the carving is similar to that found at Wroxeter in Shropshire and Acton Beauchamp in Herefordshire.

Reference

1.   Anon, *A History of St Michael's Church and Village, Cropthorne*

Other Places of Interest

- St Peter's Church, **Rous Lench** (SP014533) has, according to the church guidebook, an Anglo-Saxon carved block. However, I was unable to locate it.
- Pevsner claims that at the church of St Michael, **Stoke Prior** (SO949676) and to the left of the left capital of the south doorway there is an Anglo-Danish stone with interlace carving.

Glossary of Architectural Terms

- Abacus – Slab at the top of a capital.
- Acanthus – Leaf decoration.
- Aisle – Passage to the side of the nave of a church.
- Ambulatory – Aisle to the side of the chancel or sanctuary of a church.
- Apse – Semi-circular extension of a chancel.
- Arcade – A series of arches supported by columns.
- Baluster – A small belly-shaped pillar.
- Capital – Head of a column.
- Chancel – East end of a church where the main altar is situated.
- Clerestory – Upper part of nave walls of a church containing windows.
- Crypt – Underground room beneath a church.
- Double Splayed Window – Slit window with both the internal and external jambs angled to allow more light to enter the building.
- Gothic – Medieval architecture typified by pointed arches. Sub-divided, chronologically into Early English, Decorated and Perpendicular.
- Herringbone masonry – Masonry with zig-zag courses.
- Hood Mould – Projecting moulding above an arch.
- Impost – Moulding at point where arch rises from its support
- Jamb – Straight side of an opening.
- Lesene – A flat relief against a wall, also known as a pilaster strip.
- Long-and-Short Work – Quoins with their stones placed with long sides horizontal and then vertical.

- Lozenge – Diamond decoration.
- Motte – Earthen mound.
- Nave – Main body of a church, west of the crossing.
- Pilaster – Flat relief against a wall.
- Piscina – Basin for washing mass vessels.
- Porticus – Small side room, projecting north or south of a church, usually containing an altar and similar to, but smaller than, a transept.
- Quoins – Dressed stones at the corner of a building.
- Reredos – Screen behind an altar.
- Romanesque – Norman architecture of 11ᵗʰ and 12ᵗʰ century.
- Rood – Cross, typically over the entrance to the chancel.
- Saxo-Norman – Romanesque style with Anglo-Saxon and Norman features.
- Single Splayed Window – Slit window with the internal jamb angled to allow more light into the building.
- String course – Stone moulding separating stages of a wall.
- Tympanum – Surface between a lintel and the arch above it, typically over a door.
- Voussoirs – Wedge shaped stones forming an arch.

Bibliography

Abels, Richard, *Alfred the Great* (Longman, 1998)

Anglo-Saxon Chronicle

Bailey, Richard N., *Viking Age Sculpture* (Collins, 1980)

Barlow, Frank, *Edward the Confessor* (Eyre Methuen, 2nd Edition, 1989)

Bede, translated by Leo Sherley Price, *A History of the English Church and People* (Penguin Books, 1968)

Blair, John, *The Church in Anglo-Saxon Society* (Oxford: Oxford University Press, 2005)

Buchanan, James J., and Davis, Harold T., *Zosimus: Historia Nova, The Decline of Rome* (San Antonio, Texas: Trinity University Press, 1967)

Campbell, James, John, Eric, and Wormald, Patrick, *The Anglo-Saxons* (Phaiden Press, 1982)

Dictionary of National Biography (Oxford: Oxford University Press, 2004)

Faith, Rosamund, *English Peasantry and the Growth of Lordship* (Leicester University Press, 1997)

Fisher, D.J.V., *The Anglo-Saxon Age* (Longman, 1973)

Fletcher, Richard, *Who's Who in Roman and Anglo-Saxon England* (Shepheard Walwyn, 1989)

Foot, Sarah, *Aethelstan, the First King of England* (Yale University Press, 2011)

Frodsham, Paul, *Cuthbert and the Northumbrian Saints* (Northern Heritage, 2009)

Griffiths, Bill, *An Introduction to Early English Law* (Anglo-Saxon Books, 1995)

Higham, Nicholas, *The Death of Anglo-Saxon England* (Sutton, 1997)

Higham, Nicholas J., and Hill, D.H., eds., *Edward the Elder* (Routledge)

Higham, Nicholas J., and Ryan, Martin, *The Anglo-Saxon World* (Yale University Press, 2013)

Hill, David, ed., *Ethelred the Unready* (BAR Series, 1978)

Howard, Ian, *Harthacnut, the Last Danish King of England* (History Press, 2008)

Howarth, David, *1066, the Year of the Conquest* (Collins, 1977)

Johnson, Stephen, *Late Roman Britain* (Routledge & Kegan Paul, 1980)

Kendrick, Sir Thomas, *Anglo-Saxon Art to AD900* (Metheun, 1938)

Kendrick, Sir Thomas, *Late Saxon and Viking Art* (Metheun, 1949)

Keynes, Simon and Lapidge, Michael, eds., *Alfred the Great, Asser's Life of King Alfred and Other Contemporary Sources* (Penguin Classics, 1983)

Keynes, Simon, *The Council of Clovesho, Brixworth Lecture* (University of Leicester, 1993)

Kirby, D.P., *The Earliest English Kings* (Routledge, 1990)

Lang, James, *Anglo-Saxon Sculpture* (Shire Publications, 1988)

Lapidge, Michael, *Archbishop Theodore, Commemorative Studies on his Life and Influence* (Cambridge University Press, 1995)

Lapidge, Michael, ed., *The Blackwell Encyclopaedia of Anglo-Saxon England* (Blackwell, 1999)

Lavelle, Ryan, *Aethelred II* (History Press, 2008)

Lawson, M.K., *Cnut, England's Viking King* (Tempus, 2004)

Leff, Gordon, *Alcuin of York and the Foundation of Medieval Education* (Kirkdale Lecture, 1994)

Leyser, Henrietta, *A Short History of the Anglo-Saxons* (I.B. Tauris, 2017)

Loyn, H.R., *Anglo-Saxon England and the Norman Conquest* (Longman, 2nd Edition 1991)

Mortimer, Roger, ed., *Edward the Confessor: The Man and the Legend* (Boydell, 2009)

Peddie, John, *Alfred the Good Soldier* (Millstream Books, 1989)

Points, Guy, *An Introduction to Anglo-Saxon Church Architecture & Anglo-Saxon & Anglo-Scandinavian Stone Sculpture (Rihtspell Publishing, 2015)*

Rex, Peter, *King and Saint: The Life of Edward the Confessor* (History Press, 2008)

Stenton, Sir Frank, *Anglo-Saxon England* (Oxford: Oxford University Press, 3rd Edition,1971)

Trow, M.J., *Cnut, Emperor of the North* (Sutton, 2005)

Venning, Timothy, *The Anglo-Saxon Kings* (Amberley, 2011)

Webster, Leslie, *Anglo-Saxon Art* (British Museum, 2012)

White, Newport J.D., *St Patrick His Writings and Life* (London, S.P.C.K., 1920)

Whitelock, Dorothy, ed., *English Historical Documents 500–1042* (London, Eyre Methuen, 2nd Edition, 1979)

Williams, Ann, *Aethelred the Unready* (Hambledon, 2003)

Wilson, David, *Anglo Saxon Art* (Thames and Hudson, 1984)

Yorke, Barbara, *Kings and Kingdoms of Early Anglo-Saxon England* (Seaby, 1990)

Index